The Child–School Interface
Environment and Behaviour

Raya A. Jones

CASSELL

Cassell
Villiers House   387 Park Avenue South
41/47 Strand   New York
London WC2N 5JE   NY 10016–8810

British Library Cataloguing-in-Publication Data
A catalogue record for this book is available from the British Library

ISBN 0–304–32981–9 (hardback)
     0–304–32979–7 (paperback)

Typeset by Intype, London
Printed and bound in Great Britain by Biddles Ltd, Guildford and
King's Lynn

Contents

Foreword

The books in this series stems from the conviction that all those who are concerned with education should have a deep interest in the nature of children's learning. Teaching and policy decisions ultimately depend on an understanding of individual personalities accumulated through experience, observation and research. Too often in recent years decisions on the management of education have had little to do with the realities of children's lives, and too often the interest shown in the performance of teachers, or in the content of the curriculum, has not been balanced by an interest in how children respond to either. The books in this series are based on the conviction that children are not fundamentally different from adults, and that we understand ourselves better by our insight into the nature of children.

The books are designed to appeal to *all* those who are interested in education and who take it as axiomatic that anyone concerned with human nature, culture or the future of civilization is interested in education – in the individual process of learning, as well as what can be done to help it. While each book draws on recent findings in research and is aware of the latest developments in policy, each is written in a style that is clear, readable and free from jargon that has undermined much scholarly writing, especially in such a relatively new field of study.

Although the audience to be addressed includes all those concerned with education, the most important section of the audience is made up of professional teachers, the teachers who continue to learn and grow and who need both support and stimulation. Teachers are very busy people, whose energies are taken up in coping with difficult circumstances. They deserve material that is stimulating, useful and free of jargon and that is in tune with the practical realities of classrooms.

Each book is based on the principle that the study of education is a discipline in its own right. There was a time when the study of the principles of learning and the individual's response to his or her environment was a collection of parts of other disciplines – history, philosophy, linguistics, sociology and psychology. That time is assumed to be over and the books address those who are interested in the study of children and how they respond to their environment.

Each book is written both to enlighten the readers and to offer practical help to develop their understanding. They therefore not only contain accounts of what we understand about children, but also illuminate these accounts by a series of examples, based on observation of practice. These examples are designed not as a series of rigid steps to be followed, but to show the realities on which the insights are based.

Most people, even educational researchers, agree that research on children's learning has been most disappointing, even when it has not been completely missing. Apart from the general lack of a 'scholarly' educational tradition, the inadequacies of such study come about because of the fear of approaching such a complex area as children's inner lives. Instead of answering curiosity with observation, much education research has attempted to reduce the problem to simplistic solutions, by isolating a particular hypothesis and trying to improve it, or by trying to focus on what is easy and 'empirical'. These books try to clarify the real complexities of the problem, and are willing to be speculative.

The real disappointment with educational research, however, is that it is rarely read or used. The people most at home with children are often unaware that helpful insights can be offered to them. The study of children and the understanding that comes from self-knowledge are too important to be left to obscurity. In the broad sense real 'research' is carried out by all those engaged in the task of teaching or bringing up children.

All the books share a conviction that the inner worlds of children repay close attention, and that much subsequent behaviour and attitudes depend upon the early years. They also share the conviction that children's natures are not markedly different from those of adults, even if they are more honest about themselves. The process of learning is reviewed as the individual's close and idiosyncratic involvement in events, rather than the passive reception of, and processing of, information.

Cedric Cullingford

CHAPTER 1
The Ecosystemic Metaphor

> The question of the relation of the school to the child's life is at
> bottom simply this: Shall we ignore this native setting and tend-
> ency, dealing, not with the living child at all, but with the dead
> image we have erected, or shall we give it play and satisfaction?[1]

The school is an environment designed to have an 'impact'
on children and youth. As a learning environment, it is structured to bring about behavioural and mental changes. Educational goals are fairly well defined, even if the means vary.
Often, we construct an idealized image of the child at school,
a child who would respond to the structured environment as
predicted by psychologists. Apparent failures bring forth the
'living child' to whom Dewey alludes in the above quotation:
we look for emotional disturbance, problems at home, peer-
group pressure ... The *experiential environment* comes to the
foreground.

For a child, however, there is only the school as personally
experienced. Sentiments such as expressed by the American
pragmatist philosopher and educator John Dewey gave
impetus to the ecological reform in the social sciences. Certain
psychologists, mainly in the United States, queried the
explanatory viability of statistical data and generalization from
laboratory-based experiments to ordinary human life. The
emphasis on laboratory studies in developmental psychology
has led to what Bronfenbrenner called 'the science of the
strange behaviour of children in strange situations with strange
adults for the briefest possible periods of time'.[2] Trends in a
population, or the mythical Average Person, do not explain
human behaviour. For instance, many surveys have shown that
'working class' children are more likely than their 'middle
class' peers to have learning difficulties – but a child's difficulties hardly occur 'because' of the statistical probability, no

1

more than a road accident on the M4 happens because of the annual rate of accidents on that motorway. In-depth studies of classroom interactions show how the school can inadvertently discriminate against pupils of lower social classes or ethnic minorities.

Such studies were initially conducted in sociological frames of reference. In the 1950s and 1960s, ecological psychologists began to implement a similar rationale in so far that they concentrated on systematic descriptions of children's behaviours in and out of schools. Their theoretical framework was very different from the sociological tradition. Ecologically oriented psychologists started with a conception of the child as an organism embedded in the natural world, and described relations between the physical environment and overt behaviour. More recent ecological models, especially in developmental psychology, have moved away from the strictly biological slant, and look at the child as an agent in a social world, thereby taking on board sociological and social-psychological insights.

In any case, the ecological reform has been, as Gibbs put it, a reaction to research into the 'trivial and irrelevant', coupled with 'a plea for sensitivity to the contextual continuities and potentialities of human behaviour'.[3] The appeal of an ecological perspective lies in the realistic consideration of living children in actual schools. It is not enough, however, to document children's behaviour in its natural setting; psychologists aim to understand why children behave as they do.

The living child at school is someone to whom responding to certain stimuli and not to others, and responding in certain ways and not others, is meaningful. By the late 1970s, ecologically oriented psychologists began to take into account subjective viewpoints. Unless we have an insight into subjective meanings, unless we gain an access to the 'inner world of the school' (to borrow Cullingford's phrase[4]), we cannot fully explain why or how environment influences behaviour.

This book reviews research and theories concerning environment-behaviour relations in educational settings. In contemporary education, 'whole-school' management approaches are often recommended; to be more than naive sentiment or administrative gesture, whole-school thinking should be substantiated with research evidence and an understanding of how social – and physical – environmental factors affecting the child are interconnected. It is my thesis, elaborated below, that ecosystemic thinking makes sense in educational psychology, sociology of education, and related fields. The ecosystemic metaphor holds in focus the *child–school interface* – not the child in isolation, or the school as an 'empty entity'.

Ecosystemic Perspectives in Education

The idea that an educational setting is analogous to an ecosystem has emerged independently in educational psychology and sociology of education. Educational psychologists have to understand the aetiology (causes) of pupils' problems. The ecosystemic approach to classroom problems, derived from psychiatric systems theory, looks at the network of teacher–pupil(s) interactions (the 'ecosystem' in focus) for the explanation of the problems. Sociologists of education, concerned with school effectiveness, typically quote organizational and group processes theories. The school is envisaged, implicitly or explicitly, as a network of institutional processes (the 'ecosystem' in focus in this instance).

Ecosystemic perspectives in education did not appear in academic isolation. During the late 1970s, many research domains underwent a reformulation marked by increased attention to everyday contexts in which individuals or groups act. Bronfenbrenner presented his framework for research on the ecology of child development (see Chapter 7);[5] Gibson 'departed' from psychophysics with his ecological approach to sensory perception (see Chapter 3);[6] Eggleston wrote about the ecology of the school organization,[7] and Moos evaluated educational environments on the basis of his social-ecological model (see Chapter 4).[8] Somewhat later, the term 'ecosystemic' became popular. It indicates an integration of the ecological orientation and systems theory. Whereas the strictly ecological tradition describes what an organism does in its habitat (or a child in school), systems theory describes

3

relationships between elements of systems which might exist only in an abstract sense, such as the system of interactions that evolves between a teacher and her pupils. Upton and Cooper's ecosystemic approach to behaviour problems brings this model to British special education (see Chapters 5 and 8).[9]

The upsurge of models labelled ecological, systemic, or eco-systemic coincided with a drastic elaboration of ecology in biology, physics, and geography, spurred by the development of mathematical systems theory, and with the rise of political ecologism (Green issues). The jargon might have been an intellectual fad, but it embodied a very important message. The starting-point for many ecologically oriented inquiries in psychology was the imperative to discover behavioural regularities that occur independently of experimental manipulation; hence the focus on the ecology of human behaviour. The natural complexity of everyday behaviour calls for 'systems' analyses or, at least, systemic thinking.

Nearly twenty years on, the importance of relating human behaviour, development or learning to a relevant context is widely accepted. We should continue to stress the 'ecological validity' point, but hardly need to campaign for it any more. Basic premises such as the holistic complexity of systems, hierarchies of systems and sub-systems, and the principle of reciprocal causality, are by now commonplace. What new insights have been gained as a result?

Generally, ecosystemic thinking does not invalidate knowledge generated in other frameworks; rather, it puts findings in a new perspective and opens up new inquiries. Ecological or systemic models are not 'theories' in the traditional scientific sense. That is, they do not answer *why* certain phenomena occur, but represent a way of asking *what* is occurring.

In education, an ecosystemic perspective may begin with the heuristic analogy of a school as an 'open system', but this should generate research issues, and lead to scientific description and explanation.

The analogy is readily grasped: a school is a complex, multi-levelled and multi-factorial organization; it is embedded in a wider societal context, but is autonomous in many respects.

Since a school is structured for a purpose, it may be evaluated in terms of how well it meets its purpose. It was discovered that schools associated with good rates of attainment and low incidence of behaviour problems are those which engender a sense of collaboration among staff, pupils, parents and governors:

> effective schools [are] friendly, supportive environments, led by heads who are not afraid to assert their views and yet able to share management and decision-making with the staff. Class teachers within effective schools provide a structured learning situation for their pupils but give them freedom within this framework.[10]

Much research effort has gone into isolating the crucial determinants of school effectiveness. But inherent in this process of elimination there is a danger of throwing out the baby with the bath water: ineffectual factors are not necessarily irrelevant. For example, Rutter *et al.* found no statistical relationship between the state of the school building and attainment or conduct variables.[11] Does this mean that a school building in bad repair is of no consequence?

A site perceived by staff as inadequate and restrictive can have a demoralizing effect, which 'feeds' into the school ethos. However, given sufficient motivation and dedication, staff may rise above it. A Sunday newspaper reporter described the Small School in Hartland, Devon (an 'alternative' school for 11–16 year olds):

> Once the school is empty of children you notice, for the first time, the shabby decor, make-do furnishing, battered equipment. Do such things matter? [The headmaster] thinks not. Happiness and all-round achievement of the children are more important.[12]

This aspect of the physical environment is therefore not an objective factor mediating educational outcomes, but a subjective matter. On the other hand, it is sometimes impossible to ignore environmental conditions. With the best will in the world, noise interferes with classroom activities.

In conclusion, it is not sufficient to list key 'causal' factors;

we must also state how the various factors affect each other. As proponents of systems theories are fond of saying: *the whole is different from the sum total of its parts.*

School effectiveness research concerns processes and outcomes on the level of a school population. Slightly different issues arise when behaviour, learning or development are to be explained on the level of the individual child. To those we turn next.

Explaining Behaviour

Psychologists endeavouring to explain human behaviour or development have looked at the school as one of children's habitats. In psychology, the ecologist's initial effort was to define the human environment. Bronfenbrenner observed that previously intricate analyses of properties of the person was supplemented with 'only the most rudimentary conception and characterization of the environment in which the person is found'.[13] Environmental factors have been frequently equated with demographic variables, and differences in children from diverse backgrounds were 'explained' as if due to the socioeconomic or ethnic background, family composition, etc. Even when the environment was described, it was either construed as 'a static structure that makes no allowance for the evolving process of interaction through which the behaviour of participants in the system is instigated, sustained, and developed', or else delimited to 'a single immediate setting containing the subject'.[14] More fundamentally than being understated or misconstrued in the manner pointed out by Bronfenbrenner, the environment has been regarded as a source of interference with 'pure' psychological functioning. Doise and Mackie remarked that in Piagetian cognitive development studies, the explanatory use of social-contextual variables 'when not left entirely implicit, has often been limited to almost "last ditch" attempts to account for what are considered "departures" from the "normal" path of development'.[15]

One traditional view of the child's surroundings is exemplified in Hadfield's statement: '*The environment and the material world around are the medium in and through which the potentialities*

in the child's nature are expressed and developed.'[16] In this view, the
description of child development, or of individual differences,
usually entails the identification of behaviour patterns, traits
or abilities which transcend the specific settings in which the
individuals are observed. For instance, young children's language acquisition follows a universal pattern, irrespective of
the language that the child is brought up to speak.

However, the setting specificity of behaviour is sometimes
significant. Loeber and Dishion found that adolescent boys
who fought both at home and at school displayed more severe
and more frequent violence than did boys whose aggression
was limited to one setting.[17] It might be concluded that the
consistently aggressive boys had a 'violent streak', whereas
the other boys reacted to external circumstances in the given
setting. But this hardly justifies dismissing the setting-specific
case. Evidently, if a boy fights only at school, there are problems there which need sorting out. This reasoning can be
taken further: boys who fight at home and at school perhaps
react to circumstances common to both settings. It follows that
the identification of *environmental* determinants of behaviour is
as relevant as the diagnosis of 'disorders' or traits, if not more
so. The same applies to non-problematic behaviour. The view
of the environment as the ultimate source of causal influences
has been expounded in another tradition, behaviourism, presently described in some detail.

Early theories of human motivation outlined hierarchies of
needs and drives to explain why people behave as they do
in particular settings. Theorists usually distinguished between
biological needs, which ensure the organism's survival in the
physical world, and needs for esteem, achievement, etc., to do
with psychological survival in a social world. Need- and drive-
theories, representing an attempt to conceptualize environment-behaviour relations, have since fallen out of favour
because of their explanatory limitations.

A pupil's disruptive behaviour can be seen as attention-
seeking, but to say that children seek attention because they
have an 'attention need' tells us very little about the origins
of the disruptive behaviour. Attention-seeking also manifests
itself in trying to please the teacher, so why are some attention-

seekers disruptive? It is potentially more illuminating to ask about the subjective significance of the particular behaviour: what does being the class's 'big naughty' (or being the 'teacher's pet') mean to the child? Do the ways in which the teacher and classmates react to the child's behaviour confirm its subjective function? Similarly, we might say that students who invest a lot of effort in their work have a strong need for achievement. Individuals may be (and have been) compared according to the 'strength' of their supposed achievement-need. Again, this hardly explains why success is so important for some students and not for others. Furthermore, different students may be motivated to a similar degree for different reasons: for some, education means a passport to a better life; to others, doing well means the approval of 'significant others'; and so on. Asking about the subjective implications of academic success in view of student's life circumstances is potentially more illuminating than the idea of a psychological need.

Behaviourism stands diametrically opposed to motivation theories and to the notion that the child's nature unfolds as a matter of maturation. In the latter view, the environment – home, school, the street, and other settings – is believed to make *possible* what is innately given (the 'nature' view of development) or is currently desired (need or drive theories). In contrast, behaviourists believe that the environment *determines* the child's so-called 'nature' and elicits current so-called 'motivation'.

Why do people behave as they do? With this question, the influential American psychologist B. F. Skinner began one of his books, *About Behaviourism*.[18] Skinner and his followers have expounded a view that dominated psychology until the 1980s. Although jargon-ridden, the approach is very simple (some say, simplistic): any act is at bottom a response to stimuli arising externally, in the organism's environment, or internally, in the organism's body. Responses may be instinctive, arbitrary, or learned. Radical behaviourists attribute learning to the pattern of rewards and punishments generated by the organism's environment. According to Skinner, a principal mechanism involved in organisms' adaptation to their changing environments is *operant conditioning* (also called instrumental conditioning). Operant conditioning is based on the idea that any operation on one's environment which is consistently followed with a desirable event (e.g., getting food) is likely to be repeated, and is thus *reinforced*. An action that is consistently associated with an undesirable event (e.g., feeling pain) is not likely to be repeated, and is thus *extinguished*. Behaviour patterns can be modified in infinite ways as the rewards and punishments provided by the environment, and the organism's own biological needs (internal stimuli), change.

Skinnerian explanation, deterministic as it is, presupposes that living organisms actively operate on their environments. They are not machines to be activated as drives or needs arise (the traditional psychodynamic notion), but are 'in motion' from the very start and all the time. Being overtly inactive, e.g., freezing in the face of danger, is also 'doing something' about a situation. In laboratory experiments, an accidental or random act is reinforced by its consequences (which are controlled by the experimenter). A rat, placed in a maze for the first time, finds the correct route to food by trial and error; with experience, the sequence of taking certain turns through the maze becomes associated with reaching food. It is reported in the literature that Skinner trained pigeons to walk in a figure of eight by patiently providing food every time the pigeon happened to step in the 'right' direction. Thus the pigeons developed an absurd ritual, as if they had the superstition that walking in a figure of eight produces food. As the organism's behaviour becomes progressively more attuned to the conditions of the particular environment, it gradually takes on the *appearance* of being goal-directed – but, according to behaviourists, it is merely shaped by past environmental contingencies, and reflects no real intentionality.

To paraphrase Skinner, *why do pupils behave as they do?* If a child's performance suddenly starts to improve or to deteriorate, most people intuitively enquire about recent changes in the environment (e.g., is there a new teacher?). A behaviourist might add persuasively that the observed change in performance is somehow rewarded in the new circumstances. But, regarding the explanation of human action, the behaviourist framework is unduly restrictive. As illustrated below, ecosystemic thinking may penetrate the parts that behaviourist reasoning cannot reach.

Like the unnatural walk of Skinner's pigeons, the primary school custom of standing in lines at the school playground is not an instinctive thing for children to do. The behaviour is clearly a response to a stimulus, such as the sound of a bell signalling the end of the break, and yet no amount of bell-ringing would reinforce it. To a 'lay' observer or a sociologist, lining up *makes sense* in view of its function in the school's regime (it reflects teachers' beliefs that otherwise pupils might not return to the classrooms in an orderly manner, that lining up ensures their own control over pupils, and that such order and control are necessary) – but this is not a causal explanation of the kind psychologists have sought. Behaviourists, seeking to identify scientifically the causes of behaviour, may point out that the children respond to teachers' instructions. The teachers' utterances are themselves physical events in children's environments. Over time, lining up is reinforced by the reactions of teachers and peers: 'correct' behaviour is rewarded with the avoidance of punishment, even praise, just as the pigeons' steps were rewarded by the experimenter with something that is important to pigeons. The fact that some children seem unaffected by teachers' reactions towards 'incorrect' behaviour simply means that there are stronger reinforcers in their environment; perhaps challenging the teachers is rewarded with status in the peer group.

The fact that behaviour such as pupils' lining up, which is nonverbal and takes place in the physical world, is explainable with an account of what people say to each other does not necessarily contradict the behaviourist approach. Contemporary behaviourists are increasingly interested in *rule-governed behaviour*, a technical term for a 'special case' of contingency-shaped behaviour.[19] In behaviourist jargon, 'rules' mean strictly antecedent verbal events – instructions, comments, or words of advice that people give each other and themselves. Behaviourists might dispute that there is anything essentially different about lining up in response to a teacher's instruction or because of nonverbal antecedents. Without being told, a new pupil may stand in line by following the example of others. According to *social learning theory*,[20] children learn what behaviour brings rewards in particular situations, not only through experiencing the consequences directly (operant conditioning), but also by imitating other people (modelling) and by observing the consequences of others' actions (vicarious reinforcement).

Both rule-governed behaviour and social learning underline the fact that a crucial element in the environment upon which a child operates is *other people*. But there is more to 'social context' than the overt behaviour of other people. Other schools of thought, especially in social psychology and sociology, focus on the world of shared meanings and intentions in which one is *accountable* for one's actions.[21] In lining up in the playground, children 'operate' on other people by creating impressions about themselves: *lining up quietly* means being seen as a 'good pupil' by teachers and peers alike; a rebel might try to avoid this image. If so, the context which explains the child's behaviour is not the immediate environment and the history of the response pattern, but *the situation as perceived by the child.*

Kurt Lewin, whose early work inspired later 'ecologists' such as Bronfenbrenner, argued that isolating causal connections across time (as the behaviourists do) might lead to losing sight of the significance, or function, of an event in its context.[22] Lewin envisaged the person as embedded in a *life space*, a field of subjective meanings which influence behaviour. A classroom situation is comprised of tasks and events, involving objects and other people, *the combination of which* influences a child's action.

What the child is drawn towards or wishes to avoid in the given moment is a subjective matter, determined by the child's anticipations. Any situation is the culmination of many causal influences coming together, but it is a 'system' maintained also by a-causal relations between its elements. A teacher's presence in the classroom does not 'cause' a pupil's presence there, or vice versa; their simultaneous presence, however, maintains the particular teacher–pupil relationship. According to 'ecosystemic' educational psychologists, the classroom relationship is the context in which a pupil's behaviour should be explained.

Ecosystemic thinking involves, first, the recognition of what Lewin called the 'uncertainty of historical conclusions':[23] it is unrealistic to expect to be able to account for all the causal factors that underlie ordinary human behaviour to a satisfactory prediction accuracy. Second, there is Lewin's *principle of contemporaneity*: 'any behaviour or any other change in a psychological field depends only upon the psychological field *at that time*'.[24] The quest for cause and effect thus gives way to a description of the ways in which person-environment systems evolve, and such systems, in turn, are the context in which the person's behaviour makes sense.

Defining the Child's Environment

The ecological reform in psychology represents a dissatisfaction with the reduction of the human being to a cluster of variables, be they behaviours or psychodynamic drives. In education, the ecosystemic metaphor is associated with a 'topdown' explanation, reflecting the belief that social phenomena cannot be duly explained by 'adding up' isolated processes. Instead, the phenomenon is placed at the centre of nested systems, ranging from the immediate context to progressively wider ones: a pupil's behaviour can be explained in the context of the classroom interaction; the classroom interaction can be explained in view of the school ethos; the way a school is run can be explained in the context of the local educational authority or the society it serves; and so on. When endeavouring to explain behaviour by looking at its school or classroom context, which is the environment in question?

Biology oriented, 'orthodox' ecological frameworks, such as developed by Barker (see Chapter 2)[25] and by Gibson (see Chapter 3),[26] centre on what people do in ordinary places – not on what they say they do, or why they think they do it. Workers in these frameworks refer to the human organism as embedded in a physical environment, and therefore focus on overt behaviour, not on people's accounts. Typically, observational and experimental methods used in the study of animal behaviour (ethology) are used. It may be observed, for instance, that pupils talk among themselves more often when seated around tables, and less when seated at desks arranged in rows. Quantitative observations of verbal behaviour potentially help classroom management: teachers wishing to minimize chatting should arrange the classroom in rows; teachers wishing to encourage collaborative learning should use tables. What children talk about is irrelevant in this frame of reference.

In contrast, frameworks derived from symbolic interactionist and phenomenological traditions in sociology and social psychology describe a universe populated with the contents of people's talk. Where people happen to be when they talk is irrelevant in this frame of reference. The person is seen as a social agent, whose (verbal or symbolic) actions are explained by relating them to the actions of other people. Conversations are analysed qualitatively, using the methodology of hermeneutics (originally used in the study of biblical texts). This approach was implemented by school ethnographers such as Sarah Delamont[27] and Bronwyn Davies,[28] whose studies provide key primary sources for issues discussed in Chapters 5 and 6.

In either perspective, the person is construed as an element in a larger system whose functioning can be understood by working out the person's relations to other people, objects, or events which together constitute that system. It is customary, however, to separate physical and social systems, and by implication to describe the human as either an organism or a social agent.

On the one side, there is the organism's immediate location, which can influence behaviour; on the other, there is the agent's position in a social group, a position that entails moral obligations, rights, and personal powers relative to other people, and thus influences action. On the one side, there is natural reality; on the other, the reality that people construct in their discourse.[29]

The living human does not respond to an environment divided in this way. If the prospect of failing an exam means a great deal to the student as a social agent, the exam situation might engender stress, an organism's response to threat. Noise in the lecture hall is a physical event, affecting the organism's ability to hear, but its significance depends on what hearing the lecture means to the student as a social agent. If the person is whole, so is the subjective environment.

Instead of dividing the human environment into physical versus social phenomena, we may distinguish between the world that exists independently of the person, and the world as it *exists for the person*. On the one side, there is the world of material objects, other people, external events and, more abstractly, linguistic and cultural frames of reference. On the other, there are 'psychologically critical facts of the environment, such as the friendliness or unfriendliness of a certain adult, [which] may have fundamental significance for the child's life-space without the child's having a clear intellectual appreciation of the fact'.[30]

Furthermore, personal significance can be considered on two time scales. Classroom conduct is sometimes explained best in view of pupils' perceptions of the immediate situation; academic effort is sometimes explained best in view of learners' beliefs about the relevance of education for their present and future lives: 'Environment is understood psychologically sometimes to mean the *momentary* situation of the child, at other times to mean the *milieu*, in the sense of the chief characteristics of the permanent situation.'[31]

As will be seen throughout the book, we may choose to focus on either the physical or the social milieu of the school. Either way, we may choose to describe objectively the phenomena with which the child comes in contact, or to analyse the surroundings in terms of their subjective significance to the child. Furthermore, we may look at the immediate situation or at the child's general circumstances. The environment in question may ultimately depend on what is being asked.

The Scope and Organization of the Book

An exhaustive review of the many relevant fields is hardly possible to achieve in one book. The reader may find that certain important issues, crucial to the ecology of educational settings, are summarily discussed or mentioned only in passing; namely, bullying, the 'hidden curriculum' (stereotypic messages about gender, race, etc., communicated to pupils), and similar topics. My understatement of those issues in this book is justifiable in view of the availability of excellent reviews, some very recent (as mentioned in due course). A body of literature that is less accessible to readers specializing in education comprises topics that usually come under the scope of environmental psychology, human performance or ergonomics, and health psychology. This book is meant to redress the balance, albeit in a small way. It is my contention that the 'social climate' of classrooms or schools must be understood in relation to the physical setting and biological mediators of behaviour.

Ecosystemic theorists explore a view of the individual or the group as intricately embedded in a complex environment. This holistic conception does not mean that discrete domains cannot be distinguished and investigated separately, up to a point. A child's environment at school can be envisaged as many-layered, ranging from aspects of the physical world, structured events and interpersonal interactions prescribed by general educational goals, all of which exist independently of the child, to the subjective or phenomenological environment, *the school as experienced by the child.*

Chapter 2 looks at relations between actual place and behaviour. The focus is on the spatial environment of schools and classrooms. The endeavour to describe 'behaviour in places' is epitomized in behaviour setting theory, the kernel of Barker's ecological psychology, which is evaluated in that chapter. Chapter 3 looks at the 'organism-environment fit' as applied to the child–school interface. The effects of noise, temperature and light are discussed with particular attention to stress. Learning, too, is essentially organisms' adaptation to their environments according to Skinner and Piaget, whose views are compared. Gibson's and Lewin's theories explain behaviour (or perception) by considering the external world as it exists for the individual.

Moving to the group level of analysis, Chapter 4 considers relations between the organizational environment and pupil performance, with a particular reference to the use of survey methods to probe the school as perceived by pupils. Moos' social-ecological model provides a relevant conceptual framework.

Chapter 5 begins the discussion of the social environment with a focus on teacher-pupil relationships. Social-psychological research into the effects of teachers' attitudes and expectations is reviewed. Looking at classroom communication, the sociological ideas of roles and positioning are considered, and related to research on 'child-centred' practices. The idea of the classroom group as a social system is encapsulated in the ecosystemic approach to behaviour problems. Chapter 6 continues the discussion of the social environment with a look at peer relationships. A main theme is the conflation between the environment children create for each other, on the one hand, and the adult-directed environment structured by the school, on the other. Child–child relationships are profoundly important for social-affective and intellectual development.

Chapter 7 complements some of the themes raised in the previous chapters with a focus on the 'child' side of the interface. Bronfenbrenner's ecological model provides a developmental frame of reference. Kelly's personal constructs theory offers a way to explore the private worlds of children. Chapter 8 concludes the review with a look at ways in which problems of adjustment have been approached, especially in British special education. Finally, Chapter 9 outlines general conclusions regarding research and theorizing about the child–school interface.

Notes and References

1 Dewey, J. *The School and Society*, rev. edn. Chicago: University of Chicago Press, 1943, p. 61.
2 Bronfenbrenner, U. *The Ecology of Human Development*. Cambridge, MA: Harvard University Press, 1979, p. 19.
3 Gibbs, J. C. 'The meaning of ecologically oriented inquiry in contemporary psychology'. *American Psychologist*, **34**, 1979, p. 127.

4 Cullingford, C. *The Inner World of the School.* London: Cassell, 1991.

5 Bronfenbrenner, U., 1979, op. cit.

6 Gibson, J. J. *The Ecological Approach to Visual Perception.* Boston: Houghton-Mifflin, 1979.

7 Eggleston, J. *The Ecology of the School.* London: Methuen, 1977.

8 Moos, R. H. *Evaluating Educational Environments.* San Francisco: Jossey-Bass, 1979.

9 Upton, G. and Cooper, P. 'A new perspective on behaviour problems in schools: the ecosystemic approach'. *Maladjustment and Therapeutic Education,* **8**, 3–18, 1990.

10 Mortimore, P., Sammons, P., Stoll, L., Lewis, D. and Ecob, R. *School Matters: The Junior Years.* Somerset: Open Books, 1988, p. 261.

11 Rutter, M., Maughan, B., Mortimore, P. and Ouston, J. *Fifteen Thousand Hours: Secondary Schools and Their Effects on Children.* London: Open Books, 1979.

12 *You* magazine, *The Mail on Sunday,* 5 November, 1992.

13 Bronfenbrenner, U., 1979, op. cit., p. 16.

14 Ibid., pp. 17–18.

15 Doise, W. and Mackie, D. 'On the social nature of cognition'. In Forgas, J. P. (ed.), *Social Cognition: Perspectives on Everyday Understanding.* London: Academic Press, 1981, p. 53.

16 Hadfield, J. A. *Childhood and Adolescence.* Harmondsworth: Penguin, 1962, p. 55; his italics.

17 Loeber, R. and Dishion, T. J. 'Boys who fight at home and school: family conditions influencing cross-setting consistency'. *Journal of Consulting and Clinical Psychology,* **52**, 759–768, 1984.

18 Skinner, B. F. *About Behaviourism.* Harmondsworth: Penguin, 1974.

19 See contributions in Hayes, S. C. (ed.). *Rule-governed Behaviour: Cognition, Contingencies and Instrumental Control.* New York: Plenum Press, 1989.

20 E.g., Bandura, A. *Social Learning Theory.* Englewood Cliffs, NJ: Prentice-Hall, 1977.

21 Cf. Harré, R. *Personal Being: A Theory for Individual Psychology.* Oxford: Blackwell, 1983; Shotter, J. *Social Accountability and Selfhood.* Oxford: Blackwell, 1984.

22 Lewin, K. *A Dynamic Theory of Personality: Selected Papers.* New York: McGraw-Hill, 1935.

23 Lewin, K. 'Defining the "field at a given time"'. *Psychological Review,* **50**, 292–310, 1943.

24 Ibid., p. 294; his italics.
25 Barker, R. G. *Ecological Psychology: Concepts and Methods for Studying the Environment of Human Behaviour.* Stanford, CA: Stanford University Press, 1968.
26 Gibson, J. J. *The Ecological Approach to Visual Perception.* Boston: Houghton-Mifflin, 1979.
27 Delamont, S. *Interaction in the Classroom,* 2nd edn. London: Methuen, 1983; Delamont, S. *Sex Roles and the School.* London: Methuen, 1980.
28 Davies, B. *Life in the Classroom and Playground: the Accounts of Primary School Children.* London: Routledge and Kegan Paul, 1982.
29 Harré, R., 1983, op. cit.
30 Lewin, K., 1935, op. cit., p. 74.
31 Ibid., pp. 71–77; his italics.

CHAPTER 2

The Behaviour Setting

Over a decade ago, Carol Weinstein attributed the then-increasing interest in the interplay between schools' physical environments and educational outcomes to two separate movements: the open-plan movement in primary education; and, among psychologists, a growing concern with person-environment relationships, a concern that precipitated the emergence of environmental psychology.[1] Since the time of Weinstein's review, questions about the effects of schools' spatial environments subsided in both education and environmental psychology. In education, researchers' interest decreased partly because the open-plan school ceased to be a 'burning issue'. Results of research into open-plan schools are still a source of insight into school ecologies, but arguments for or against open plan are no longer topical. Separately, the current ebb of interest in the physical environment of the school, open plan or not, might imply that pertinent questions about the person-environment relationship have been answered. Yet several issues remain undecided.

Educational research is typically driven by specific problems and subserves educational policy. Does the layout of college buildings influence students' socialization? Does the seating arrangement determine students' participation in lessons? These and similar questions have been addressed in numerous studies using a variety of methods to document the variability of behaviour, attainment, or other psychological constructs (IQ, personality type, etc.), across educational settings differing in some spatial factors. The effects of the spatial environment on learning, conduct or development can be discovered by comparing how children fare in different environments. If, among pupils whose ability and background are similar to start with, attainment rates differ after exposure to dissimilar educational environments, we can be reasonably confident that attainment is somehow dependent on the environment. But how? Further research would be necessary to discover the underlying causal mechanisms.

For some practical purposes, it may suffice to demonstrate relations between types of environment and rates or quality of pupil performance. Evidence that certain features of the environment are consistently associated with satisfactory attainment or conduct, *irrespective of individuals' tendencies,* can help school planners, administrators and staff to structure the school environment in ways that would foster good study habits and discipline in the majority of pupils. Evidence that disruptive behaviour or low attainment are more likely to occur in certain school environments will likewise help to improve educational provision. In psychology, however, the empirical inquiry typically subserves theories about human functioning. The initial phase in basic research concerns discovery, a systematic description of what people do where and when, but the ultimate aim is the explanation, *why?*

This chapter reviews research on school spatial environments, and discusses one endeavour to conceptualize behaviour patterns as place-related phenomena, namely, behaviour setting theory.

Given Spaces

There are obvious relationships between school architecture and the activities that take place within its walls. The size and shape of classrooms, school halls, corridors and playgrounds can facilitate or inhibit the scope of activities. The layout of the premises can influence the flow of routines. For example, a spare room can be turned into a woodwork workshop. If the hall is too small, whole-school assemblies cannot be held. An extended layout might mean that lesson time is wasted getting from place to place.

It is less obvious, however, that there should be a relationship between architecture and educational outcomes or personal development. Wise management can compensate for design drawbacks; or, conversely, the potential of available space might not be realized by the staff. Teachers' management of the spatial environment makes the task of separating the effects of space availability from the effects of space use difficult – but not impossible. If the frequency of a certain activity co-varies with the size of a classroom (for instance), despite identical management on the teachers' part, we may surmise that the amount of space influences the behaviour in question.

Spatial dimensions and fixed features of educational settings are designed with foreknowledge of educators' requirements, and educators' requirements are shaped by beliefs about the kinds of activities necessary for effective teaching and management. But the extent to which given spaces actually meet educators' requirements sometimes depends on activities that are inadvertently elicited by certain types of built environments.

AMOUNT OF SPACE

Smith and Connolly investigated the ecology of the preschool by setting up experimental playgroups.[2] Their research project comprised several separate investigations and took place during three consecutive school years in the early 1970s. The playgroups, located variously in two church halls and a scout hut in Sheffield, were ordinary in most respects, but for the strict selection of children's age, gender and socioeconomic background, and the systematic variations introduced by the researchers during the course of the project. Smith and Connolly manipulated available floor space, amount and kind of play equipment, staff:child ratio, and group size. In this way, they could separate the effects of floor space on the children's play and social behaviour from the effects of other resources or the sociometric character of particular groups.

The investigation into the effects of floor-space availability involved the comparison of two playgroups, identical in size and composition, which used the same church hall. The amount of space in the hall was manipulated by means of movable tall screens and curtains of a fairly uniform appearance, to provide three conditions: 25 square feet, 50 square feet, and 75 square feet per child. In conjunction with the three space conditions, Smith and Connolly varied the amount of play equipment by duplicating or triplicating a basic set of toys and apparatus. In this way, they created nine environments (3 'space' × 3 'toys' conditions), presented in sequence to each of the two groups. Children's companion choices, activity choices and behaviours were observed.

The amount of floor space consistently affected the level and kind of gross motor activity. The children utilized the larger space with increased running, chasing and fleeing, and 'unusual' uses of apparatus, such as spinning the rocking-boats around or making 'chair-trains'. When space was limited, there was a decrease in free motor activity, but an increase in vigorous use of the climbing frame. The change in activity preference associated with the spatial variations, however, was not accompanied with changes in the overall level of social contacts and choice of companions, nor in the amount of aggressive behaviour. Although more visual and physical contact among children were observed when space was limited, the increase was mainly in incidental contact – for example, a child brushing against another in passing, as distinguished from holding hands. Neither group play nor parallel play increased as a result of limited space; smiling, holding hands or object exchange did not increase. A 'ceiling' effect – i.e., a limit to the extent to which spatial conditions affect behaviour against children's motivation to pursue a certain activity – can be glimpsed in the children's use of the tricycle. Smith and Connolly report that the tricycle was 'the most popular item of the play equipment, being constantly in demand and almost invariably occupied'.[3] There was no decrease in the use of the tricycle when space was limited, despite the fact that the riders had to negotiate carefully around tables and apparatus, and had less freedom for rapid movement.

In all, these findings show a direct relationship between spatial environment and physical activities, on the one hand, and the absence of relationship between space availability and social interaction, on the other. Smith and Connolly related floor-space availability to *spatial density*, which they equated with crowding. Other research, especially with animals, had shown that crowding is associated with increased aggressive behaviour. Although aggressive behaviour in the playgroups did increase when less toys were available, it was not related to spatial limits *per se*: the children competed for the toys.

Stokols pointed out a certain confusion between 'crowding' and 'spatial density',[4] terms that are frequently used interchangeably: density is a physical condition involving spatial limitation, whereas crowding is an experiential state 'in which the restrictive aspects of limited space are perceived by the individuals exposed to them'.[5] As Stokols proposed, for spatial density to become salient and unpleasant enough to engender an experience of crowding, several other factors must be present. Social interference or competition with others heightens the salience of spatial constraints, as does the restriction of movement when engaging in tasks requiring the co-ordination of one's activity with those of others. Competitive feelings may be aroused if the presence of others is perceived as threatening and intrusive. In sum, crowding 'appears to rise through the juxtaposition of density with certain social and personal circumstances which sensitise the individual to the potential constraints of limited space'.[6]

Although pupils might experience crowding at school, their experience could have more to do with their perceptions of the school environment, their own goals and relations to other people, than with the amount of space. The children in Smith and Connolly's playgroups might have become acutely aware of spatial limitations when they had to steer the tricycle carefully around tables and apparatus. At the tables or apparatus, preschool children might become aware of others pushing in to use the same facility.

Regarding an objective evaluation of space availability, then, the fundamental criterion is the *space requirements* of educational activities. The play activities that a preschool aims to provide for obviously have different space requirements than do the activities necessary for the education of older children or adults.

COHESIVE V. ISOLATED LAYOUTS AND PLAYGROUNDS

The subtle influence of school layout on behaviour was noted in a 1968 report prepared for the US government by Myrick and Marx.[7] They studied two schools housed in one or two buildings, a layout which they labelled *cohesive*, and one school housed in several separate buildings, a layout which they labelled *isolated*:

> The cohesive layout facilitated the formation of larger student groups, which promoted student conversations that were less in keeping with the goals of the school administration . . . An isolated design discourages interaction because of its extended layout, lengthy corridors, and alternate routes for getting from one place to another.[8]

The layout evidently regulated the flow of students and affected the kind of social contact that took place at school, but wider or lasting effects on socialization are not self-evident.

Does increased social contact, facilitated by the cohesive design, extend into enduring friendships outside school? Is there a greater ethnic integration in the population of 'cohesive' schools than in the population of 'isolated' schools? If mingling freely with a large number of peers can be shown to have developmental or social benefits, a cohesive school design may be recommended – but the desirability of being part of a crowd, as opposed to being a member of a small social group, is debatable. In a study reviewed in detail in Chapter 4, Barker and Gump discovered that junior students in small schools experienced more often satisfactions related to personal improvement, to challenge and action, to close co-operation with peers and to 'being important', than did their counterparts in large schools.[9]

The preferability of a structured 'habitat' over featureless open spaces is best illustrated with a look at school playgrounds. While open-plan school interiors are hardly left empty, and children's activities there are structured under teacher guidance, school playgrounds seldom involve more than their basic spatial features, and thus allow observations of children's spontaneous interactions with the spatial environment. Unlike the cohesive school layout, a cohesive playground, being a single open area, is perhaps in keeping with administrative goals: the supervision of large numbers of pupils is easier or requires less staff than when pupils are dispersed in several areas around the building (i.e., in an isolated playground design).

However, it is naive to assume that a shared area must lead to social integration. The Opies, who applied an anthropological framework to observations of British schoolchildren in the 1950s and 1960s, noticed that children's play in school playgrounds is markedly more aggressive than when the children are in the street or 'wild places'.[10]

Some drawbacks of cohesive playgrounds were made obvious to me during regular visits to junior schools in Cardiff. Suffice it to compare the playgrounds of two schools. School A is an old-fashioned, austere building with several levels and wings, maze-like corridors and numerous stairwells. The building is surrounded by asphalt playgrounds, a patch of grass and some trees. This means that during breaks, groups can disperse around the building and play in relative seclusion. In School B, a newer building, most classes, the hall and the offices are housed in a U-shaped building; a few classes and the canteen are located in another building, situated across the 'top' of the U. Visually, School B's playground is cut off from the surrounding streets. In the U-shaped building, most corridors run along the inside of the U, so windows overlook, and doors open to, an asphalt yard. The school is thus turned inwards. During lessons, teachers and children take short-cuts across the playground area to get to different parts of the building. Organized activities in the playground can be observed by anyone passing in the corridors. During breaks, most children are out there. Typically, several groups carry out separate, though spatially interwoven, play activities. Visitors to the school negotiate what seems like a whirlpool of boisterous children. Mishaps and conflicts are inevitable. During the couple of weeks I visited School B, children with scratched knees, fight instigators and their victims regularly lined up outside the head's office, often in numbers exceeding those I saw in any other school. Some children occasionally sneaked in 'for no reason', and would be ordered back out to the playground, which offered no privacy, and little opportunity for quiet pursuits.

Clearly, the main problem was the playground's inadequate

size. However, its lack of 'landscape', too, limited the opportunities for play and social interaction. This impression was reinforced by children's comments. In the context of my research at the time, 27 children in School A and 16 children in School B were asked to name something that they liked to do in the playground. In both schools (and two others), the question elicited predominantly mentions of group activities ('play football', 'talk to my friends'), and fewer mentions of solitary or relatively withdrawn activities (e.g., 'eat my crisps', 'play on my own', 'drawing'). Social orientations or play dispositions, as indicated by the frequency of group-activities versus withdrawn-activities preferences, did not differ significantly among children attending Schools A and B.

The same responses can be categorized, alternatively, in terms of their *space requirements*: team sports and certain games which require considerable space, i.e., 'field' activities, on the one side, and pursuits that do not require much space (whether social or solitary), i.e., 'corner' activities, on the other. In School B, the school with the cohesive playground, only one boy mentioned a 'corner' activity ('eat my crisps'); his fifteen schoolmates mentioned 'field' activities (mostly, football). In School A, thirteen children mentioned 'corner' activities, and the other fourteen children mentioned 'field' activities. The distribution of 'field' v. 'corner' activities preferences across the two schools is statistically significant, a result suggesting that the difference in the response pattern was due to the fact that these children attended different schools.

Other data collected at the time indicate that the children who attended School A were also less concerned with bullying than their counterparts in School B and two other schools. It may be surmised that children had an altogether happier time – greater play diversity and less aggravation – in the isolated playground of School A, than did children in the cohesive playground of School B. But caution is necessary in drawing conclusions about the role of the spatial environment, especially since my study was not designed to test hypotheses about a relationship between playground features and play-time activities (the study essentially looked at children's perceptions of school in general). Factors other than playground layout could account for the difference. A better school ethos could well 'spill over' to the children's experiences in the playground.

A further difference is worth noting here. Several School A pupils mentioned a preferred play *location* ('play on the grass/ in the trees'). In School B, the children did not have such playground features to relate to. The fact that grass and trees are elements of the living environment could be incidental to the children's attraction to those areas. In a third school which participated in the same study, the 'playground' question elicited several mentions of playing 'on the yellow lines', referring to game markings. The children spontaneously utilized the spatial demarcation for their own games (e.g., touch).

The eagerness with which children relate their play activities to environmental features was noted by Robin Moore, a professional city-planner, who investigated children's everyday urban surroundings by asking 9–10-year-old children in London, Stevenage and Stoke-on-Trent to take him around their favourite places.[11] Moore discovered that school grounds, which are typically expanses of mown grass, were hardly used by children (except for team sports), and did not feature in the children's drawings and interviews. Moore attributes the children's lack of interest to the large size and the monotonous appearance of those areas. Only the grounds of a new primary school were used by children in their free time: the children were attracted to peripheral features, such as ditches and mounds. Throughout his guided tour of childhood's domain, Moore noticed children's attraction to varied topography and visual characteristics of the environment, i.e., 'rough' ground.

In contrast to the 'rough' ground favoured by children,

> Most school playgrounds are bleak sites – empty spaces between buildings and perimeter walls which do not invite or encourage creative play and which lower the spirits until filled with the noise and bustle of children released from the classroom.[12]

Elinor Kelly and other researchers are currently taking a close look at the breaktime 'bustle': those bleak sites are arenas not only for games and ritual, a world rich in folklore, but also, sadly, for bullying and harassment – an issue discussed in more detail in Chapter 6.

Design mistakes are difficult to rectify. Even if School B were to be rebuilt, its site (situated on a street corner) is restrictive. On a site that size, placing the building more or less centrally might create isolated playground areas that are too narrow for games and landscaping. Nevertheless, an imaginative architect can overcome such constraints; for instance, the classrooms can be lifted off ground level on columns, thus creating a sheltered hard-surfaced play area and leaving the surrounding unsheltered areas free for landscaping. The importance of playground landscapes must first be acknowledged.

Awareness is rising: Blatchford reviews ways in which schools have tried to make their playgrounds more interesting and also used as resources for learning.[13] Lucas describes a charity project, Learning Through Landscape, launched in the late 1980s in Britain, which aims to promote widespread improvements to the quality of school grounds.[14]

Installing play equipment and involving children in gardening are not new ideas in the nursery and infants school sector; teachers of young children are well aware of the developmental importance of play. As children grow older, however, their play seems to be regarded as leisure, to be tolerated rather than provided for by the school. It is perhaps assumed that older children and adolescents fulfil their recreation and social needs elsewhere. Most do. Some do so instead of attending school.

INTERIOR ENCLOSURES

Addressing architects, Sommer summed up a dismal picture of prison-like American schools: 'high schools provide few places for students to linger, so they congregate in the corridors, outside the locker rooms, or in the stairwells, seeking refuge from crowd pressures and impersonal authority'.[15] Notwithstanding appearances, the lack of freedom implied by Sommer's description could be a matter of opinion. In my children's comprehensive school in South Wales, which is hardly 'prison-like', pupils are not allowed to linger freely in the corridors during breaks; social interaction must take place in the playground or (in bad weather) in the classroom. Yet corridors offer different opportunities than do playgrounds or classrooms. The various stretches, corners and alcoves can accommodate quiet alternatives to outdoors playtime pursuits and relative privacy (though they may raise problems of supervision).

Particular activities require not only a certain amount of space, but also a certain topography or layout. Hide and seek cannot be played on a football pitch. Spatial features do not determine children's play or social preferences, but can lead to frustration, boredom and discontent – or to richer childhood experience and a happier time at school.

Quite aside from children's happiness, school enclosures might affect educational activities. A need to know more about the impact of schools' physical environments on learning was perceived following the popularity of open-plan (open-space) design. The architectural innovation lies in the relative lack of interior enclosures:

> Traditional school construction provides enclosed, even sealed, spaces for each class. A typical arrangement provides classrooms along each side of a corridor. The term *egg-carton schools* often labels this spatial pattern. Open schools, on the other hand, have larger interior spaces without walls and corridors.[16]

In Britain, the number of open-plan schools rose steadily from the middle 1960s and through the 1970s (but declined in the 1980s). By 1976, about 10 per cent of all primary schools were open plan, and a new school of conventional design was a rarity.[17]

The open-plan school was meant to facilitate modern teaching practices, based on the premise that children learn best through self-organized exploration. The teaching practices associated with open education, such as flexible groupings and individualized instruction, were deemed best served by physical openness. Critics felt that this was primarily a response to economic pressures: building schools without interior walls cuts down construction costs considerably. Either way, it was necessary to evaluate the effectiveness of open-plan design, and this necessity generated numerous comparisons of outcomes in open-plan versus conventional schools.

Canter and Donald note in their review of British research that most comparisons of outcomes in open plan vs. conventional schools failed to find significant differences in IQ gains, attainment, personality factors, friendship patterns or numbers of social isolates.[18] They attribute this failure to want of information about the extent to which teachers implemented or disregarded the ethos of open education, and conclude that teachers' philosophy was a primary factor. The fact that a school is housed in an open-plan building does not mean that its staff practises open education. Bennett *et al.*, in an extensive study into open-plan schools, found that 'many more teachers claim to be working independently, as they would in conventional classrooms, than cooperatively, irrespective of the age of their pupils'.[19]

Teachers may override the open-plan design to suit their own pedagogic and management purposes, and according to their perception of opportunities in the available space. In contrast with the vision of a free flow of children, imagined by advocates of open-plan design, Cooper observed children in open-plan schools to be most frequently immobile, seated at desks or tables, or standing still, their behaviour dominated by only a few activities which occurred with any great frequency.[20] Children's contacts during lesson periods were most consistently with inanimate teaching resources than with people, and their spatial locations were limited to the class-base for most of the school day. The behaviour patterns in the open-plan settings visited by Cooper were hardly distinguishable from those in conventional classrooms.

In open-plan schools, teachers might have adhered to conventional management basically because of practicality, not so much out of habit or teaching philosophy. The ecology of the open-plan setting turned out to be counter-productive. Noise and distraction lowered pupils' performance of educational tasks. The importance of knowledge about how environmental variables interact with pupil behaviour and with educational goals cannot be stressed enough.

Use of Classroom Space

The 'mismatch' between spatial opportunities and the use to which spaces are put is widely noted. Like many researchers who compared different types of classrooms, Rolfe[21] found that most teachers in small classrooms complained that their rooms were 'too crowded, noisy, cramped, inflexible, and unsuitable for a variety of activities', whereas teachers in larger (and newer) classrooms expressed satisfaction with the class environment. And yet Rolfe 'was quite discouraged by the sameness': the pattern of teaching or the range of activities did not seem to be affected by the size of the room, the type of furniture (fixed-row seating or movable chairs), or the amount of storage space.[22]

How teachers organize their classrooms' environment depends on what they want to achieve. In a recent handbook for primary school teachers, Pollard and Tann assert: 'Space in a classroom is always limited; yet what space there is must be utilised in such a way that the wide-ranging activities which form essential elements of the primary-school curriculum can occur without major disruptions.'[23] This may say more about our beliefs concerning primary education than about the reality of our classrooms: it reveals that we consider wide-ranging activities to be essential. In reality most of these activities are accommodated in one room and supervised by one teacher. This calls for a high degree of organization, usually on the teacher's part: separate activities must be co-ordinated so that individuals or small groups can proceed with their tasks without interference. The degree to which individuals' activities require co-ordination with those of other occupants of a limited area heightens the experience of crowding, irrespective of the physical openness of the room or the arrangement of activity centres.[24] Not surprisingly, most teachers feel that the given space is inadequate for the use to which they must put it.

Teachers' actual use of space in open-plan schools may

explain why conclusive evidence for psychological correlates of school design was not forthcoming, as seen in the previous section. Teachers' inclination to reorganize the setting to suit their teaching approach is by no means limited to open-plan settings. Sommer, testing a hypothesis about seating location and participation in college settings, allocated two psychology seminars to a laboratory room.[25] As the laboratory tables could not be moved, the room seemed an excellent example of a straight row arrangement, and promised an interesting comparison with seminar-style arrangements. However, Sommer admits:

> We still had to reckon with the ingenuity of our [teaching assistants], one of whom typically sat at the front of the instructor's desk rather than behind it and the other who encouraged her students to bring their stools up to the front bench in a vain attempt to approximate a semi-circular arrangement.[26]

It is inherent in teachers' professional commitment that they should organize their classrooms as they believe best serves the learning process. Observations confirming that this is the case are less pertinent here than observations of relationships between pupil behaviour, classroom arrangements, and educational goals. Again, it is difficult to separate the effects of space use from those of teaching methods, teachers' skills, and the social atmosphere of particular classes. Nevertheless, a relatively clear view of space-use effects may be possible in college lectures and seminars, since in those settings the teaching is based on a very narrow range of activities. Do different seating arrangements affect communication between teacher and students?

SEATING ARRANGEMENTS

A classroom is first of all a place for learning, and its physical organization reflects beliefs about the learning process. Getzels considered the divergent expectations about the learner that are implied in different arrangements of classroom furniture.[27] The traditional classroom with chairs bolted to the floor in straight rows, and the teacher's desk at the front, discloses a notion of the learner as an empty organism, who must be taught. A classroom with movable chairs, and in which the teacher's desk is situated in a corner, conveys an image of an active organism, who collaborates in the learning process. The classroom without a teacher's desk, in which desks are trapezoid so they can form a circle when placed adjacently, suggests a social organism, who learns from peers. Finally, the open classroom, comprising several activity and resource centres, reflects an idea of a stimulus-seeking organism, who learns by exploration. Classroom layout is thus shaped by prior assumptions or a teaching philosophy – but does it affect actual learning?

Classroom seating has attracted more attention than any other aspect of the classroom environment, although the body of research is by no means extensive. Most studies refer to traditional lecture-style classes, with row-and-column seat arrangements. Often, college or university settings were preferred on grounds that in primary and secondary schools, teachers 'use nonrandom seating for disciplinary, interpersonal or instructional purposes',[28] a fact that undermines the investigation of an interaction between individuals' attitudes, motivation, or personality factors and their seating selection, participation and attainment.

When students are free to select their seats, a relationship between attitudes and location seems obvious: 'In the front row is a plentiful sprinkling of over-dependent types, mixed perhaps with a number of extraordinarily zealous students. In the back row are persons in rebellion . . .'.[29] Walberg found that high school students who placed a high positive value on learning said that they preferred a front seat; students who revealed a high need for affiliation and sensitivity to criticism liked to sit near friends; those who preferred to be at the back of the room or to be near the windows had negative attitudes towards learning and their own ability.[30] Similarly, Becker et al. asked college students from three classes who met in the same room to indicate their typical seat, current course grade and overall grade point average.[31] They found that course grade (but not the overall average) decreased as physical distance from the teacher, towards the rear and the sides, increased. These findings support anecdotal evidence that 'classroom space can be divided into zones containing people who behave differently',[32] and also point to the way that people tacitly equate physical distance with personal or social remoteness. Haber, for instance, noticed that blacks and Hispanics in predominantly white colleges chose marginal seats.[33]

The self-selection hypothesis states that keener and brighter students (who are therefore more likely to participate in lessons and get better marks) choose to sit near the teacher. Classroom observations, as well as students' self-reports, have repeatedly shown that in row-and-column arrangements, occupants of front centre seats participate more and obtain higher grades than do occupants of side and back seats. Wulf demonstrated that students who chose to sit in front centre seats participated more than those who chose to sit in peripheral seats; when students were allocated seats, there was no relationship between location and participation.[34]

The evidence that students who prefer different zones display divergent attitudes or personalities suggests that the seating position in itself does not determine participation or attainment. Nevertheless, as Gump points out, 'One may assume that the seat position does have qualities, independent qualities, that attract persons with particular motives.'[35] If that is so, then the seating location might influence attainment after all – possibly by making it easier or more difficult for students to pay attention and get involved in the lesson. The idea that participation and attention (and, consequently, attainment) may be determined by the seating location is called the environmental hypothesis. There is a growing body of evidence in favour of the environmental hypothesis. Stires, for example, compared two psychology classes taught by the same team of instructors.[36] In one class, students chose permanent seats on the second day of the course, whereas in the other class, students were assigned seats alphabetically. Stires found strong location effects in both choice and no-choice conditions: seating location seemed to affect attendance, grades, attitudes towards the course, and even a personality test administered mid-term. Only one measure, extra credit, seemed related to choice of seating alone.

ACTION ZONES

About thirty years ago, Robert Sommer began to explore the idea that certain seating locations may have different qualities, due to the interaction of physical and social-behavioural factors.[37] In the first study of its kind, he investigated participation patterns among undergraduates in six discussion groups, led by two teaching assistants. Four of the groups alternated between three rooms. One seminar room contained a horseshoe arrangement of tables and chairs and additional chairs placed along the walls. In another seminar room, the tables were arranged to form a hollow square, and students sat on all four sides, as well as on chairs along the walls. The third room was the laboratory mentioned earlier, chosen because its straight-rows arrangement of high tables provided a contrast with the usual seminar rooms. The other two groups met in conventional small classrooms with three or four rows of portable chairs. One of those rooms had 'starkly modern décor but no windows',[38] whereas the other had a wall composed almost entirely of windows. In each class, an observer sat inconspicuously at the rear of the room and recorded student participation on a prepared seating chart.

In all room conditions and groups, the average number of voluntary statements per person was higher in the middle seats than in the side seats. In the seminar rooms, students sitting directly opposite the teaching assistant participated more than those sitting at the side tables. Students sitting away from the tables participated less than those sitting at the tables. Sommer attributed this effect to eye contact between students and the teaching assistant. In the laboratory, students in the front row participated the most; but students around the walls participated more than those in rows other than the first. As Sommer pointed out, this was consistent with the eye-contact hypothesis, as only occupants of the front row and the sides had a clear view of the teaching assistant.

Sommer noted that the choice of seats was not random. As already mentioned, later studies would bear out a connection between personality variables and seat selection. But Sommer related individuals' preference also to the actual conditions in the room. For example, in the laboratory, the noise and

35

inconveniently high tables meant that the choice seats were at the front; latecomers were relegated to the rear. In contrast, in the conventional classrooms, students tended to avoid the front rows, perhaps because the rooms were very small, and seating in the front would place the students too near the teaching assistant; most latecomers ended up in the front. In those rooms, although students in the front seats spoke more times than others, the difference was not statistically significant. Summarizing the same study elsewhere, Sommer concluded:

> When the desirable seats are in front, increased participation results because the greater stimulus value of the instructor reaches the most interested students. When the favourable seats are in the middle or rear, the increased expressive value of the instructor for students in front will tend to cancel out the fact that the most interested students are in other rows, and there will be no clear relationship between row and participation.[39]

At least two implications are relevant here. One is that individuals' motivation, interest in the particular course, confidence and similar variables are not sufficient conditions for seat selection and participation. Rather, personal inclinations interact with the individuals' evaluation of the opportunities in the particular environment. The other point is that although the initial selection of seats, at least by early comers, may be largely determined by personal factors, once the lesson is in progress, environmental factors (notably, the physical proximity between teacher and pupil) become prominent.

In the traditional seating arrangement, the front centre seems to be the *action zone*, where teacher–pupil interaction is concentrated. The term action zone was coined by Adams and Biddle,[40] who videotaped 32 classes, taught by 16 teachers, in primary and secondary settings. Their observations concur with Sommer's: most verbal interaction took place in the front centre, and in a line directly up the centre. Other studies have substantiated Adams and Biddle's findings, although the precise location of the action zone and its degree of advantage for participation have varied.

The variability of action-zone location implies that teachers differ in their inclinations to direct attention to certain parts of the room. Moore and Glynn studied the effects of seating positions on the frequency with which teachers addressed questions to their pupils in two primary school classes in Papua New Guinea.[41] Pupils were seated at individual desks, the overall seating pattern was determined by the teachers: the one class had five rows across the room, whereas in the other class there were five clusters of four to six desks. Prior to the study, the teachers positioned individual pupils on the basis of their experience with the pupils, so as to reduce disruption and maximize the class's attention to lesson activities. As a baseline measure, the researchers identified areas, in each classroom, in which pupils were most or least likely to be addressed by the class teacher. In the course of the study, the researchers systematically shifted pupils in and out these areas, while monitoring the frequency with which the pupils received questions. Their results suggest that location within the classroom is in itself a causal factor in the pattern of teacher–pupil interaction.

Moore and Glynn's study highlights a relatively neglected determinant of the action-zone effect. Most studies have looked at individuals' voluntary participation. Environmental explanations usually emphasize the way that physical proximity means optimal conditions for attention (i.e., a clear view, easy hearing, less distraction from peers) and for communication with the teacher (e.g., eye contact), all of which, in turn, increase individuals' interest in the lesson. Moore and Glynn draw attention to the fact that teachers actively elicit interest.

However, all the seating-arrangement studies described so far envisage a stationary teacher and lecture- or seminar-style instruction. In British primary education, at least, straight-rows seating has been long abandoned; classwork has been largely replaced with child-centred, 'integrated day' practices which involve a considerable emphasis on independent work. Although teachers regularly address the class as a whole, learning is assumed to occur primarily when individuals or small groups work on tasks assigned by the teacher. Completing 'pieces of work' seems more important than participating in teacher-led sessions. Furthermore, the primary classroom is usually divided into specialist areas (art, sand, water, library or reading corners), besides tables for general work.

Ironically, perhaps, seating location has taken on a different significance in British primary classrooms. Roy Nash observed that in most non-streamed classes in his study, the seating allocation reflected ability groups.[42] 'Streaming by tables' was still prevalent in the late 1980s, in my experience. There are direct implications for the child's self-concept and academic attitudes, as children readily get the message about their own academic status relative to peers. Being relegated to the 'lazy table' or the 'swots' table' has clear messages for children.

Behaviour In Places

Sommer commented that the absence of empirical evidence concerning the impact of the spatial environment on human functioning perpetuated the 'fuzzy thinking about behavioural aspects of school design'.[43] As long as such 'fuzzy thinking' prevails, design policies may be swayed with fads, as the case of open-plan schools suggests. Often, the emotive arguments for a particular approach to design are based on anecdotal evidence and personal values (and my case for landscaping school playgrounds, argued earlier, is no exception). It goes without saying that more empirical research is called for, especially research that may increase school-planners' appreciation of children's cultures as essential contexts for personal development. However, in the decades since Sommer made his comment, environment–behaviour relations have received unprecedented attention.

The studies reviewed so far in this chapter suggest clear relations between place and behaviour, but not to the extent that they make a major impact on educational outcomes. In particular, research has failed to establish a correlation between school design and educational outcomes. However, most studies typically test hypotheses, such as the prediction that students in certain seating locations might be more inclined to participate in seminars. To formulate a hypothesis, we must first have reasons to suspect a relationship between specific environmental and behavioural variables, on the basis of either a theory or anecdotal evidence. Plausibly, potentially important dimensions of the educational setting might not enter the range of specific theories, or be overlooked in informal observations. Barker's ecological psychology, reviewed below, represents an attempt to formulate a framework for systematic observations of what people actually do, and where and when, in everyday life.

THE DISCOVERY OF THE BEHAVIOUR SETTING

In the 1950s, a team of researchers led by Roger Barker and based at the Midwest Psychological Field Station in Oskaloosa, Kansas, set out to discover the 'kinds of habitats children live and grow up in and what they do and encounter there'.[44] They described human behaviour systematically and objectively, suspending their personal knowledge of behaviour in habitats such as schools, shops, parks or hospitals. This was the beginning of eco-behavioural science,[45] the precursor of contemporary environmental psychology.

Barker and his associates, known as the Kansas school of ecological psychology, drew attention to the fact that a geographical location, such as a town, comprises units definable by spatial and temporal boundaries. A school has well-defined spatial boundaries: there are its buildings, playground, playing fields. There are also temporal boundaries: the school is populated for definite periods of the day, week, and year. Within these boundaries, teachers and pupils carry out activities which would appear out of context elsewhere or at other times. Furthermore, a school comprises several molecular units, each with its own spatio-temporal boundaries, typical activities, and a relatively limited range of functions: the classroom during lessons, the playground during breaks, the hall during assembly or (another micro-setting) during a PE lesson, and so on. The school is therefore a behaviour setting in every sense of the term, and indeed features conspicuously in Barkerian research.

Using a technique of naturalistic observation known as the behaviour setting survey, Barker and his associates painstakingly recorded streams of behaviour in everyday settings. For instance, 10-year-old Anne was observed in a music lesson at school.[46] The observer recorded Anne's ongoing behaviour, minute by minute: having entered the room, she sat down, picked up the music book, listened to the teacher, watched other pupils, put up her hand in response to the teacher's question, and so on.

Pertinently, certain actions – such as Anne's raising her hand – tell us more about behavioural norms in school lessons than about Anne or children in general: 'The school class where [a child] is a pupil, the game in which he plays, and the street where he walks all function according to laws alien to those that govern his behavior as a person.'[47] The lack of dependence on particular persons to maintain the behaviour setting makes this research approach potentially useful: 'we could predict some aspects of children's behavior more adequately from knowledge of the behavior characteristics of the drugstores, arithmetic classes, and basketball games they inhabited than from knowledge of the behavior tendencies of particular children'.[48]

In a behaviour setting analysis, the individuals under observation, referred to as *setting inhabitants*, are not unlike actors who have their entrances and exits. They inhabit a setting by carrying out activities in keeping with the place's function.

Behaviour settings research concerns

(1) the *fit* between the structural features and arrangement of physical objects of a location and people's activities there;
(2) the behaviour *programme* of a setting, that is, 'a time-ordered sequence of person–environment interactions that leads to the orderly enactment of essential setting function'.[49]

This seems apt in our sphere of interest, in so far that children at school are confronted with a complex system, in the shaping of which they have little say, and to which they must adjust by 'behaving appropriately'. But if we adopt a simplistic Barkerian approach, we are in danger of losing sight of both the individuality of setting inhabitants and the social construction of settings such as schools.

When sociologists of education and educational psychologists investigate the ways in which individuals fit (or fail to fit) into the school's organization, they keep the goals of the educational establishment, and individuals' attitudes, motivation, ability, etc., very much in mind. The application of behaviour setting analysis to educational settings has taken a very different slant: the ecological psychologists observed children at school as if they, the observers, had no prior knowledge about the function and norms of a school. The scientific detachment practised by the ecological psychologists was meant to ensure that their reports are not biased by their own preconceptions. But the 'coarse-grain' analysis and reliance on narrative commentaries in the behaviour setting survey perhaps offset this endeavour. This can be seen in behaviour setting analysts' inferences about setting inhabitants' moods or mental states. Arbitrarily to pluck a few instances from Barker's survey data (my italics throughout the following): a girl, observed in a drugstore, 'seemed *fascinated* by the procedure [of serving soda]; she *took in every detail* of the situation';[50] the girl observed in a music lesson 'watched [the teacher] *solemnly*'; a little later, '*with interest* she watched [another pupil] demonstrate the way to lead the song'; two minutes later, as she raised her hand to volunteer to conduct the class, 'on her face was a look of *expectancy*'.[51] Such descriptions seem no more (nor less!) reliable than any lay observations.

However, the above quibble is perhaps unfair: Barker's ecological psychology merely draws attention to the *distribution* of responses across places, to the fact that activities are clustered in fairly standard ways within small places. Behaviour setting theory is not meant to tell us why Anne raised her hand, instead of shouting out or doing something else to attract her teacher's attention; the theory simply states that raising hands is among the response patterns that distinguish a school lesson setting from other social contexts. Barker saw behaviour programmes as a setting's *maintenance mechanisms*, i.e., processes which keep the setting distinguishable from others, make it a systemic whole.

As Kaminski dramatically states in his critique of the Barkerian approach, this was 'an incredibly courageous, adventurous and ambitious undertaking and an enormous step forward in the history of psychology to let psychologists be affected immediately by everyday life in all its variety and diversity'.[52] Its innovation lies in the emphasis on settings' internal order. 'Thus dynamic, superindividual systemic wholes were discovered', as Kaminsky affirms, although 'the natural individual', whose behaviour ecological psychology had set out to record and report, 'now appeared to be confronted with a super- or extraindividual, autochthonous reality which contains its own order'.[53]

Several methodological and theoretical criticisms have been raised against the Barkerian approach by contemporary environmental psychologists. Notably, Wicker has expounded a dynamic view of behaviour settings as social constructions, 'the result of sense-making and interactive behaviours of the participants'.[54] As a complete theory of human psychology, Barker's paradigm leaves much to be desired. Clearly, explanations of human behaviour in places must go beyond the immediate environment-behaviour congruence (we want to explain why a congruence exists). But the concept of a behaviour setting is a very good start to any discussion of location-specific activities.

An empty classroom is not a behaviour setting, it is just a place. A behaviour setting clearly means more than a location. The Kansas school of ecological psychology underestimated the importance of relationships among setting inhabitants. For example, Anne's active participation in the music lesson (she is described by Barker raising her hand several times) must have a significance in the context of the teacher–pupil relationship. We may wonder, for instance, how Anne took the fact that every time she, Anne, raised her hand, the teacher chose someone else. Questions of this sort have been addressed exhaustively in social psychology and sociology, as will be reviewed in later chapters. Typically in those frameworks, however, social interactions are investigated as if happening in a physical vacuum.

PRIVATE SPACE

Pupils usually have something at school that is labelled theirs for the duration of the school year: a coat-peg in the infants school cloakroom, a tray for one's books, perhaps a locker in the secondary school or college. Pupils are also likely to have their usual seat; and if the choice of seat is their own, individuals' preferences suggest that they feel more comfortable in one zone of the classroom than in others. Eggleston asserted that 'On first entering school, the child is likely to be concerned with the spatial aspects of his environment... identifying his personal space and its resources'.[55] More precisely, Eggleston's description refers to what Altman defined as *territoriality*, 'the personalizing, ownership, and defence of geographical areas'.[56] *Personal space* is 'an area immediately around the body; intrusion into this space by others leads to discomfort or anxiety'.[57] Personal space is thus closely related to the experience of crowding.

The tendency in environmental psychology is to look for objective influences of environment on behaviour, and while the importance of subjective implications of a place is duly recognized, it is often assumed that the spatial environment has a direct impact on the individual. For example, Gould proposed that a school's architecture determines pupil behaviour through its implications for personal space or opportunity for privacy (i.e., physical seclusion).[58] Her thesis implies physical determinism, a concept rejected even at the time, and notably by architects such as Lipman (whose Commentary follows Gould's paper). Imagine a man in a very small room: the physical dimensions restrict his activities in a very concrete sense; but without knowing anything else about him, we cannot tell whether he is frustrated by the spatial limitations, disturbed by the confined space, or, on the contrary, finds it cosy. The information we need in order to describe and explain the impact of the room's size on the man's behaviour does not exist in any way in the physical dimensions of the room.

Second, Gould's thesis rests on a belief in 'a powerful need felt by the individual to personalize his environment'.[59] Fact or fiction? If it is fact, what is the significance of pupils' territorial behaviour? It seems too simplistic to assume that this is innate, as is animal territorial behaviour, although there is probably an evolutionary basis to feeling secure in an environment we recognize as predictable and controllable. New environments are associated with stress – and this stress can be reduced by familiarizing ourselves with the place, even putting our mark on it, ultimately 'owning' it. But could pupils' apparent territoriality reflect simply a frustrated need for elbow room? I recall marking 'my half' of a school-desk shared with another girl; if I didn't, her books would take over my limited work area.

If, as Altman proposed, the concept of privacy is central to understanding environment and behaviour relationships,[60] then pupils' privacy-related behaviour should tell us something about their relation to the classroom environment. Weinstein carried out an experimental study of privacy-seeking behaviour by setting up privacy booths in an elementary school class-room.[61] For the purpose of her study, she defined 'privacy' as self-elected physical isolation. Fourth grade pupils were given the option of using these booths. But once the novelty abated, the children quickly declined from taking advantage of the opportunity. Interestingly, no correlation was found between the children's actual privacy-seeking (declining use of the booths) and the desire for privacy they expressed in a questionnaire. One of the explanations for this attitude–behaviour discrepancy, noted by Weinstein herself, is that retreating into a booth is not in keeping with fourth grade children's habituation into the classroom environment, which means learning to live in a crowd and to carry out individual tasks by minimizing interaction, not necessarily by physical seclusion.

The absence of privacy-seeking in a classroom, in Wein-stein's study, may be taken as evidence for socialization into the school's milieu. The need for privacy is itself a cultural construct. Notwithstanding Weinstein's experiment, most evidence for a desire for privacy is derived from self-reports, and thus reflects basically people's beliefs, not objective person–environment relations. Moreover, desiring privacy implies that the person perceives other people in the immediate environment as undesirable company, a source of anxiety or interference with his or her activities. It may be that the children in Weinstein's study were not inclined to use the booths because they did not regard their classmates as intruding on their personal space.

Studies of children's awareness of personal space show a clear relation between a child's perception of others' social identity and spatial proximity. In one series of studies,[62] the perception of personal space in elementary school children was investigated by asking the children to place manipulable silhouette figures, representing 'self', in relation to several printed peer figures, labelled 'a best friend', 'an acquaintance', 'a stranger', 'someone liked very much', 'someone neither liked nor disliked', 'someone disliked very much', 'someone feared'. The children consistently placed the 'self' figure closer to figures representing interpersonal closeness. Koslin *et al.* used line drawings of figures to track children's developmental patterns with respect to personal space: in the early school grades, children tended to place opposite sex figures farthest apart from themselves; after the fourth grade, racial differences seemed more important than gender.[63] We can also expect considerable individual differences, partly due to upbringing and cultural background.

However, those studies investigate spatial proximity as if detached from actual settings. We tolerate the proximity of strangers in lifts, on crowded buses, in queues, shops, and so on, but we might object if the same strangers were just as close to us in other places. Individuals' perceptions of the place, as well as of interpersonal relations, should be taken into account.

What is the utility of the personal-space concept in education? Does children's appraisal of classmates' spatial proximity affect or reflect their adjustment to life at school? These and similar specific questions, to my knowledge, have not been explored in empirical research. Altman regarded *privacy* as 'an interpersonal boundary process by which a person or group regulates interactions with others'.[64] Territoriality, personal space and privacy have more to do with the social environment than with the spatial, and reflect individual-based cognitive and affective processes more than objective environmental influences. The environmental psychologists Proshansky and Fabian have proposed to view *place identity* as part of the self-concept.[65] That is, we define who we are partly by our beliefs and knowledge about the places we inhabit – home, school, work, shops, bus-stops, etc. – and our relations to these places. If so, private space seems to be in the mind.

LOCATIONAL FUNCTIONING

Individuals usually pattern their behaviour in accordance with the perceived function of the particular setting; but a description of a setting's behaviour programme must allow for individual differences within a setting, and for variations across settings of an identical function. For instance, students in a lecture follow a simple behaviour programme: they listen, take notes, occasionally ask questions. In any given lecture, individuals differ in attentiveness, note-taking, or asking questions. Therefore, dissimilar rates of certain behaviours, observed in different classes, could be due simply to the different mixture of individuals in those classes, and/or to differences in the lecture settings, from room architecture to lecturers' style. Statistical analyses can help distinguish variations in behaviour tendencies that relate to features of settings from variations that reflect individual differences. In this way, empirical relationships hitherto unnoticed, nor predicted by theories, may be discovered.

In a large-scale study, Solomon and Kendall collected data about classrooms, teaching practices, children characteristics and attainment, in 50 fourth grade classes across 26 schools in one county, during one academic year.[66] Using factor analysis to discover which physical characteristics accounted for most variance between classrooms, they isolated five principal factors, as follows. The strongest factor referred to the physical openness and the accessibility to resources for students. A related item was the background noise: classes characterized by physical openness also had a relatively high level of noise. The second factor referred to wall displays: classrooms differed in the ratio of 'commercial' versus 'student-made' displays. The third factor was the presence and amount of plants, inanimate objects from the environment, and animals. The fourth factor represented a combination of 'gradedness and crowdedness': classes including two or more grade levels that were judged uncrowded, versus single-graded classes that were judged crowded. Finally, the least discriminative factor was the number of children and adults in the class area (which simply means that most classes in the study were of a fairly similar size). However, none of these physical-setting factors entered Solomon and Kendall's final categorization of classroom types; their observations, backed up with teachers' reports, disclosed that the classes differed most importantly in terms of social atmosphere.

However, while school design seems to have negligible impact on educational outcomes, most of the research described here reveals a clear relationship between individuals' immediate surroundings and the actual stream of behaviour; activities may not be determined by the physical environment, but behaviour 'flows' in places. In the classroom, on the 'child' side of the child–school interface, there are activities such as listening to a teacher, chatting with peers, borrowing a pencil or doing sums. Each is a *molar activity*. Although molar activities merge with each other, an observer can discern goal-directed episodes, involving discrete interactions with physical objects or with other people in the immediate classroom surroundings. The objects within reach and the people around, with whom the child does or may interact, can be envisaged as a sphere surrounding the child. Thus, on the 'school' side of the interface, there is a field comprised of objects and people, existing independently of the child, but which come in contact with him or her. This is the *molar ecological environment*, as defined by Barker.[67]

The interaction between children's molar activities and their molar ecological environment was the subject-matter of Barkerian ecological psychology, and has remained a major focus in contemporary environmental psychology. However, it has been increasingly conceded that what children do in classrooms is determined primarily by their awareness of how such places are used, when and by whom, and by their perception of their own relation to the place. This idea is not new, nor alien to behaviour setting theory. Barker discussed people's perceptions of a place, their sensitivity to their own needs, and similar subjective factors, as *input*, something that setting inhabitants bring with them into their transactions with the place. Partly, the concession represents a shift of opinion regarding what should be studied.

In an early review of research into school environments, Gump identified three 'foci of convenience':

(1) the objective setting environment, regarded as eliciting behavioural programmes;
(2) the objective individual environment, or the interface between inputs arising in the settings and a child's action and reaction to these;
(3) the subjective individual environment, a set of changes or developments in the child, related to interfacing with the school environment, such as emotional reactions, and enduring attitude changes.[68]

Gump's definition of the subjective environment implies that the input a child brings into transactions with particular settings or micro-settings in school is derived from previous transactions.

As seen, research into the ecology of schools or classrooms does not so much answer specific questions, as lead to a tacit realization that the causal influence of the physical environment on human behaviour was overestimated in the early literature. Consequently, a more subtle view of people's relation to their environments has emerged. The contemporary focus is exemplified in Taylor's description of what he calls 'human territorial functioning': 'an interlocked system of attitudes, sentiments and behaviours, regarding small-scale or delimited spaces of the environment, concerned with who has access to the space in question and what activities go on there'.[69] Taylor's thesis concerns specifically the progressive association of some urban areas with crime and social deviance, but its central premises are applicable to our area of interest:

(1) there are location-specific behaviours;

(2) prior assumptions about the location influence people's impression-formation (and hence influence their responses to the setting);

(3) social pressures, beyond the level of individuals' immediate interactions with the setting, guide their perception of the place and their actions there.

These premises are well-substantiated in the research reviewed throughout this book.

Following Taylor, a concept of *locational functioning* may be suggested: locational functioning refers to a convergence of place features, and behaviours and perceptions of the people who interact with it. The implicit message is that instead of seeking to delineate causal relationships between spatial features and educational outcomes, the focus should be on identifying optimal environments for educational activities. On the whole, the awareness that behaviour programmes depend on the physical characteristics of their location and on the *perceived* meanings of both location and behaviour, was not accompanied by a revised interest in children's relation to their school environments.

Notes and References

1 Weinstein, C. S. 'The physical environment of the school: a review of the research'. *Review of Educational Research*, **49**, 577–610, 1979.

2 Smith, P. K. and Connolly, K. *The Ecology of Preschool Behaviour.* Cambridge: Cambridge University Press, 1980.

3 Ibid., p. 125.

4 Stokols, D. 'On the distinction between density and crowding: some implications for future research'. *Psychological Review,* **72**, 275–277, 1972.

5 Ibid., p. 275.

6 Ibid., p. 276.

7 Myrick and Marx, 1968, reviewed in Moos, R. H. *Evaluating Educational Environments.* San Francisco: Jossey-Bass, 1979.

8 Moos, R. H., 1979, op. cit., p. 7.

9 Barker, R. G. and Gump, P. *Big School, Small School.* Stanford, CA: Stanford University Press, 1964.

10 Opie, I. and P. *Children's Games in Street and Playground.* London: Oxford University Press, 1969.

11 Moore, R. *Childhood's Domain: Play and Place in Child Development.* London: Croom Helm, 1986.

12 Kelly, E. 'Racism and sexism in the playground'. In Blatchford, P. and Sharp, S. (eds), *Breaktime and the School: Understanding and Changing Playground Behaviour.* London: Routledge, 1994, p. 63.

13 Blatchford, P. *Playtime in the Primary School: Problems and Improvements.* Windsor: NFER-Nelson, 1989.

14 Lucas, W. 'The power of school grounds: the philosophy and practice of Learning Through Landscape'. In Blatchford, P. and Sharp, S. (eds), *Breaktime and the School: Understanding and Changing Playground Behaviour.* London: Routledge, pp. 80–89, 1994.

15 Sommer, R. *Personal Space: The Behavioural Basis of Design.* Englewood Cliffs, NJ: Prentice-Hall, 1969, p. 100.

16 Gump, P. V. 'School and classroom environment'. In Stokols, D. and Altman, I. (eds), *Handbook of Environmental Psychology,* Vol. 2. London: John Wiley and Sons, 1987, p. 693; his italics.

17 Bennett, N., Andrea, J., Hegarty, P. and Wade, B. *Open Plan Schools.* Windsor: NFER for the Schools Council, 1980.

18 Canter, D. and Donald, I. 'Environmental psychology in the United Kingdom'. In Stokols, D. and Altman, I. (eds), *Handbook of Environmental Psychology,* Vol. 2. London: John Wiley and Sons, pp. 1281–1310, 1987.

19 Bennett, N., *et al.,* 1980, op. cit., p. 233.

20 Cooper, I. 'The maintenance of order and use of space in primary school buildings'. *British Journal of Social Education,* **3**, 267–279, 1982.

21 Rolfe, 1961, reviewed in Sommer, R., 1969, op. cit.

22 Sommer, R., 1969, op. cit., p. 103.

23 Pollard, A. and Tann, S. *Reflective Teaching in the Primary School: A Handbook for the Classroom.* London: Cassell, 1987, p. 112.

24 Cf. Stokols, D., 1972, op. cit.

25 Sommer, R. 'Classroom ecology'. *Journal of Applied Behavioural Science,* **3**, 489–503, 1967.

26 Ibid., p. 495.

27 Getzels, J. 'Images of the classroom and visions of the learner'. *School Review,* **82**, 527–540, 1974.

28 Montello, D. R. 'Classroom seating location and its effect on

course achievement, participation, and attitudes'. *Journal of Environmental Psychology*, **8**, 1988, p. 150.

29 Waller, 1932, quoted in Rivlin, L. G. and Weinstein, C. S. 'Educational issues, school settings, and environmental psychology'. *Journal of Environmental Psychology*, **4**, 1984, p. 352.

30 Walberg, H. 'Physical and psychological distance in the classroom'. *School Review*, **77**, 64–70, 1969.

31 Becker, R. D., Sommer, R., Bee, J. and Oxley, B. 'College classroom ecology'. *Sociometry*, **36**, 514–525, 1973.

32 Sommer, R., 1969, op. cit., p. 111.

33 Haber, G. M. 'Spatial relations between dominants and marginals'. *Social Psychology Quarterly*, **45**, 219–228, 1982.

34 Wulf, K. M. 'Relationships of assigned classroom seating area to achievement variables'. *Educational Research Quarterly*, **21**, 56–62, 1977.

35 Gump, P. V., 1987, op. cit., p. 699.

36 Stires, L. K. 'Classroom seating, location order effects and reactivity'. *Personality and Social Psychology Bulletin*, **8**, 362–364, 1982.

37 Sommer, R., 1967, op. cit.

38 Ibid., p. 490.

39 Sommer, R., 1969, op. cit., p. 115.

40 Adams, R. S. and Biddle, B. J., *Realities of Teaching: Explorations with Video Tape*. New York: Holt, Rinehart and Winston, 1970.

41 Moore, D. W. and Glynn, T. 'Variation in question rate as a function of position in the classroom'. *Educational Psychology*, **4**, 233–248, 1984.

42 Nash, R. *Classrooms Observed*. London: Routledge and Kegan Paul, 1973.

43 Sommer, R., 1969, op. cit., p. 108.

44 Kaminski, G. 'The enigma of ecological psychology'. *Journal of Environmental Psychology*, **3**, 1983, p. 86.

45 Barker, R. G. *Ecological Psychology: Concepts and Methods for Studying the Environment of Human Behaviour*. Stanford, CA: Stanford University Press, 1968; Barker, R. G. (ed.). *Habitats, Environments and Human Behaviour*. San Francisco: Jossey-Bass, 1978.

46 Barker, R. G., 1968, op. cit., pp. 12ff.

47 Ibid., p. 6.

48 Ibid., p. 4.

49 Wicker, A. W. 'Behaviour settings reconsidered: temporal stages, resources, internal dynamics, context'. In Stokols, D. and

Altman, I. (eds), *Handbook of Environmental Psychology*, Vol. 2. London: John Wiley and Sons, 1987, p. 614.

50 Barker, R. G., 1968, op. cit., p. 146.

51 Ibid., pp. 13–14.

52 Kaminski, G. 1983, op. cit., p. 87.

53 Ibid., p. 87.

54 Wicker, A. W., 1987, op. cit., p. 616.

55 Eggleston, J. *The Ecology of the School.* London: Methuen, 1977, p. 104.

56 Altman, I. *The Environment and Social Behavior.* Monterey, CA: Brooks/Cole, 1975, p. 5.

57 Ibid., p. 6.

58 Gould, R. 'The ecology of educational settings'. *Educational Administration*, **4**, 14–27, 1976.

59 Eggleston, J., 1977, op. cit., p. 107.

60 Altman, I., 1975, op. cit.

61 Weinstein, C. S. 'Privacy-seeking behaviour in an elementary classroom'. *Journal of Environmental Psychology*, **2**, 23–35, 1982.

62 Guardo, C. I. 'Personal space in children'. *Child Development*, **40**, 143–151, 1969; Guardo, C. I. and Meisels, M. 'Factor structure of children's personal space schemata. *Child Development*, **42**, 1307–1312, 1971.

63 Koslin, S., Koslin, B., Paargament, R. and Bird, H. 'Children's social distance constructs: a development study'. *Proceedings of the Annual Convention of the American Psychological Association*, **6**, 151–152, 1971.

64 Altman, I., 1975, op. cit., p. 6.

65 Proshansky, H. M. and Fabian, A. K. 'The development of place identity in the child'. In Weinstein, C. S. and David, T. G. (eds), *Spaces for Children: The Built Environment and Child Development.* New York: Plenum Press, pp. 21–40, 1987.

66 Solomon, D. and Kendall, A. J. *Children in Classrooms: An Investigation of Person-Environment Interaction.* New York: Praeger Publishers, 1979.

67 Barker, R. G., 1968, op. cit.

68 Gump, P. V. 'School environments'. In Altman, I. and Wohlwill, J. F. (eds), *Children and Their Environment.* New York: Plenum Press, pp. 131–174, 1978.

69 Taylor, R. B. 'Toward an environmental psychology of disorder: delinquency, crime and fear of crime'. In Stokols, D. and Altman, I. (eds), *Handbook of Environmental Psychology*, Vol. 2. London: John Wiley and Sons, 1987, p. 954.

CHAPTER 3

The Direct Environment

This chapter considers pupils or students in educational settings as organisms embedded in physical environments. The discussion draws from separate research fields – human performance, health psychology, ecological perception theory, and others – which, despite their divergent applications, set out from the premise that humans evolved to perceive and operate on the world in certain ways, and to function best under finite optimal conditions, departures from which impair performance, induce stress, and might damage health.

External conditions or events, such as excessive heat or loud noise, obviously interfere with performance of given tasks through their physical or physiological effects. It is also clear that internal states such as anxiety or fatigue can interfere with performance. Human performance research endeavours to pinpoint the precise effects of specific external or internal variables. Theories of stress take the issue further. Richard Lazarus, in particular, has forwarded the well-substantiated claim that physiological states which arise in response to situational demands depend on individuals' cognitive appraisal of their own relations to the particular environment or event. For example, background noise interferes with classroom communication in a physical sense; but its impact on individuals depends partly on what the interference means to them. A teacher who plans to cover important material might become frustrated and 'stressed out'; pupils might be indifferent.

The scientific account of the world, including human psychology, in terms of natural forces and causal relationships is called *naturalism*. The naturalist perspective is not the only frame of reference in which human behaviour can be understood, and (according to some theorists) might not even be the most appropriate. Indeed, the rest of the book draws chiefly from perspectives in sociology and social psychology, which describe the human solely as an agent in a social world. However, can we dismiss the biological dimension of the child-school interface? Education can benefit from research based on naturalist premises both pragmatically and conceptually. Pragmatically, empirical observations about processes such as the effects of noise on attention and memory can help us understand how environmental conditions might affect the teaching/learning process. Separately, models of person–environment relations, forwarded by theorists of a naturalistic inclination, can arguably help us to conceptualize pupils' subjective environments.

Human Performance and Stress

Research into the effects of situational demands on performance of cognitive and motor tasks is usually carried out with occupational settings in mind. Typical studies are laboratory experiments with adult subjects, whose performance of specially designed tasks under manipulated conditions may bear on the efficiency and health of people in ordinary employment. Not unlike adults at work, children and young people in full-time education spend relatively long periods in a designated place, during most of which they are required to perform prescribed tasks. The case of the learner differs from that of a worker in one important sense: the tasks are designed to bring about change in the person who performs them, the learner. For present purposes, however, suffice it to ask whether situational variables are conducive or inimical to the teaching/learning process.

Research on relations between situational variables and performance in educational settings consists chiefly of field observations and correlational studies, demonstrating a statistical relationship between educational or behavioural outcomes and aspects of the classroom environment, either specific stimuli or ambient conditions. Noise is by definition interference, the 'acoustic by-product' of incidental events in the immediate environment. A sound becomes 'noise' only in relation to individuals' activities. Heat or cold are not stimuli as such, but ambient conditions in relation to the organism, which can adversely affect performance. An interesting aspect of the organism–environment fit is revealed in a study of the effects of natural light in classrooms, described presently: denying natural light, as is the case in windowless classrooms, can affect the children's metabolism, and consequently their behaviour and attention. Some of the findings about noise, temperature, and daylight are reviewed below. Among additional environmental factors which might affect performance, health and education, is air pollution (e.g., the effects of lead fumes); but at present the research evidence is sparse and results are contradictory. In contrast, diurnal variations are fairly well established: measures of human performance show fairly predictable fluctuations in efficiency over the day and night. Children's performance on perceptual-motor tasks generally improves over the school day; in contrast, short-term memory seems to reach its peak at about 11 a.m., and then declines during the rest of the day.[1]

Time-of-day effects on arousal, memory, and other physiological and psychological processes, have obvious implications for the scheduling of school timetables. These daily, cyclic variations are believed to reflect the so-called biological clock, or circadian rhythms. This phenomenon reinforces the idea that we cannot consider the effects of an environment on an organism without taking into account the state of the organism. In the same vein, health psychologists conceptualize stress as a function of the person–environment interface. On the environment side, there are situations which demand readjustment, *stressors*, such as unexpected, unpleasant or threatening conditions, changes brought about by major life events, or daily hassles. On the person side of the interface, there is the *stress response*, a complex yet specific pattern of physiological and cognitive changes, to do with the mobilization of resources in preparation for action to meet situational demands. Implications for the child–school interface are indicated towards the end of the section.

NOISE

Noise, probably one of teachers' commonest complaints, can be generated inside the school or come from the outside.

Whatever its source, noise interferes directly with classroom communication in two ways:

(1) the decibel (dB) level of the background noise may be such that the teacher's voice is simply not heard; the interference of noise with the detection of wanted signal is called *masking*;

(2) a pupil's attention may shift to other sources (peers' talk, laughter, or street sounds), even when their dB rating is moderate, i.e., *distraction*.

Noise can vary in dB intensity, can be continuous, intermittent, or a sudden blast. Continuous noise does not necessarily cause enduring changes in pupil motivation or competence, but might affect academic attainment through the disruption of educational activities.

The level of normal speech, in the absence of competing sounds, lies in the range of 50–65 dB, depending on the distance between speaker and listener. For sustained discourse at a distance of about one metre, communication becomes unsatisfactory when background noise is over 70 dB; if the distance is six metres or over (as may be the case in large classrooms and in lecture theatres), shouting is necessary, and communication becomes very difficult.[2] Cohen *et al.* investigated the effects of aircraft noise on children in a school near a busy airport.[3] With flights passing over about every two minutes, pupils and staff were exposed to peak levels as high as 95 dB – with obvious implications for normal communication. Noise caused by traffic, trains or aircraft is associated with less attentiveness, less student participation, and a shift from discussion to lecturing, and (as several field studies have shown) consequently results in lowered educational progress. In the laboratory, the effect of masking on speech is well-documented, although the implications for ordinary situations are not straightforward.[4] Speakers naturally respond to background noise by raising their voice, but not in proportion: elevations of vocal effort are typically about 3–5 dB for every 10 dB increase in the level of background noise. Factors such as the acoustic quality of the room, and whether the discourse is brief or sustained, should be taken into account. Intelligibility depends not only on the ratio between speech (signal) and noise levels, but also on the listener's familiarity with the speaker's voice or the transmitted information. The laboratory studies show that the effects of masking are relatively low if the material is familiar or predictable – hardly the case in university lectures!

Besides interference with communication and signal-detection, noise can affect performance by inducing stress-related changes in attention and information processing. An illustrative study is reported by Schönpflung.[5] Four groups wrote an essay on a news item, while exposed to noise varying in intensity. With increased noise, the quantity of words and sentences increased, but linguistic quality decreased. Under quiet conditions, subjects wrote sentences like, 'After addressing the council the secretary brought forward a motion'; whereas under noise, subjects would write, 'The secretary first addressed the council. Then he brought forward a motion.'[6] These findings are consistent with knowledge about cognitive correlates of stress. Arousal is associated with a characteristic pattern of electrical activity in the brain: there is desynchronized cortical activity, involving beta waves. When there is a high beta activity, attention is very selective, memory capacity is reduced, work-rate is high but the responses are stereotyped – a pattern of cognitive function that is ideal in a situation involving uncertainty and danger. In contrast, in a more relaxed state, the cortical activity is more synchronized, involving theta and alpha waves, attention is less selective and reactions are slower, but creative problem-solving or lateral thinking increase. If the task that Schönpflung set his subjects were an exam paper, an essay written under noise might get lower marks, and create a poorer impression of the student. A consideration of the conditions under which an exam is taken rarely enters educational assessment.

Noise is a noxious stimulus: people try to remove the source of unacceptable noise or to avoid being exposed to it. Failing that, they are likely to experience frustration and anger. Long-term exposure to uncontrollable noise can lead to learned helplessness, and thus affect academic motivation. The educational, behavioural and emotional effects of noise were demonstrated in an innovative field experiment by Ward and Suedfeld, aimed to evaluate the consequences of a proposed highway extension that was to pass by Rutgers University.[7] The researchers recorded traffic noise of an existing highway elsewhere, at different times of the day. With the aid of a sound playback equipment, students were exposed to realistic high and moderate round-the-clock noise environments in their dormitories and classrooms. Classroom behaviour was observed for three days under noise conditions, and a week later for three days without noise. Under noise, there was less student participation in lessons, less attentiveness, and reported difficulty in hearing. Moreover, some students were so annoyed by the noise that on a couple of occasions the cable to the sound equipment was cut. Observations and questionnaires revealed changes in interpersonal interactions: under noise, disagreement was more frequent, and there were more negative emotional reactions. Students exposed to a week of noise in their dormitories reported changes in their sleep patterns, in studying and social relationships, and in judgement, alertness, and nervousness.

Ward and Suedfeld's study has demonstrated what happens when a population is suddenly exposed to increased traffic noise. Typical affective reactions are annoyance and anger; typical behavioural reactions are threats and actual attempts to remove the source of the noise. Long-term exposure might be associated with adaptation, but of kinds that are not necessarily benign from a psychological viewpoint: people can learn to put up with noise, becoming habituated to it, but still suffer chronic stress; depression and generalized dissatisfaction might replace the initial anger.

HEAT AND COLD

Extremes of temperature are rarely, if ever, experienced in educational settings. If the school's boiler fails on a cold winter day, pupils are usually sent home; growing up in the subtropics, I recall being sent home when the weather was too hot! Nevertheless, well within the tolerable range, an overheated or underheated classroom might cause discomfort and affect performance. The human body maintains heat balance within narrow limits around 37°C (98.6°F), and although people can function in temperatures ranging from −30°C (22°F) to +80°C (176°F), a variation of more than 4°C (7°F) in the body's core temperature will impair physical and mental capacity.[8]

Relatively high temperature might induce fatigue or drowsiness, leading to reduced industry. In a British study, Humphreys related teachers' observations of their 7- and 8-year-old pupils to the temperatures in primary school classrooms.[9] The teachers rated the children's behaviour four times a day for a fortnight during June, and again during July the following year. Fluctuations in room temperature seemed responsible for about 1 per cent of the variation in the children's activity (but the time of day accounted for 6 per cent of the variation in the children's industry).

Interestingly, there is some evidence for a correlation between a subjective feeling of thermal comfort and individuals' performance on perceptual-motor tasks: most people seem to perform continuous, repetitive mental tasks best when the temperature lies in the range they consider as comfortably cool.[10] Studies aimed at establishing the optimal temperature range for thermal comfort have relied greatly on self-reports. In Humphreys' study, mentioned above, the children reported that the classroom felt 'just nice' or 'nice and warm' when the temperature, indoors, ranged between 19°C and 21°C. However, factors besides the room's actual temperature can affect people's sensations of comfort. One study found that children wanted a warmer classroom when the weather was warm, and a cooler room on cold days[11] – perhaps because they wore light clothes on warm days, and were wrapped warm in cold weather. Seasonal acclimatization could also affect perceptions of warmth. Furthermore, perception of thermal comfort is relative: students coming into a lecture hall from the cold outdoors are likely to find it warmer than would a lecturer coming down from an overheated office. The kind of activities people perform, and the duration of their stay in the building, should also be taken into account.

Several studies establish a relationship between attainment and classroom temperature. In an extensive field study during the early 1970s, Pelper compared attainment in air-conditioned and non-air-conditioned grade schools, junior high and senior high schools in Oregon.[12] Test scores were obtained each week for spelling classes at the grade schools, social studies and Spanish classes at the junior high, and Latin and maths at the senior high school. Students' performance in the non-air-conditioned schools showed more variability when indoor and outdoor temperatures were high. In the air-conditioned schools, attainment varied to a lesser degree. The benefits of air-conditioning were clear on very warm days, although the students felt that the classrooms were too cool on those days. Experimental evidence for a relationship between heat and attainment is reviewed by Wyon.[13] In one study, the performance of 13-year-old children, given routine reading speed and comprehension tests in a language laboratory, deteriorated by more than 30 per cent when the temperature was raised from 20°C to 30°C. Other studies reported by Wyon showed that performance was affected by temperature variability more in the afternoon than in the morning, and also that less able pupils were more affected than bright students.

DAYLIGHT

In the United States, at least, windowless classrooms were built for reasons such as reducing heating costs. Early studies did not yield conclusive evidence for long-term effects of lack of windows in classrooms.[14] On the face of it, there seems to be little reason to suspect interference with school work: artificial lighting, after all, is quite adequate for vision. However, there is now evidence that natural light has profound physiological and emotional effects.

In Sweden, Küller and Lindsten discovered that daylight deprivation in windowless primary schools can upset children's basic hormone pattern, which in turn influences their industry and sociability, and may also have an impact on body growth and general health.[15] Küller and Lindsten selected four classrooms which differed in the access to natural daylight and two types of artificial light, one of which has properties similar to the properties of natural light. At regular intervals during the school year, the researchers observed children's behaviour in those classrooms, and recorded the presence of an arousal-related hormone, cortisol, in urine samples. The secretion of cortisol normally follows a diurnal pattern, regulated by day-light (it is generally high during daytime, and low during the night). Differing levels of arousal, or stress are known to promote different behaviours; therefore, the researchers expected that variations in levels of cortisol would be accompanied by behavioural changes. Second, since metabolism is regulated partly by daylight, the researchers also compared the children's body growth during that year. Third, relatively prolonged periods without daylight can affect health and may be associated with depression; the researchers therefore compared the rates of sick leave across the four classes during the year of the study.

The impact of light on cortisol secretion was apparent in the results. In the three classrooms that had access to *daylight* (either natural or artificial), there were seasonal variations in levels of cortisol; high values were recorded in September, the minimum in December, then a gradual increase in the spring, the maximum reached in February, before decrease. The class that had access to neither natural nor daylight-type fluorescent light showed a marked delay in the annual pattern: the level of cortisol secretion kept on falling after December, and the minimum was reached in February, before a sharp rise. The comparison of body growth rates suggested that children with high cortisol levels grew less than other children; there were no significant differences in sick leave.

Most interesting here are the effects on classroom behaviour. Küller and Lindsten compared the number of times common behaviours were observed in each classroom. Eight behavioural items occurred the most frequently: 'sits at desk without working', 'motoric unrest', 'turns over leaves absent-mindedly', 'works independently', 'talks with schoolmate', 'inquires, gives/gets help', 'other relevant activity', 'yawns, sucks thumb, reclines on desk'.[16] Küller and Lindsten noticed that children in the different classrooms differed in two salient respects: their ability to concentrate, and their sociability.

Children's ability to concentrate was measured by the frequency with which they sat at a desk without working, turned over a book's leaves absent-mindedly, displayed motoric unrest, or (on the positive side) worked independently. This varied across the school year: it was low for the first two months after the summer holidays, 'with noticeable elements of motoric unrest',[17] then increased and reached a peak in November and December; there was a slight decrease again after the Christmas holidays, but the children's ability to concentrate remained generally high during the spring term. Although this pattern varied somewhat across the four classrooms (in classrooms with access to natural light, ability to concentrate remained high until February; in windowless classrooms, it decreased in November and picked up again in February), it is difficult to relate the variations specifically to light. Küller and Lindsten point out the possibility that differences in room temperature might have accounted for some of the results.

A general seasonal variation was also noticed in the children's social behaviour, measured by the frequency with which they talked with classmates, inquired, offered or received help, and (on the negative side) worked independently. There was a general decrease during September–December, then a gradual rise until May. But there were sharp class differences in this respect. On average, sociability was higher in the classrooms with non-daylight fluorescent tubes (though one of those classrooms also had ordinary windows); we may surmise that the effects of the particular artificial lighting were prominent here.

The issue of windowless classrooms does not arise in some countries (British traditions in school design show a preference for large windows), but Küller and Lindsten's findings are interesting in two general respects. First, the study tells us something about how the many levels of the organism–environment interrelate: work in classrooms without daylight upsets a basic hormone pattern, which in turn influences children's ability to concentrate or to co-operate and participate in lesson activities – and hence influences educational outcomes. Second, the behaviours that Küller and Lindsten class as 'sociability' may be associated, positively, with co-operation and active participation in lessons – but can also be associated, negatively, with restlessness and misconduct when quiet work is called for. Therefore, the *educational* implications of behavioural correlates of biochemical processes can be understood only in relation to normative expectations and pedagogical aims.

STRESS-INDUCING ENVIRONMENTS

Most of the studies mentioned above report independent effects of a particular variable. At some stage, it is necessary to ask how noise, heat, etc., interact in real life. Imagine an exam being held in the afternoon in an overheated, stuffy classroom, while road works are in progress outside. Is there a cumulative impact which is greater than the isolated effects of the time of day, heat, poor ventilation, and noise? Or does adaptation to one stressor moderate the impact of another? Could drowsiness induced by heat and stuffiness reduce arousal in response to the intermittent noise outside? And what about individual differences?

Hans Selye, who pioneered research on physiological stress, described a set of bodily changes associated with arousal and preparation for action.[18] These include increased secretion of adrenaline and other hormones which facilitate rapid action, and changes in the pattern of the brain's electrical activity, associated with focused attention. Such changes occur whenever a situation demands readjustment. Selye coined the term *Generalized Adaptation Syndrome* (GAS) to refer to this specific set of the body's reaction to non-specific stimuli. It is the totality of changes in the structure and chemical composition of the body; while some of these changes are signs of damage, physiological wear and tear, others indicate adaptive reactions. The concept of GAS relates to the observation that the major purpose of physiological functions is to maintain homeostasis ('steady state'). The body's internal environment is kept in a state of chemical and thermal stability in the face of actual or potential change in the external environment. Some of this control takes place in the cells of the body, the functions of which are modified through hormones secreted by various glands (the endocrine system). Overall control and co-ordination is carried out via the central nervous system and through the work of the autonomic nervous system. When a change in the external environment is detected or anticipated through the sensory system, the neuroendocrine control system is mobilized to get the appropriate organs into taking whatever action is needed to restore or maintain the equilibrium.

Behavioural correlates of transient stress, such as listlessness and poor concentration, have obvious implications for academic performance. But how predictable are such effects?

Rabbitt and Maylor point out the limitations of models in which people are posited as 'steady-state' systems which are supposedly affected in invariable ways by given stimuli on different occasions.[19] There are at least three reasons why this is not the case: the complex impact of multiple stimuli, individual differences, and within-individual change. Rabbitt and Maylor contend that useful models for human performance must describe change, account for individual differences, and complement models for stress and our knowledge about the neuropsychological bases of individual differences. As Rabbitt and Maylor assert, even the simplest laboratory task reveals striking individual differences in initial competence; an individual's competence improves with practice, and deteriorates with fatigue or the onset of old age. They call for the development of 'functional models that do not merely predict patterns of performance indices in single paradigms but across many different tasks' and, ultimately, 'the overall effects of stressors and individual differences in terms of their differential patterns of effects on particular functional subsystems [i.e., cognitive processes]'.[20] We may then be able to describe how rates and styles of pupils' problem-solving, attention, and so on, reflect the effects of a complex environment in combination with the dynamics of individuals' competences and states.

If reactions to situational factors that are extrinsic to given tasks can interfere with children's ability to concentrate, cooperate or participate in lesson activities, even more conspicuous effects can be expected to result from stress associated with individuals' feelings about the given tasks and their own competence to perform them. Empirical research is yet to provide a full description of the interaction between various environmental, personal and task-related variables, but there is nothing new in the assertion that an environment or a situation can be very demanding for a combination of reasons. Saegert has distinguished several classes of stress-inducing qualities of environments, a classification loosely followed below.[21]

Some environments are physically threatening. Environmental threats to well-being elicit physiological stress reactions; the immediate effects of sudden noise, temperature extremes, or noxious odours, fall into this category. Although the extent to which pollution, unsafe buildings, etc., induce stress may depend on sensing danger, the physiological stress response can occur irrespective of the person's conscious awareness of the nature of the threat. An illustrative anecdote was told by one of my students, who once worked in a jewellery factory. She hated that job, and soon developed what she correctly recognized as stress symptoms; she assumed that her stress was brought about by her unhappiness. Only when several other workers complained of similar symptoms, it was in fact discovered that toxic fumes seeped into the workshop from an adjacent storage room.

Sometimes, however, the personal significance of situational factors can be the crucial determinant of stress. Environments perceived as incompatible with one's intended or preferred activities can induce stress in the same way that hazardous environments do. In the scene pictured in this subsection's introductory paragraph, students trying to concentrate on exam questions might find the noise of the road works outside, or their discomfort due to the heat and stuffiness of the classroom, highly frustrating. A related type of stress-inducing situation arises from the perceived demand on personal resources required for one's *transactions* with the environment (not necessarily with aspects of the environment as such); that is, a disparity between individuals' concept of how they would ideally function, and their perception of the options actually open to them.

Alternatively, since exams themselves generate stress, and stress is associated with heightened selective attention, students might become virtually unaware of the noise, heat, etc., as they focus on the questions. Indeed, stimuli need not be perceived as threatening to induce stress: novel stimuli demand attention, and elicit physiological arousal. In Selye's view, stress is inherent in being alive, since life is an ongoing process of adaptation to events; he frequently stated that complete freedom from stress is death! Arousal caused by novel environments can have positive implications: cognitive development is enhanced through exposure to, and exploration of, novel environments – and stimulus deprivation, associated with the experience of boredom, is also known to induce stress. On some occasions, however, the sheer quantity, intensity, suddenness or simultaneity of stimuli might lead to attentional overload. Long-term detrimental consequences of attentional overload depend on the degree to which the environment is unpredictable or uncontrollable, which prevents habituation.

An environment contains not only stimuli signifying threats, or novel stimuli demanding attention, but also reminders that the place is hostile and uncontrollable: 'the psychologically and socially meaningful messages associated with particular physical environments'.[22] Social status or stigma are often attached to the places where we live, work, or are educated. Living in a slum could be stressful because of the social stigma and its implications for self-esteem, in addition to physical dangers. Attending a school where one is bullied, rejected or is seen as a failure, can be stressful for similar reasons. Threats to the psychological self are as powerful as physical danger, and their impact can be more enduring.

THE ROLE OF COGNITIVE APPRAISAL

A person's appraisal of a situation or an environment is inevitably biased by previous experiences. A victim of bullying might become sensitized to the possibility of assault, anticipate hostility even when none is intended, and overreact to slight taunts (often to the amusement of his tormentors, who might continue to tease him to see the reaction). For the victim, innocuous aspects of the school building or yard could become painful reminders. The prospect of going to school might itself become a stressor (and can have psychosomatic effects, such as stomach pains or headaches). One coping strategy, avoidance, involves truancy or school refusal. Another strategy involves angry, disruptive conduct. Less conspicuously, yet perhaps more commonly, stressful unavoidable situations can lead to learned helplessness and depression.

Current models of stress in health psychology attribute a central role to people's cognitive appraisal of situational demands and of their own abilities to cope. In this view, stress arises from an imbalance between *perceived* demands and *perceived* personal resources, irrespective of whether individuals' beliefs about their circumstances are accurate or misplaced in some objective sense. Students might get unduly apprehensive about an exam for which they are adequately prepared, for instance. 'The cognitive appraisals that shape our emotional reactions can distort reality as well as reflect it realistically.'[23] Cognitive appraisal is not a rational process of sifting through information, but the instant evaluation of something as a threat or as not threatening, or as something we like or dislike. This evaluation is inherent in the person-environment interface, for, as Lazarus puts it, 'humans are meaning-oriented, meaning-creating creatures who constantly evaluate events from the perspective of their well-being and react emotionally to some of those evaluations'.[24] That is, we do not respond passively to environmental stressors; we are motivated to find out what events mean to us, to our physical well-being and self-esteem, and so on. The subjective appraisal of threat leads to physiological and cognitive stress responses which prepare the body for action. Behavioural outcomes of the stress response are actions designed to remove the threat ('fight'), remove oneself from the situation ('flight'), or neutralize one's part in the situation ('freeze'). If direct action is perceived as not possible or advisable (exams cannot be, or are best not avoided), cognitive defences, such as denial and rationalization, may come into play; alternatively, the person might resort to actions aimed at minimizing the *experience* of stress (e.g., through drugs, alcohol, etc.).

Having perceived an actual or potential threat, we might feel anger, fear, or despair. Lazarus construes emotion as 'a result of an anticipated, experienced, or imagined outcome of an adaptation relevant transaction between organism and environment'.[25] However, emotional states can precipitate stress. If cognitive appraisal is a constructive process (as Lazarus suggests), a process that involves individuals' anticipation of what an event might mean to their well-being, self-esteem, future, etc., then their interpretation of the actual event must be biased by their expectations: the actual event either confirms or disconfirms the expectations. If the circumstances are entirely new, the person might feel *uncertainty*, itself a powerful stressor. Anxiety or apprehension arising from uncertainty about a situation can bias cognitive appraisal.

Since the stress response is a reaction to threats detected on any level of perception, it can be provoked by the sheer anticipation of aversive consequences, justified or groundless. But while the neurophysiology of stress due to immediate danger or its anticipation may be the same, the respective emotional responses are different. An immediate danger might cause fright, whereas an anticipated danger is associated with anxiety: 'anxiety always involves symbolic threats (probably to the self), is anticipatory, and occurs under conditions of ambiguity, whereas fright is immediate, concrete, and concerns survival-related dangers'.[26]

A correlation between anxiety and school failure is well established.[27] A distinction is made in the literature between a state of anxiety, which is situation-specific, and a trait, or chronic anxiety, which is more generalized. Doubts about one's competence in a particular subject and the personal implications of anticipated failure may evoke a state of anxiety: for instance, anxiety was associated with pupils' poor performance in maths more than with their performance in reading, and more so in the upper primary and secondary school levels than in the lower level.[28] Chronic anxiety is associated with inhibited problem-solving competence, with obvious implications for schooling.[29] Anxiety is usually discussed as a problem of the individual child. However, neither anxiety state nor trait can be fully understood without taking into account the child's environment as perceived by the child.

Environmental Selection

So far, in this and the previous chapter, the environment has been described as *regulating* behaviour. Physical dimensions or conditions facilitate or constrain goal-directed activities: spaces in the school yard are used by children according to their play preferences; external noise interferes with students' listening to a lecture; and so on. The physical setting is thus posited as a stage upon which goal-directed activities are performed. This section draws attention to the role of the environment also as *selecting* behaviour patterns.

Exemplars of this idea can be drawn from opposing traditions in psychology. One view of the material world as the medium for all psychological functioning is explicit in radical behaviourism, a philosophical perspective outlined by B. F. Skinner.[30] This perspective centres on principles of learning, discovered and verified in laboratory experiments. According to Skinner and his followers, organisms adapt to their changing environments principally (but not only) through *operant conditioning*. Operant conditioning explains the acquisition of behavioural repertoires by linking the response pattern to rewards or punishments generated in the organism's environment. Although the Skinnerian explanation is highly deterministic, it underlines the fact that organisms actively operate on their environments: there must be some initial activity, however random, to be reinforced. Behaviourist explanations are also called learning theories, for they pertain to stable changes which occur after exposure to environmental contingencies.

Separately, the idea of children's learning through operations on their environments was expatiated by the Swiss biologist and child-psychologist Jean Piaget, who claimed 'Intelligence is an adaptation. In order to grasp its relation to life in general it is therefore necessary to state precisely the relations that exist between the organism and the environment.'[31] Piaget refers to the development of internally represented knowledge of the world, brought about through organisms' operations on their environments. His model of

69

the origins of intelligence embodies 'mentalist' assumptions which behaviourists eschew.

Piaget's work has had an enormous impact on primary education, especially science teaching, and on developmental psychology. Skinner's ideas, too, are likely to be familiar or readily accessible to readers pursuing education and psychology courses. To do justice to either theory would take us well beyond the scope of this chapter, but their common denominator and a few crucial differences are relevant to the present topic; those are looked at in the following subsection. Furthermore, both Skinnerian and Piagetian perspectives are broadly compatible with ecological or systemic thinking in psychology, in so far that they explain psychological functioning by describing the individuals' relations to their environments.

Workers in strictly ecological frameworks, however, endeavour to identify the principles of organism–environment relations *per se*. An implicit idea in ecological theories is pre-established harmony: the organism–environment fit or environment–behaviour congruence. An apt metaphor is the river, which flows in a channel already there, but in doing so, it modifies its environment (the channel deepens, the shape of its banks is altered, and so on); likewise, behaviour is regulated by what is possible in the immediate environment, and at the same time shapes the environment. This view is encapsulated in a precursor of ecological thinking in psychology, Kurt Lewin's field theory,[32] reviewed later in this section.

It is clear why water flows where it can, given the laws of gravity, but the laws for human action are less unequivocal. Behaviour could depend on the person's perception of what is possible (or advisable) to do. In a review of research on children's environmental cognition, Heft and Wohlwill point to a certain disparity between theory and evidence:[33] most studies, broadly supported by the Piagetian model, describe the development of mental representations of the world. Yet actual findings suggest that the reference system employed by the child to act on its environment is determined not simply by the child's cognitive ability, or 'objective' knowledge of the world, but by environmental conditions confronting the child at that particular time, and their emotional implications for the child (evidence that ties well with Lazarus' concept of cognitive appraisal, mentioned in the previous section). This concurs with James Gibson's ecological approach to perception.

Like Lewin, Gibson proposed to chart an environment in terms of its action possibilities for a particular organism, though (unlike Lewin) his chief interest was in the senses, especially in visual perception.[34] The aspect of Gibson's theory that is most relevant here (and discussed later in this section) can be illustrated as follows: consider a student looking at the clock in the lecture hall. The sensory input is 'objectively' processed into the knowledge that, say, there are 20 minutes to the end of the session; but this input would have a very different impact on a student who is bored or hungry, and on a student sitting a difficult exam.

Following Gibson, we would infer from the student's reactions the subjective significance of the visual input (the clock's face); we would focus on the experiential environment. Following either Skinner or Piaget, we may be interested in finding out how a person comes to associate this visual input with a measure of time, and to infer what it means in the given situation; we would focus, then, on the learning environment. This dichotomy of the learning vs. the experiential environment pervades the literature on educational settings.

LEARNING AND PLACE

Piaget and Skinner construed learning in general, and concept forming in particular, as the organism's adaptation to its surroundings. Their theories point to a process involving changes in individuals' operations as a result of experience; these changes usually (but not always) enhance the individuals' fitness for a particular environment. However, Piaget's and Skinner's basic premises foster divergent views on the learning environment.

The Darwinian concept of natural selection underlies both Piaget's and Skinner's theories, but in a very different sense. Charles Darwin proposed natural selection as the major evolutionary force that shapes a species' physiological and behavioural characteristics. According to this principle,

71

individuals who possess traits that happen to be advantageous in their particular habitats live longer, thereby increasing the number of their offspring, who since they inherit the adaptive trait, render it ubiquitous in succeeding generations. Human intellect, according to Piaget, is one such trait; and he studied intellectual development in children partly in order to understand the evolutionary origins of intelligence. According to Piaget, children acquire abstract concepts as they refine their operations according to feedback from their manipulation of things:

> [Intelligence] is not at all an independent absolute, but it is a relationship among others, between the organism and things. If intelligence thus extends an organic adaptation which is anterior to it, the progress of reason doubtless consists in an increasingly advanced acquisition of awareness.[35]

Skinner considered the human ability to form concepts and solve problems as an extension of discriminative learning.[36] He disputed the utility of constructs such as 'intelligence', 'awareness' and 'reason' in scientific explanations of human behaviour. Learning to discriminate stimuli, and to associate situations with particular consequences, is a universal capacity of all animal species; the uniquely human is acquired (according to Skinner) as a result of the child's interactions with other people: 'intellect' is culturally, not biologically, derived.

Skinner proposed that 'mechanics' analogous to those of Darwinian natural selection shape behaviour patterns on the level of the individual organism.[37] Operant conditioning is, in his view, a second kind of selection by consequences, which works in conjunction with natural selection. Thus, some behaviour patterns are selected in the course of a species' evolution, and become the innate repertoire of an individual member of the species. Other behaviours are acquired in the lifetime of the individual. Skinner proposed a third kind of selection, 'the evolution of social environments or cultures', which is facilitated by verbal behaviour.[38] A culture evolves when practices which originate in a group contribute to the group's successful adaptation to its environment. In sum,

> human behavior is the joint product of (i) the contingencies of survival responsible for the natural selection of the species and (ii) the contingencies of reinforcement responsible for the repertoires acquired by its members, including (iii) the special contingencies maintained by an evolved social environment.[39]

It is important to bear in mind that Skinner focused on the survival of discrete units of behaviour (responses) in the organism's repertoire. In a Skinnerian interpretation, a child's knowledge of a multiplication table simply means that the correct answers have survived in the child's repertoire. Moreover, problem-solving is defined by Skinner as a behaviour that 'changes another part of the solver's behaviour and is reinforced when it does so'.[40] Critics would say that this definition not only over-simplifies problem-solving, but also confuses behaviour and reasoning processes.

For behaviourists, then, learning means a stable change in the way an organism is likely to respond to given stimuli. In contrast, cognitive psychologists, including Piaget, postulate self-organizing mental networks (schemas) which mediate input and output; when arithmetic problems are correctly answered, it is assumed that the algorithms are somehow represented in the child's mind.

Behaviourists focus on the evolution of stimulus-response (S–R) bonds. These bonds do not originate 'in' the organism, nor do they exist transcendently as environmental 'forces', but are intrinsic to the organism–environment *relationship*. It is not disputed that learning has a neurophysiological basis; learning depends on processes to which Skinner referred as events within the skin. Since experiences are encoded by the brain, repetitious or powerful interactions with the external environment are believed to bring about changes in the internal environment (e.g., brain biochemistry). In subsequent encounters with similar stimuli, the organism would be prone to respond in a way that was effective on previous occasions, since its brain has been altered to produce that effect.

73

Both Skinner and Piaget focused essentially on the individual organism. People with whom a child interacts are regarded as 'objects' in his or her world, albeit uniquely salient. Thus we may speak of the social environment as we speak of the thermal environment, the acoustic environment, the spatial environment, and so on, all of which combine to create the child's natural environment. Skinnerian and Piagetian perspectives, however, lead to radically different views on the role of other people in the child's learning. According to Piagetian cognitive conflict theory, children's concept forming can be speeded up when they observe how more competent individuals solve practical problems (although, as will be discussed in Chapter 6, this is not always the case). Clearly, concept forming can be slowed down when other people deny the child access to the necessary experiences. But what and when a child learns, in the Piagetian view, follows a logical sequence; progress is induced or hindered by other people. In the Skinnerian view, other people control the consequences of a child's behaviour by rewarding some responses, and punishing or ignoring others. Thus other people, according to Skinner, determine what and when the child learns.

For Piaget, cognitive development is goal-directed: it unfolds in a predictable way towards abilities selected during the species' evolution. Piaget outlined sequential stages which lead from practical intelligence to formal logico-mathematical operations. For Skinner, learning has no predictable culmination, it is the result of ongoing operant conditioning; he refrained from making pre-emptive assumptions about the developmental sequence or outcomes. Skinner wrote about education, suggesting programmes for effective instruction, but he did not comment on the curriculum. Decisions about what people ought to learn reflect cultural beliefs and values, and therefore lie outside the science of behaviour as Skinner defined it. Piaget's theory, in contrast, implies that certain educational environments are more in keeping with the natural direction of cognitive development; Piaget and his colleagues looked for evidence of certain strategies and age-related competences in children's problem-solving. Their thinking bears directly on the curriculum. Who is right? It is difficult to find empirical evidence that does not lend itself to alternative explanations.

For example, Piaget observed that when water is poured from one beaker to another of a different shape, preschool children expect the volume of water to change. Older children know that the volume of water remains the same. In cognitive parlance, we say that the older children have acquired the concept of liquid conservation. The educational implications are clear: providing for water play in the nursery ensures that children have the hands-on experiences from which to derive their understanding of liquid conservation, at a stage in their development when they are ready to begin forming this concept. Perret-Clermont asked children in a nursery class to share out orange juice in beakers of different sizes; she observed that they did try to make sure that the juice was equally shared.[41] This demonstrates that children appreciate liquid conservation on a practical level before they can extrapolate this understanding to more abstract contexts, as Piaget assumed. But does Perret-Clermont's finding really show a precursor of the scientific understanding – or an early sense of 'fairness', a precursor of moral values? Does the likelihood that equal sharing was reinforced by teachers' and peers' approval in the nursery have anything to do with the finding? Regarding the learning environment, Skinner's message is to arrange 'a world in which behavior that is important to you actually occurs [in so far that] by noting the conditions under which we work well and by making every effort to maintain them, we can maximize the probability of the behavior that is important to us'.[42] Nursery staff structure an environment in which behaviours which we hold to be important, both socially (e.g., fair sharing out of juice) and educationally (e.g., liquid conservation), are reinforced.

Skinner's message applies also to self-study. Students may prefer to work on an essay in the library for a number of obvious extrinsic reasons (books and journals are available there, the place is quiet, and so on). Consequently, better work is produced. This consequence is intrinsically rewarding, and reinforces the students' preference for the library. In time, the place becomes associated with studying, so that the students might find themselves working more efficiently there than elsewhere.

Lewin's famous formula, $B = f(P,E)$, captures the idea that behaviour (B) is a function of a personal state (P) and environmental possibilities (E).[43] Lewin's explanation of behaviour in terms of a field of possibilities surrounding the person at a given moment was influenced by the biologist von Uexküll, who, in the early 1900s, drew attention to the experiential world of the animal. Von Uexküll's conception of the biological environment as a complex of foods, enemies, means of protection, etc., inspired Lewin to assert that things and events in the child's environment are defined 'partly by their appearances but above all by their functional possibilities'.[44]

Lewin, who originally wrote in German, mapped the environment in terms of *Aufforderungscharakter*, which roughly translates as 'invitation qualities'; his translators preferred *valences*: 'Objects are not neutral to the child, but have an immediate psychological effect on its behaviour... These imperative environmental facts – we shall call them valences – determine the direction of the behaviour.'[45] The emphasis is on the pull or push of environmental objects or features. Some objects or features have appealing qualities (positive valences), while other aspects of the environment are obstructive or threatening (negative valences); respectively, the child's actions are characterized by either *approach* or *avoidance* (or a combination of both). Lewin proposed that valences can be measured in terms of velocity and vector, like physical forces. For instance, we speak of a gravity field; in the same way, we can imagine a psychological field, the *life space*. Just as gravity does not exist independently of falling objects, so the forces postulated by Lewin are 'defined empirically and functionally, excluding all metaphysical problems, by their effect upon the behaviour of the child'.[46]

Similarly, Gibson's theory of *affordances* describes an environment in terms of perceiver-dependent qualities: 'the affordance of anything is a specific combination of the properties of its substance and its surfaces taken with reference to an animal'.[47] It is meaningless to talk of an environment (surroundings) without taking into account what is being surrounded. Likewise, it is meaningless to describe perception without specifying the perceiver and the perceived object. Direct perception, the process by which the organism maintains contact with its environment, is characterized by selective attention to something that is important to the organism. Internal states may determine what is subjectively important at a given moment, and the external world determines what it is objectively possible to do. For example, thirst primes an animal to detect water (information pick-up), or actively to seek it (behaviour); the thirsty animal perceives external objects in terms of 'drinkability'. It is important to stress that, like Skinner, Gibson and his followers strongly object to mentalism.[48] That is, they do not believe that a thirsty animal has, in any way, a mental representation of its world and its own need for water. Intentional action (e.g., seeking water) arises directly from the animal's present being-in-the-world.

When Gibsonians consider an organism's perception of its environment, they ask, in a sense, what it is like to be that organism in that place. What is it like to be a boy in a school yard during a break? If we adopt a Gibsonian stance, we would observe what the boy does there. Let's say that we see him run around and kick a ball. An 'orthodox Gibsonian' might sum up the observations by saying that the boy picked up the yard's affordance for these body-scaled activities. The fact that he calls it 'playing football' is trivial; to the Gibsonian, the relevant point is that the yard space and other features of the immediate environment (including peers with whom to play), complement a boy's intentional state. We may speak of the football-playing affordance of the setting to indicate the kind of activities it facilitates.

Unlike Lewin's valences, Gibsonian affordances do not allude to the attraction or repellence of environmental features. Gibson sought merely to chart environmental qualities that exist for an organism. A football-playing affordance is an objective ecological fact that holds for all able-bodied children in suitable school yards (and favourable school rules), but only individuals for whom playing football has personal significance would pick it up – would experience a positive valence, if they are keen, or a negative valence, if they dislike football but are coerced into playing it as a school sport.

Barker, whose behaviour setting theory was reviewed in the previous chapter, described an episode in a music lesson, that will serve to elucidate the point made here:

> Miss Madison said, 'Now we want one person to get up in front of the class and conduct.'
> Anne immediately raised her hand very eagerly straight up into the air.[49]

The teacher's request created an affordance that only Anne and a few of her classmates picked up. How to explain differences in pupils' responses to a teacher's request? The Gibsonian focus on the pick-up of sensory information cannot account for Anne's eagerness. Gibson's critics regard the epistemological gap between information available to the senses and people's actions as a major flaw in his theory of human perception.[50] Lewin's formula merely describes the observed facts, it does not explain why conducting the class might be important for Anne.

TOWARDS DISCURSIVE AFFORDANCES

This chapter has expatiated on the naturalist belief that there is no 'ghost in the machine': a child's behaviour in the classroom is not the effect of some intrapsychic dynamics, cognitive processes, or some other mental entities; all there is, is happening out there in the real world, in the child's interactions with the classroom environment. But a naive interpretation of this philosophical position is hardly tenable. It does not make human sense to explain Anne's response to the teacher's request, described earlier, with no reference whatsoever to what conducting the class might mean to Anne's perception of herself as a person – although both Gibsonian direct perception and Skinnerian learning principles undoubtedly underlie Anne's action (Anne not only heard the teacher's request, but selectively attended to it instead of attending to other events or day-dreaming; she previously learned that raising her hand was more likely than jumping up or shouting out to get the teacher to choose her). We must concede, then, that people pick up information that is relevant to their perceptions of their relationships with other people. In other words, we must consider *discursive affordances.*

Gibson's definition of affordances has been introduced earlier with the example of a thirsty animal. In the same vein, we may consider a child, for whom adults' attention and approval are very important, as 'primed' to detect classroom opportunities in that respect, perhaps behaving as Anne did in the music lesson. A boy may enjoy playing football for a number of reasons, among which are the social images and status it carries (e.g., 'being one of the boys'). Thus features of the immediate, physical environment can have affordances which effect not the state of the organism, but the social position of the individual. A very similar idea underlies the social-psychological concept of positioning, introduced in Chapter 5.

Notes and References

1 Folkard, S. 'Diurnal variation'. In Hockey, G. R. J. (ed.), *Stress and Fatigue in Human Performance.* Chichester: John Wiley and Sons, pp. 245–272, 1983.

2 Jones, D. M. 'Noise'. In Hockey, G. R. J. (ed.), *Stress and Fatigue in Human Performance.* Chichester: John Wiley and Sons, pp. 61–95, 1983.

3 Cohen, S., Evans, G. W., Krantz, D. S., Stokols, D. and Kelly, S. 'Aircraft noise and children: longitudinal and cross-sectional evidence on adaptation to noise, and the effectiveness of noise abatement'. *Journal of Personality and Social Psychology,* **40**, 331–345, 1981.

4 Jones, D. M., 1983, op. cit.

5 Schönpflung, W. 'Coping efficiency and situational demands'. In Hockey, G. R. J. (ed.), *Stress and Fatigue in Human Performance.* Chichester: John Wiley and Sons, pp. 299–330, 1983.

6 Ibid., p. 302.

7 Ward, L. M. and Suedfeld, R. 'Human responses to highway noise'. *Environmental Research,* **6**, 306–326, 1973.

8 Ramsey, J. D. 'Heat and cold'. In Hockey, G. R. J. (ed.), *Stress*

and Fatigue in Human Performance. Chichester: John Wiley and Sons, pp. 33–60, 1983.

9 Humphreys, M. A. 'Relating wind, rain and temperature to teachers' reports of young children's behaviour'. In Canter, D. and Lee, T. (eds), *Psychology and the Built Environment.* England: The Architectural Press, pp. 19–28, 1974.

10 Ramsey, J. D., 1983, op. cit.

11 Auliciems, 1969, cited in Moos, R. H. *The Human Context: Environmental Determinants of Behavior.* New York: John Wiley & Sons 1976.

12 Moos, R. H., 1979, op. cit.

13 Wyon, D. P. 'Studies of children under imposed noise and heat stress'. *Ergonomics,* **13**, 598–612, 1970.

14 Weinstein, C. S. 'The physical environment of the school: a review of the research'. *Review of Educational Research,* **49**, 577–610, 1979.

15 Küller, R. and Lindsten, C. 'Health and behaviour of children in classrooms with and without windows'. *Journal of Environmental Psychology,* **12**, 305–317, 1992.

16 Ibid., p. 310.

17 Ibid., p. 312.

18 Selye, H. *The Stress of Life,* rev. edn. New York: McGraw-Hill, 1976.

19 Rabbitt, P. M. A. and Maylor, E. A. 'Investigating models of human performance'. *British Journal of Psychology,* **82**, 259–290, 1991.

20 Ibid., p. 260.

21 Saegert, S. 'Stress-inducing and reducing qualities of environments'. In Proshansky, H. M., Ittleson, W. H. and Rivlin, L. G. (eds), *Environmental Psychology: People and Their Physical Settings,* 2nd edn. New York: Holt, Rinehart and Winston, pp. 218–223, 1976.

22 Ibid., p. 221.

23 Lazarus, R. S. 'Thoughts on the relations between emotion and cognition'. In Scherer, K. R. and Ekman, P. (eds), *Approaches to Emotion.* Hillside, NJ: Laurence Erlbaum Associates, 1984, p. 253.

24 Ibid., p. 249.

25 Ibid., p. 255.

26 Ibid., p. 254.

27 E.g., Gaudry, E. and Spielberger, C. D. *Anxiety and Educational Achievement.* Chichester: John Wiley and Sons, 1971.

28 Ibid.

29 Kinsbourne, M. and Caplan, P. J. *Children's Learning and Attention Problems*. Boston: Little, Brown, 1979.
30 E.g., Skinner, B. F. *About Behaviourism*. Harmondsworth: Penguin, 1974.
31 Piaget, J. *The Origin of Intelligence in the Child*. Harmondsworth: Penguin, 1977, p. 15.
32 Lewin, K. *A Dynamic Theory of Personality: Selected Papers*. New York: McGraw-Hill, 1935.
33 Heft, H. and Wohlwill, J. F. 'Environmental cognition in children'. In Stokols, D. and Altman, I. (eds), *Handbook of Environmental Psychology*, Vol. 2. London: John Wiley and Sons, pp. 175–203, 1987.
34 Gibson, J. J. *The Ecological Approach to Visual Perception*. Boston: Houghton-Mifflin, 1979.
35 Piaget, J., 1977, op. cit., pp. 31–32.
36 E.g., Skinner, B. F., 1974, op. cit.; Skinner, B. F. *Verbal Behaviour*. New York: Appleton Century Croft, 1957.
37 Skinner, B. F. 'Selection by consequences'. *Behavioural and Brain Science*, **7**, 477–502, 1984.
38 Ibid., p. 478.
39 Ibid., p. 478.
40 Skinner, B. F. 'An operant analysis of problem solving'. *Behavioural and Brain Science*, **7**, 1984, p. 583.
41 Perret-Clermont, A. *Social interaction and cognitive development in children*. European Monographs in Social Psychology, Vol. 19. London: Academic Press, 1980.
42 Skinner, B. F., in an interview with *Omni* magazine, September 1979.
43 Lewin, K., 1935, op. cit.
44 Ibid., p. 77.
45 Ibid., p. 77.
46 Ibid., p. 79.
47 Gibson, J. J., 'The Theory of Affordances'. In Shaw, R. and Bransford, J. (eds), *Perceiving, Acting and Knowing: Towards an Ecological Psychology*. New Jersey: Lawrence Erlbaum, pp. 67–82, 1977. See also Gibson, J. J., 1979, op. cit.
48 E.g., Heft, H. 'Affordances and the body: an intentional analysis of Gibson's ecological approach to visual perception'. *Journal for the Theory of Social Behaviour*, **19**, 1–30, 1989; Heft, H. 'Perceiving affordances in context: a reply to Chow'. *Journal for the Theory of Social Behaviour*, **20**, 277–284, 1990.
49 Barker, R. G. *Ecological Psychology: Concepts and Methods for*

Studying the Environment of Human Behaviour. Stanford, CA: Stanford University Press, 1968, p. 14.

50 E.g., Chow, S. L. 'An intentional analysis of "Affordance" revisited'. *Journal for the Theory of Social Behaviour*, **19**, 357–365, 1989.

CHAPTER 4
Organizational Ethos

> The individuality of a man is achieved within a social environment, so to explain the individual we must, among other things, consider the structure of the social system in which he operates.[1]

The school organization creates an environment to which individuals must adapt. Schools vary widely in scale, regime, social composition. Does the size of the school (or the class) matter? Does the way a school is organized and managed influence educational and social outcomes? What are the implications for individuals' development? This chapter considers some of the issues relating to the evaluation of school organizations and their effects.

School and Class Size

The number of pupils enrolled in a school is meaningless on the level of individual pupils, but the enrolment scale can create or deny certain opportunities, and calls for management strategies, all of which directly affect individuals' schooling. School and class size are unrelated in so far that large schools, affording to cater for 'speciality' interests, accommodate small classes (believed to be better for learning). Small schools tend to be friendlier as a whole, but might mean larger classes and less educational variety. Separate psychological processes underlie the effects of school size and of class size. However, similar questions may be raised. What are the implications of school/class size for management of resources? What are the implications for learning and attainment? What are the implications for pupils' social-personal development?

BIG SCHOOL, SMALL SCHOOL

Large schools are increasingly the norm, reflecting primarily administrative and financial considerations. The trend is a political issue, especially in rural education, where the closure of small schools, often due to costs, can have adverse effects on the community.[2] Issues related to the quality of education and the implications for personal development, too, are not free of political undertones. In Britain, Human Scale Education (HSE), an educational charity, represents a reaction to recent trends in the state sector. In 1993, seven small schools were registered with the HSE, and five more were due to open. HSE supporters are teachers and parents dedicated to humanistic ideals of education. These values, they feel, are ill-served by current practices. In addition to small schools, HSE promotes alternative schemes such as flexischooling and minischools (the latter involving the restructuring of a large school into smaller units sharing a campus).

The emotive argument against large schools is that the 'person' is lost in the educational machinery. The sheer size of a large school poses administrative problems that have little to do with the nitty-gritty of educating children and young people. Good teachers are not necessarily good administrators, and efficient school administrators do not have to be good teachers (in the same way that in industry, factory managers do not have to be skilled production workers). But, needless to say, the 'produce' of schools is unlike any industrial output. The analogy of factories is usually applied to schools in a derogatory sense, the implication being that pupils are treated like objects processed in a production-line manner, instead of as human beings whose individuality ought to be nurtured.

Is depersonalization an inevitable consequence of largeness?

The most illuminating study on the matter was carried out over thirty years ago by the ecological psychologists whose approach was introduced in Chapter 2. The study is reported in detail by Barker and Gump, in a book entitled *Big School, Small School*.[3] Barker and his associates investigated thirteen schools in Kansas, ranging in enrolments from 35 to 2,287. The researchers set out to record the differentiation of children's behaviour patterns in different educational 'habitats', and supplemented their field observations with inventory-based inquiries about affective consequences for pupils.

In his summary of the study, Gump focused on findings concerning the implications of size for school institutions and their populations, in terms of the variety of instruction and extracurricular provision, and in terms of students' participation in school affairs.[4] The bigger the school, the more types of academic and vocational courses were available. But the increase in variety was not in proportion to the increase in school size: 'it takes a lot of bigness to add a little variety. On average a 100 percent increase in size yielded only a 17 percent increase in variety'.[5] A further qualification to the assumption that a big school offers more is the actual range of courses available to individuals. When Gump and his co-workers looked into the opportunities open for the average student in a particular term, they found that students in four of the small schools in their study in fact had slightly more kinds of classes than did students in the largest school. Furthermore, even what was available in the large school was often not used by considerable segments of the student population. On the positive side, the large schools offered more opportunities for individuals who were particularly interested in one area, such as music or maths. Therefore, the question about size, regarding instruction, may boil down to the preference of either more opportunity for 'specialists' or a wider academic experience for the general student body.

Looking at the junior classes of the largest school (enrolment: 2,287) and four small schools (average enrolment: 110), the researchers investigated the provision of extra-curricular activities, in terms of quantity, rates and nature of student participation, and the kinds of satisfaction that students derived from the activities. Over a three-month period in each school, the researchers made a complete inventory of what they termed 'nonclass behaviour settings': sport events, fund-raising projects, concerts, library, canteen, etc. During the period in focus, the large school provided 189 nonclass settings open to juniors, and the small schools averaged 48.5 settings. However, it must be asked, to what extent these opportunities were picked up and by whom. After the researchers listed all the school's extracurricular activities, they asked the junior students to indicate which of these they had attended over the previous three months. The *number* of participations was slightly greater in the large school – but the variety of participation was clearly greater in the small schools. That is, in the large school a student may go to more events, but those events tended to be of the same type (e.g., all sports matches or clubs), whereas in the small schools, a student might attend less sports events, but would go also to concerts. A related finding was that in the large school there was a sizable minority who participated in very few extracurricular occasions, usually the compulsory ones (e.g., assemblies).

As Gump asserted, 'It is important to know what students did in these settings, not just whether they were there or not.'[6] Almost every extracurricular activity had openings for active participation: players in a football match, performers in a concert, a chairperson in a meeting, and so on. The researchers referred to the students who filled such positions as 'operatives'. Although operatives in particular settings may have a different degree of importance, they all have some responsibility: if an operative quits, some readjustment is necessary, whereas the absence of an audience member seldom affects the running of the event. The psychological and developmental implications of *being needed* cannot be over-stated. As operatives, students gain leadership experience, acquire a sense of worth and obligation, and meet challenges.

As there were fewer settings per student in the large school, it is simple arithmetic that particular settings would be more crowded in the large school than in the small school (sometimes about three times as much, according to the figures quoted by Gump.[7] Obviously, the more people there are, the less chances there are to become an operative. On the basis of the junior students' reports, the researchers worked out that during the three-month period, the average large-school student was an operative in 3.5 settings, whereas the small-school counterpart was operative in 8.6 settings. Also, 28 per cent of the large-school juniors, compared to only 2 per cent of the small-school juniors, did not perform as an operative at all. This, again, highlights the fact that a large school tends to produce a sizable minority of 'outsiders', students who gain little from the facilities provided by the school.

Finally, the researchers investigated the students' own feelings about the extracurricular activities in which they had participated, especially the kind of satisfaction they derived from particular nonclass settings. Large-school and small-school juniors alike mentioned vicarious or 'secondary' pleasures (e.g., watching a good game or an interesting play), and the pride of belonging to a particular crowd or a school. But, in addition, the small-school students mentioned more often the satisfaction of increasing one's competence (e.g., getting fit by playing football, learning new things on school trips), experiencing the sense of challenge, competition and success (e.g., discovering one's abilities or shortcomings, achieving something worthwhile), and the positive experience of being part of a team or an action group.

In sum, the small-school students experienced more often satisfaction related to personal improvement, to challenge and action, to close co-operation with peers and to 'being important'. The kinds of satisfaction experienced by the large-school students were typically those derived from somebody else's action, and connected with 'belonging to something big'.[8] Wicker draws attention to other explanations for the differences found by Barker's team:[9] one possibility is that the small schools, located in rural communities, provided most of the leisure opportunities available to students, whereas the city students found many other opportunities outside school.

The *Big School, Small School* study remains important, for it demonstrates the discontinuities between objective measures of educational provision and what the school actually offers to the individual pupil. The findings seem to substantiate a case for small schools, although the potential benefits of a large school should not be ignored. The greater scope for academic, vocational or artistic specialization that may be offered by a large school is not a trivial advantage. Socially, a large-school student has more chances of meeting people who share similar interests and attitudes, as well as mixing with people from different backgrounds, than a small-school student has. Some of the less desirable implications of largeness can be overcome by schemes such as minischools, which create 'human scale' environments for learning and development within a large school.

Summing up other research on the matter, David[10] contended that school size is not an independent variable. Changes in school organization or educational and social outcomes do not occur simply as a result of varying the size; neither large schools nor small schools guarantee the quality of education. As David pointed out, size cannot be divorced from context. Size can give no more than an inkling about the internal environment of a school.

CLASS SIZE

Teachers and parents commonly believe that children learn best in small classes. Research evidence generally backs up this belief; critics point out that the advantages of small classes are not substantial enough to justify employing more teachers. In an ideal world, where costs are not an issue, is there sufficient evidence to recommend small classes? The apparent variability of class-size effects is not random: first, it indicates that the needs of certain pupil populations – the youngest and the socially disadvantaged – are best met in small classes. Second, the evidence suggests that simply reducing the pupil: teacher ratio is not sufficient: teaching methods are a crucial factor.

Studies, mainly in the United States, indicate that small classes can lead to increased gains in learning in the first years of schooling. For instance, in a state-wide intervention project in Tennessee, project STAR (Student Teacher Achievement Ratio), a comparison was made of attainment in three types of classes: small (13–17), regular (22–25), and regular size with a full-time teacher aide. The pupils were followed from the kindergarten (age five) to the third grade (age eight). The results show consistently that children taught in the smaller classes for the first four years outperform those taught in larger classes, and maintain their academic advantage two years later.[11] Moreover, disadvantaged minority children seem to benefit the most from small classes. In Britain, Mortimore *et al.* found that pupils in junior schools where the classes averaged 24 or fewer generally made better progress in maths than did pupils in schools with classes averaging 27 or more.[12]

The class-size effect discovered by Mortimore *et al.* was statistically significant only in the first year. Critics take the decrease in differences between the progress of children taught in large and small classes over the school years as sufficient reason for dismissing class-size considerations. However, the decrease may suggest that pupil age is a relevant factor. It is common sense that younger children depend on adult guidance more than older pupils; but, due to the ways schools are resourced, class sizes tend to be higher in primary schools than in the secondary schools, and post–16 classes are the smallest.

Another reason for the limited benefits from small classes is underlined by Mortimore and Blatchford in a Briefing on class size issued by the National Commission on Education (an independent commission of inquiry into education and training):[13] some studies found that teachers used to teaching in large classes did not take advantage of the opportunities offered by small classes, and maintained their old methods. As Mortimore and Blatchford point out, it makes little sense to consider class size in isolation from teaching practices; but research is lacking as to what aspects of classroom ecology are most influential:

> It is difficult to know whether the opportunity for more individual attention for pupils, more opportunities for pupils to become involved in practical learning tasks, or enhanced teacher motivation and satisfaction in small classes, which indirectly benefit pupils.[14]

Recent work by Ingram and Worrall, reviewed in the next chapter, demonstrates what can be achieved in a small class.[15] Mortimore and Blatchford recommend that, in order to maximize potential benefits, reductions in class size should always be accompanied by a review of teaching methods and classroom management, providing in-service training if necessary. In secondary schools, they recommend that the principle of 'fitness for purpose' should be applied in order to determine the best use of teacher time and group size.[16]

Finally, if the effects of class size on attainment are understated in educational research, at least in Britain, the psychological and social implications are virtually untouched. Mortimore and Blatchford conclude their Briefing with this comment:

> Unfortunately, few studies have sought to elicit the views of pupils, possibly because, unless they had *experienced* different sized classes, it would be difficult for them to make an informed judgement. Yet such a judgement could be very illuminating, not only from the point of view of whether pupils learn more easily in classes of a particular size, but also as to whether they feel happier, believe they are less likely to be bullied and are more confident about speaking up for themselves and participating in practical activities.[17]

The research difficulty mentioned by Mortimore and Blatchford is spurious. We need not ask pupils to judge classes of different sizes. There are research tools to assess whether pupils in different classes feel happier and less worried about being bullied; classroom observations can reveal whether pupils in small classes participate more, and more confidently. The real problem is raising awareness that 'A carefully controlled British research on the long-term effects of different size classes on the attitudes, achievement and behaviour of pupils is long overdue....'[18]

School Structure

The understanding that human behaviour and development takes place within structured situations calls for the description of those situations. Can descriptions of organizations explain human behaviour? If dissimilar school organizations are consistently associated with different behaviour patterns or educational outcomes, we may attribute the differences to 'something' about the way the schools are organized; subsequent studies can focus on defining that crucial 'something'.

A similar rationale underlies *school effectiveness* research, discussed below.

SCHOOL EFFECTIVENESS

A school's worth is often judged by 'results': exam passes, rates of attendance, prevalence of disruptive behaviour. In educational research, these measures are conventionally referred to as *pupil outcomes*, though of course these are outcomes of complex interactions between intake characteristics and the ways that staff implement educational goals. Since the 1970s, substantial evidence for the role of school organizational factors as determinants of pupil outcomes has been amassed by initially isolated groups of researchers in Britain, the USA, Canada, Australia, Holland and Scandinavia, who now comprise the school-effectiveness speciality in the world of education.[19]

The early studies sought to ascertain the existence of school effects. If a school is notorious for poor academic results and delinquency, an intuitive inclination may be to look at the school's catchment area: is it an area of urban decay, poverty and high crime? A consistent association between social disadvantages and poor academic performance has been shown in several wide-scale surveys in the 1960s and early 1970s. But could the school itself exacerbate educational failure and social problems? Several British studies show that substantial differences in outcomes between schools cannot be attributed entirely to the academic and social background of their pupils. The conclusion that the school must make a difference became the central thesis of the School Differences Research Group in Britain.[20] Further research has probed related questions: the size of school influences (compared to family and community influences); the consistency of school effects over time; which aspects of pupil development are most affected; individual differences in pupils' susceptibility to school influences; and the characteristics of 'effective' or 'ineffective' schools.[21] More recent studies did not find school differences of a scale similar to those reported in the 1970s.

Qualitatively, a clear picture emerges regarding the factors underlying school effectiveness. Mortimore *et al.* carried out a detailed investigation of 50 junior schools in Inner London over four years, reported in a book pithily entitled *School Matters*[22] They compared the schools in terms of pupil intake characteristics, educational outcomes (reading and maths tests), pupil behaviour (assessed by class teachers), pupils' attitudes towards different types of school activities, classroom and school organization and policies (information obtained through interviews with staff), teacher strategies (observed in the classroom), and parents' views. Twelve key factors were identified:

(1)   Purposeful leadership of the staff by the headteacher
(2)   The involvement of the deputy head
(3)   The involvement of teachers
(4)   Consistency among teachers
(5)   Structured sessions
(6)   Intellectually challenging teaching
(7)   The work-centred environment
(8)   Limited focus within sessions
(9)   Maximum communication between teachers and pupils
(10) Record keeping
(11) Parental involvement
(12) Positive climate.[23]

The importance of a *structured* learning environment is conspicuous. Mortimore *et al.* discovered a positive impact on progress in schools where teachers followed guidelines in the same way; a lack of consistency in teacher approach had a negative effect. In effective classes, pupils were guided into areas of autonomous study, rather than being given unlimited responsibilities, and received relatively more feedback about their work.

A *structured* environment does not mean a regimental, authoritarian set-up. The importance of a learning environment in which the child has 'personal powers' is another corollary of the findings reported by Mortimore *et al.* Progress was greatest in classes where pupils were encouraged to use their creative imagination and powers of observation. In terms of communication, successful teachers had a flexible approach, blending individual, class and group interaction.

The *School Matters* study backs up a common-sense 'blue-print' for the effective primary school; but why does it work? By research design, this and similar correlational studies can locate the key processes, but not explain them. Unlike most other research fields described in this book, school effectiveness is indigenous to education: the origins of the field in the United States are traced to the work of a school-board superintendent, Ron Edmonds; in Britain, although the very first studies were conducted under the auspices of bodies such as a social medicine unit and an institution of psychiatry, the thrust of research and theorizing has been *educational* implications, to do with school management and improvement. Reynolds and Parker identify a pressing need to relate school-differences findings to psychology, psychiatry and other disciplines concerned with interpersonal relationships.[24] David Reynolds, a foremost figure in British school effectiveness, has claimed in an earlier review: 'We still do not have . . . any real idea as to *how* the process factors actually generate outputs, which may be through effects upon peer group processes or upon individual self-conception, for example.'[25]

It is not a case of simply lacking such knowledge. There is a vast reservoir of research and theories on human relations within organizations. When explanations for school effectiveness are offered, they typically draw from occupational psychology and sociology, with particular reference to leadership and decision-making processes. But the psychological impact of the organizational milieu on pupils is virtually ignored in the school effectiveness literature (unless psychological impact is mistaken for the incidence of disruptive behaviour or rates of academic performance). Reynolds' comment, above, perhaps implies that as yet nobody has found a neat way to relate psychological and sociological inquiries to the problems and controversies that currently define the school effectiveness field.

The difficulty may be illustrated with a simplified example, the hypothetical case of two same-grade classes in one school, who produce different attainment rates by the end of the school year. To explain what causes the different outcomes, we would obviously investigate the quality of teaching that each class received during the year, the mixture of ability levels in the respective groups, classroom conditions, and any other likely factors. If we approach the issue with pragmatic educational goals in mind, we would be most interested to know which factors, out of several plausible ones, account for the variance in attainment. Let us say that in this hypothetical case we discover that, in the main, the teachers' styles were different. If we conduct the research in an educational frame of reference, our efforts will be invested in recommending that teachers implement the style associated with better outcomes. To make such a recommendation realistic, we may need to consider the wider context of teachers' styles: consistency in teacher approach within the school policy (one of the key factors for effectiveness identified by Mortimore *et al.*,[26] local authority attitudes, teacher training, and so on. The question, why this style and not the other is more effective, although germane, lies outside our immediate concern to promote effective teaching and optimal attainment.

If, on the other hand, we approach the difference between the two classes in psychological or sociological frames of reference, we would seek to explain why certain teaching styles lead to differential performances. Does the effective style 'work' by increasing pupil motivation, for instance? If we suspect that this is the case, we would need to defend our thesis with a reference to a theory of human motivation. Our efforts will be invested in describing the mechanics of classroom interactions or pupil intrapsychic processes (according to theoretical persuasion). In general, then, evidence for school differences in pupil outcomes sends psychologists seeking causes 'inside' classroom groups or individuals, and sends education-oriented researchers seeking implications in the wider contexts. It is difficult to look both ways at the same time.

For psychologists, school effectiveness data are invaluable in indicating processes in need of explanation. For instance, involving pupils in decision-making could be a key to school effectiveness. Reynolds in South Wales and others elsewhere found that the effective and ineffective secondary schools in their samples differed, crucially, 'in the ways they attempted to mobilize pupils towards the acceptance of their goals'.[27] Reynolds distinguishes between two major strategies, *coercion* and *incorporation*. The more effective schools utilized an incorporative strategy to some extent, which amounted to giving pupils the sense of responsibility, control over their environment, and shared goals with their teachers. This discovery concurs with theories about the psychological significance of perceiving one's environment as controllable and about the importance of shared goals in interpersonal relations.

For the moment, suffice it to note that if incorporation is indeed the key to school effectiveness, psychology can explain why. But the role of incorporation in the making of an effective school might depend on how 'effectiveness' is defined. Cuttance spells out the use of the term:

> schools are described as *effective* if their pupils perform at a higher average level than the average school, and *ineffective* if their pupils perform at a lower average level than the average school. The *average school* is usually taken to refer to schools in the system which perform at about the mean average level, in a statistical sense, for all schools in the school system under consideration.[28]

In other words, there are no absolute criteria for an ideal school. Not surprisingly, studies in different regions and eras, let alone different countries, yield discrepant results. What counts as high performance in one sample might be closer to the average level, or below it, in another sample. A school where 5 per cent of leavers lack basic literacy skills might be regarded effective if the incidence of school-leaver illiteracy is greater in other schools under comparison. Surely, however, this means that the school in focus is *less ineffective* than the others; a truly effective school will be associated with zero illiteracy. Beyond the basics, the issue is confounded by curriculum development logistics. A very low rate of failure in a GCSE subject, for instance, would mean that the curriculum grossly underestimated the ability level of the age group in question; consequently, a more advanced course will be devised. Moreover, what seemed to work for making an effective school in one society might not be accepted well in other social and economic climates, in which vocational training priorities might be perceived differently, and some discipline measures (viz., corporal punishment) might be unacceptable. 'What worked in the 1970s is simply unlikely to travel well to the educational world of the 1990s.'[29]

If viewed against the constant flux of society, the search for the effective school seems beset with insurmountable problems. We may ask, however, whether unwarranted emphasis is placed on discontinuities across generations (and countries), while the continuities of human psychology are understated. Curricula require ongoing update; children in the developed world today may be open to some concepts at an earlier age because of technological and societal changes. What is regarded as 'essential knowledge' also varies over time; it is no longer considered important to learn Latin, whereas computer literacy is fast becoming one of the basics. But whatever is being taught, pupils' pride of achievement or shame of failure, beliefs about causes of their success or failure, reasons for accepting or rejecting school values, all indicate universalities of human adaptation to a social environment.

THE ORGANIZATION AS ENVIRONMENT

How can an organization be an environment in the ecological sense? Imagine children in a classroom. In ecological thinking, an individual's environment is the complex system of external conditions impinging *directly* on the individual. Children's environments comprise objects and people with whom they can interact. Where exactly does a child 'interface' the *institution*? Nevertheless, it is a common impression that schools and classrooms have a distinct atmosphere, reflecting the kind and quality of activities associated with them.

There is a 'feel' to a classroom, even in the absence of its inhabitants. Weinstein and Woolfolk showed photographs of vacant elementary school classrooms, which were either neat or messy, to 10-year-old children and to college students.[30] The children and students alike assumed that pupils in the neat classroom would be happier and better behaved than their counterparts in the messy classroom. They also attributed different personality and behavioural traits to the teachers of those classrooms. The clear consensus emerging in Weinstein and Woolfolk's study does not necessarily mean that the respondents inferred correctly the character of unknown pupils and teachers from the state of the room. Above all, the results indicate that there are common *expectations* about educational settings.

Do such expectations influence the behaviour and self-image of individuals finding themselves inhabiting messy or neat classrooms? First, the question points to the school organization as perceived by its members. The *school climate* approach to evaluating schools represents an early descriptive effort based on pupils' and teachers' perceptions of organizational practices. Second, the question alludes to the causal significance of shared expectations in the explanations of behaviour and educational outcomes. The concept of *school ethos*, discussed later in this section, represents an early attempt to 'switch' from description to explanation.

School climate research was inspired by organization theory, which emphasized 'the twin organizational tasks of social needs satisfaction and task accomplishment, as seen through the eyes of the junior members of the organization'.[31] Early 'school climate' studies, concerned with the definition of a good work environment, regarded the school as no different from any industrial organization: 'Children in general seem to be assigned a status as organizational products rather than as important members of the organization in their own right.' Later studies show a greater sensitivity to the peculiarities of the school as an institution, and acknowledge the fact that pupils form the majority of its population, and their behaviour patterns, which differ markedly from those of staff, 'are probably the major influence on the attitudes of those adults towards the school, and also one of the most strikingly obvious features of the institution to any outsider'.[33] Therefore, more recent studies introduced pupils' perceptions of teachers and school practices, explored through surveys, as a key variable. In this vein, Finlayson identified four relevant areas applicable to the British secondary school:

- pupils' perceptions of the behaviour of peers and teachers;
- teachers' perceptions of the behaviour of colleagues;
- teachers' perceptions of the behaviour of heads of departments;
- teachers' perceptions of the behaviour of the head.[34]

Thus schools may be described, compared and contrasted, according to groups' perceptions of peers and others as incumbents of institutional roles.

However, the notion of school climate embodies a belief that pupils' and teachers' reciprocal perceptions describe the actual psychosocial or 'affective' climate of the educational setting under investigation. Taken further, the assumption is that the 'climate' somehow affects the individual pupil (or teacher). This makes intuitive sense: when I had the misfortune to teach an unenthusiastic seminar group of undergraduates, I felt that the few keen students were 'holding back', as if impelled to conform to the general apathy of the class. Regularities in the ways individuals' perceptions of the behaviour of others influence their own behaviour and attitudes are well known in social psychology, and have been described in experimental research on conformity, bystander apathy, and similar social phenomena.[35] Is a concept of 'climate' necessary?

A related concept is that of *school ethos*. In a major British survey of secondary schools, reported in the book *Fifteen Thousand Hours*, Rutter *et al.* found a variance in pupil behaviour across schools.[36] Rates of attendance and antisocial behaviour in those schools did not correlate with their pupils' behaviour in the primary schools, were not associated with catchment area differences, nor with physical or administrative features of the school. Instead, the differences had the strongest associations with *overall school process*. That is, school effects on pupils' behaviour could not be attributed to isolated factors about the school regime, size, etc., but to within-school processes taken as a whole, a 'systemic entity' that Rutter *et al.* called *school ethos*.

Rutter *et al.* suggested that 'individual actions or measures may combine to create a particular *ethos*, or set of values, attitudes and behaviours which will become characteristic of the school as a whole.'[37] The researchers concluded that 'school processes constituted the *predominant* influence on children's behaviour in the classroom and the playground'.[38] Furthermore,

> the association between the *combined* measure of overall school process and each of the measures of outcome was much stronger than any of the associations with individual process variables. This suggests that the *cumulative* effect of these various social factors was considerably greater than the effect of any of the individual factors on their own.[39]

Rutter and his co-workers substantiate their case for 'ethos effects' with the finding that single outcome variables (e.g., attendance rate) correlated more strongly with the *overall* measure of school processes than with any single school process. They briefly discuss three reasons why the whole should differ from the sum of its parts.

Two points refer to teacher–pupil relationships. When visiting the schools, the researchers observed that occasionally the same action by different teachers (e.g., leaving a class on its own) led to dissimilar class reactions in the different schools. They surmised that 'something' about the way children had been generally treated influenced their contrasting conduct in ostensibly similar situations. A second point was that many of the variables in the study did not refer to teacher actions which bore directly on individual children. The authors assumed that the way a teacher responds to an individual child has an effect on the rest of the class.

The main point forwarded by Rutter *et al.*, however, alludes to the peer group. They noted that most school process variables in their study had only indirect connection with the pupil outcome variable with which they correlated. For instance, attendance rates correlated with school features that did not involve teacher response to pupil absenteeism. Therefore, the relation could not be explained by psychological reward/punishment mechanisms, but as an effect of school ethos. Their measure of attendance referred to the school's average rates, not to the attendance records of individual pupils; even if sick leave were omitted from the data, there may be a number of reasons why a school's reaction to truancy has little effect on some pupils. Nevertheless, it is likely that in schools where truancy is rife, individuals might find it easier to truant themselves. Truancy becomes the norm.

In general, Rutter *et al.* supported their concept of ethos with the theory that 'any relatively self-contained organisation tends to develop its own culture or pattern'.[40] People tend to form groups which have distinct codes of conduct, which in turn prescribe group members' behaviours. Rutter *et al.* proposed that the chief mechanisms underlying the impact of 'ethos' on individual pupils may be found in three areas: (1) teacher expectations about pupils' work and conduct; (2) models provided by the teachers' own behaviour and by the behaviour of other pupils; and (3) the feedback pupils receive on what is acceptable behaviour at the school.

The phrases 'school climate' and 'school ethos' feature prominently throughout the contributions to a 1980s review of the school effectiveness field,[41] and both are absent from the Subject Index of the follow-up review.[42] The reason for dropping them in the space of seven years may be glimpsed in the explanation forwarded by Entwistle *et al.* for developing a new instrument for tapping pupils' perceptions of teachers and schools.[43] For the purpose of their research, it was 'necessary to explore pupils' perceptions of the school which, presumably, would involve those all too elusive concepts of "school ethos" and "school climate" '.[44] But the global definitions of 'ethos' and 'climate' did not provide the researchers with sufficient discrete dimensions upon which to build instruments for more-probing inquiries:

> the variables measured in [school climate] studies describe the 'macro-level' of school organisation and the social composition of pupil intakes. Our concern was at the level of interaction between pupils and teachers and of the *qualitative* effects that learning environments are expected to have on pupils' learning.[45]

The next section describes the rationale for using scales, and the dimensions found useful when evaluating educational environments.

The historical significance of school ethos and school climate lies in sparking interest in the ecology of schools and their effects on the education and development of children and youth. Although the terms may have outlived their utility in empirical research, what they convey arguably remains viable.

Measures of Educational Environments

Classroom environment research, arising notably from the work of Rudolf Moos in the United States and Barry Fraser in Australia, parallels the school effectiveness field in many respects. Both arose from the need to evaluate educational environments. Their survey-based methodology is identical, though different inventories are used. Workers in both fields implicitly regard the school as an ecosystem, and construe statistical correlations between school processes and pupil outcomes as indicative of pupils' adaptation. The fact that there are virtually no cross-references, nor shared theoretical grounds, between school-effectiveness and classroom-environment workers is perhaps due to the disparate disciplinary pathways into the respective areas: there is a strong sociological bias in the school effectiveness literature, whereas classroom environment is a distinctly 'psychological' enterprise.

This section generally concerns the use of surveys in research on educational environments, with a particular reference to 'classroom environment' instruments. But what exactly do surveys measure?

THE SUBENVIRONMENT

The ways in which teachers communicate educational values to pupils, and pupils' acceptance or rejection of those values, are among complex internal *school processes* which constitute the organizational ecosystem. Pupil outcomes (attainment, attendance, behaviour) are believed to reflect individuals' adaptation to environments created by administrative decisions and the ways in which staff implement such decisions. School processes

101

are conventionally posited as *independent variables*, and pupil outcomes as the *dependent variables*. The 'paradigm' embodies the general assumption that changes in school processes lead to change in pupil outcomes; it is a matter for the empirical investigation to determine which school processes affect outcomes, and to what extent. Many studies in this framework compare educational environments on the basis of pupils' (and teachers') reports. Using surveys is argued to have 'the dual advantage of characterising the class through the eyes of the actual participants and capturing data which the observer could miss or consider unimportant'.[46] Survey data are taken as the objective measure of school or classroom processes.

Ironically, the threefold interplay between classrom processes, educational outcomes and participants' perspectives has attracted little attention. The neglect is perhaps partly due to the fact that the implications for school improvement are not as direct as the implications of correlations between processes and outcomes. Conclusive evidence, say, that pupils attain better grades when taught in small classes would urge a policy in favour of keeping classes small; but pupils' liking of small classes has little bearing on educational policy – unless it can be demonstrated that the pupils' appraisal mediates performance in ways not predictable by the earlier delineation of independent and dependent variables.

There is evidence that positive perception of the classroom environment is associated with better academic performance,[47] but the preference might reflect individual differences or age factors. Hattie and Watkins linked secondary school pupils' preferences of environments to the pupils' approach to learning ('deep' versus 'surface').[48] Similarly, Ramsden *et al.* report correlations between sixth-form students' learning approaches and their perceptions of school.[49] In a cross-cultural study, Entwistle *et al.* related pupils' perceptions of the learning environment to motivation.[50] Marjoribanks discovered a relation between pupils' perceptions of the classroom environment and personality type.[51] These findings query the asumption that pupils' perceptions of school are simply reports of objective environmental features. Furthermore, Lee *et al.* investigated the developmental dimensions of children's personal expectations about school environments, and discovered that as children progressed through the elementary school grades, so the gap widened between their notions of the ideal school and their ratings of their actual school.[52] Although younger and older children responded to the identical questions about their actual school, they seemed to use different scales to weigh it. As pupils grow older, their perceptual processes change – and change plausibly as a result of their interactions with school environments.

Pupil outcome variables may be best regarded as dependent on *person–environment* interactions, a view epitomized in Moos' social-ecological model (outlined towards the end of the chapter). Fraser and Fisher interpret the positive correlation they found between (perceived) classroom environment and student achievement in terms of the *person–environment fit*: achievement rates are a function of the dynamic interaction between pupil characteristics and the quality of the educational environment.[53] However, they carried out their analysis on the group level of explanation, and have advised that their conclusions might be unsuitable on the level of the individual pupil. Surveys designed to bring out trends in school populations can shed little light on the adaptation of an individual child to the educational environment.

It is assumed in survey-based studies that pupils' and teachers' responses to questionnaires reflect the *psychosocial environment* of the educational setting. Phrases such as 'school climate', 'school ethos' and 'psychosocial environment' imply subjective reality, but profiles of settings as drawn on the basis of survey data are not accurate descriptions of those schools or classrooms as they exist for individuals. Researching industrial organizations, Lawrence and Lorsch coined the term *subenvironment* to refer to a department as perceived by its personnel.[54] If the accent is put on the prefix, *sub*environment suggests a domain 'underlying' the organizational ecosystem (not individuals' subjective environments).

The following illustration shows the incompatibility between group and individual levels of analysis. As part of my research on children's perceptions of school, 73 junior school pupils were asked open-ended questions about various aspects of school (this was not a survey, but part of a procedure called the School Behaviour Game, described in Chapter 7). Two questions referred to pupils' behaviour towards teachers, and four questions addressed peer relationships. The answers reveal a clear pattern on the group level. Regarding pupil–teacher relationships, 64 per cent of the sample thought that a pupil would please a teacher by working quietly or producing good work; 52 per cent of the sample thought that disruptive behaviour would displease the teachers. The three questions regarding *positive* peer interactions elicited mostly references to playing together (40, 44 and 53 per cent of the sample, per question); bullying in various forms was mentioned by 73 per cent of the sample in response to the question about *negative* peer interactions. We may reasonably conclude, then, that pupils hold '*working* v. *misconduct*' as a fundamental criterion in evaluating pupil–teacher relationships, and '*playing together* v. *bullying*' as fundamental in evaluating peer relations at school. As it happened, no single child in my sample gave precisely this pattern of responses.

The views of the Average Pupil, then, did not represent the viewpoint of any individual. While my respondents described their *subjective* environments, when the data were pooled and processed, their average responses have come to reflect the *subenvironment*, a statistical construct. Profiles of subenvironments can, and have been, used to compare different schools or classrooms. The potential for comparing schools on the basis of pupils' average perceptions of their environments can be demonstrated by expanding the above example. The children participating in the study were drawn from four schools in Cardiff. In three of the schools, the emphases were as stated above; but in one school, the distribution of answers was different: 50 per cent of this group thought that the teacher would be most displeased if pupils produced 'messy work' or did not work. Asked to name something that a friendly child does, 60 per cent of the same group said 'helping' (whereas in the other schools, the common answer was 'plays with you'). The same group also differed when asked to name something they do themselves which makes other children happy: 'being friends' was mentioned more times than any other response (whereas the common answer in the other groups again referred to playing together). In sum, the Average Pupil in the one school held slightly different views than its counterparts in the other three schools, in so far that academic performance *per se*, rather than 'conduct', was regarded as the fundamental criterion in evaluating pupil–teacher relationships, and positive peer relationships were evaluated in the 'psychological' terms of friendship and help-fulness, rather than by the overt behaviour of playing together. Without further information, we cannot attribute the findings to differences in the ways teachers promoted performance and peer relations (which would indicate school effects), or to intake characteristics (given that the 'odd' group was the only multicultural one in my sample) – or simply to the fact that the 'odd' group (10 children) was about half the size of any of the other three (16, 20 and 27 children). The findings merely define the kind of questions that should be asked in further research; indeed, the kind of questions asked in the classroom-environment and school-effectiveness frameworks.

ASSESSING EDUCATIONAL ENVIRONMENTS

Surveys are the most widely used method for assessing edu-cational settings in terms of the subenvironments. The con-struction of a reliable instrument requires rigorous validation procedures. Interested readers may refer to Fraser's very detailed critique of five instruments, developed by him and other researchers in Australia and the United States.[55] Three of those have been designed for the secondary school level: Learning Environment Inventory (LEI); Classroom Environ-ment Scale (CES); Individualized Classroom Environment Questionnaire (ICEQ). Of the other two, My Class Inventory (MCI) has been developed for use in the primary school, and the College and University Classroom Environment Inventory (CUCEI), as the name suggests, is aimed for the tertiary level.

The basic rationale is simple. A first step is to obtain an inventory of activities, practices and attitudes typical of most educational environments. This calls for exploratory pilot research, involving field observations and interviews with a representative sample of teachers and pupils. Distinct dimensions are derived from the data, representing the aspects of locational functioning which were emphasized in the pilot sample. The final inventory is a fusion of the exploratory findings and a theoretical perspective (reflected in the categorization scheme and labelling of derivative dimensions). The next step is to transpose the inventory into a questionnaire format. This will then be used to elicit pupils' opinions on the frequency or applicability of provided items in their own classroom environment.

For instance, we may want to find out whether children's perceptions of teacher–pupil relationships differ across types of classroom environments, or whether 'types' of pupils (e.g., with and without behaviour problems; boys/girls; high- and low-ability) construe teacher–pupil relationships differently. We know that some children consider the quality of a pupil's work to be a major cause for teachers' pleasure or displeasure: this is an empirical datum, discovered in the exploratory study mentioned earlier. Therefore, individuals or groups can be compared according to the extent to which they endorse work quality as a fundamental criterion in that respect. If we regard the work-quality dimension as *theoretically* viable (i.e., we can argue that a child's notion of 'work quality' explains something about his or her performance), we may include statements to that effect in a questionnaire, and instruct respondents to state their agreement or disagreement with our statements. Clearly, it is best to include several statements which emphasize different aspects of the same dimension. The My Class Inventory includes a dimension of Difficulty, concerning the extent to which pupils find class work difficult; in the MCI (short version) questionnaire, this is represented in the five following items:

4. In our class the work is hard to do.
9. Most children can do their schoolwork without help.
14. Only the smart pupils can do their work.
19. Schoolwork is hard to do.
24. Most of the pupils in my class know how to do their work.[56]

The child is asked to circle either 'yes' or 'no' against each item. In the Individualized Classroom Environment Questionnaire, similar items are rated on a five-point scale from 'almost never' to 'always'.

Whatever the format, respondents gauge their own reality according to areas which researchers believe to be both descriptive of school environment and theoretically meaningful. Useful insights can be gained by nothing which specified areas are emphasized by certain groups, and whether an emphasis on one domain of the educational environment is consistently associated with the emphasis or with the understatement of other domains. This selected dimensions, however, make an instrument most suitable for some inquiries and not for others. For example, none of the five scales of the MCI – labelled Cohesiveness, Friction, Difficulty, Satisfaction, and Competitiveness – concerns pupils' perceptions of teacher–pupil relationships. There is evidence that, for most children, their interactions with teachers are less important than peer relations; if so, the MCI may be adequately descriptive. But using the MCI alone, we could not pick up the 'odd' classroom, where most pupils happen to hold interactions with the teacher as exceptionally salient; we could not learn to what extent teachers' behaviours and attitudes might shape pupils' subenvironment; nor would we be able to find out whether teachers' classroom practices influence pupils' *preferences* of classroom environments.

Classroom environment instruments have been used principally to assess actual classrooms, but in some recent studies, modified questionnaires were used to compare pupils' actual and preferred classroom practices. In terms of instrument construction, the inquiry about pupils' preferences affects little more than the wording of items and the instructions to respondents. For instance, the ICEQ has both actual- and preferred-environment versions.[57] The following item in the actual-environment version, '16. The teacher helps each student who is having trouble with the work' becomes, '16. The teacher would help each student who is having trouble with the work' in the preferred-environment version. In the former, pupils indicate how often this practice takes place in their actual classroom; in the latter, they indicate how often they would like to see this practice take place. They cannot bring up any novel ideas they might have for classroom improvement.

Limitations granted, inventories are a powerful tool for comparing the subenvironments of different groups sharing the same setting (e.g., teachers vs. pupils), for comparing pupils' perceptions of school in different settings (e.g., cross-culturally), and for discovering relations between aspects of the educational environment and pupil motivation, attainment, or other person-related variables. The utility of an inventory-based instrument is an interplay between the extent to which its dimensionality achieves a comprehensive representation of the setting in focus, and the extent to which it is conducive for probing issues which are salient outside that setting, i.e., issues bearing on education policies.

DIMENSIONS OF EDUCATIONAL SETTINGS

Studies entailing surveys of pupils' subenvironments tend to embody one or two orientations. In one perspective, the main interest is in the learning environment; therefore, the dimensions of the inventory (or *scales*) address classroom practices which serve or influence educational goals. Teachers and (to a lesser extent) pupils feature in those 'subenvironments' as incumbents of their institutional roles. In the other perspective, the main interest is in the experiential environment; the scales allude to sociability and affect among the inhabitants of the setting. These perspectives are not mutually exclusive, and more or less the same scales my serve both.

Finlayson pinpointed four factors as the most crucial in determining pupils' evaluation of their school:

- *concern*: the degree to which teachers were perceived as sensitive to pupils' individual needs;
- *social control*: the degree to which teachers were perceived as imposing their expectations on pupils, and as requiring excessive power to ensure pupil compliance;
- *emotional tone*: the degree to which peers were perceived as deriving social and emotional satisfaction from participation in school activities;

- *task orientation*: the degree to which peers were perceived as accepting and applying themselves to academic tasks.[58]

This knowledge can provide impetus for questions about either educational or psychosocial implications. But the divergent inquiries are likely to pick up Finlayson's dimensions in different ways. In an education-oriented inquiry, we may seek to correlate pupils' perceptions of teacher concern with educational outcomes, the hypothesis being that effective teaching depends partly on teacher concern. In a psychology-oriented inquiry, we may seek an association between teacher concern and measures of self-esteem or personality type, to test a hypothesis that pupils who emphasize teacher concern are more dependent (for instance).

Educational psychology represents a convergence of the two perspectives, and many psychologists design their inquiries with educational problems in mind. As already mentioned, Entwistle *et al.* sought and discovered relationships between pupils' perceptions of school and teachers, levels of motivation, and approaches to learning in British and Hungarian schools.[59] Although they wanted to assess the 'climate' or 'ethos' of the schools they intended to compare, Entwistle *et al.* felt that the available school-climate scales were not sufficiently focused on the *learning* environment, and they have delineated four dimensions, subdivided as follows:

(1) *School Ethos*: Aims of School (viz., extent to which the school is perceived as trying to promote positive social values among pupils); Friendliness; Relevance (personal salience of educational provision); Discipline.

(2) *Learning Environment*: Formality; Workload; Factual Assessment (emphasis on 'fact learning'); Openness (teachers' interest in pupils' views); Facilitating Learning (extent of help with study skills).

(3) *Teaching Effectiveness*: Explaining; Simplifying; Organizing; Holistic (teaching is too global or vague); Serialist (endless facts and details).

(4) *Teacher–Pupil Relationships*: Enthusiasm (on the teachers' part, as perceived by the respondent); Support; Control; Criticism.[60]

Results obtainable by these scales can reveal a great deal about pupils' evaluation of educational practices and goals, but somewhat less about what school personally means to children and youth.

In contrast, Lee *et al.* were chiefly interested in how children perceive 'selected conventions that organize the everyday social life of the school'[61] and whether children's perceptions change as they grow older. Lee *et al.* derived general aspects of children's experience of school from pilot interviews with elementary school teachers and pupils. Their selected areas represent two major domains, 'actions' and 'values' in school. The action domain refers to 'the child's *overt actions* in school and . . . more or less tangible school dimensions'; the value domain refers to 'children's evaluations of intangible, though salient, aspects of school environment – that is, the structure of beliefs and values associated with the school'.[62] The ten areas are:

(1) *territoriality*: the amount of classroom space allotted to each child and the customary degree of mobility;
(2) *privacy*: the availability of 'personalized' space and time alone;
(3) *custodial decision-making*: participation in everyday decisions about practical routines (e.g., seating arrangements);
(4) *instructional decision-making*: participation in decisions of curricular or pedagogical nature;
(5) *governance decision-making*: the distribution of decision-making power in the classroom;
(6) *responsive environment*: responsiveness to the child needs;
(7) *important environment*: relevance of the school to the child in the child's view;
(8) *liked environment*: favourability towards school;
(9) *just environment*: fairness with respect to disciplinary measures and children's grievances;
(10) *safe environment*: safety of the child's person and possessions at school.

Broadly, the dimensions discerned by Lee *et al.* allude to the extent to which a child finds the school an accommodating environment. All the areas discerned by Lee *et al.* arguably fall within the range of Entwistle's *school ethos* dimension, mentioned earlier, and thus greatly elaborate the concept of 'ethos' in the British research literature.

While the lists used by Lee *et al.* is comprehensive regarding person–environment relationships, children's perceptions of *social relationships* in school are not included. In contrast, three of the five dimensions used in Fraser's My Class Inventory focus on peer relationships among primary school classmates:

(1) *Cohesiveness:* 'Extent to which students know, help and are friendly towards each other':
(2) *Friction:* 'Amount of tension and quarrelling among students';
(3) *Difficulty:* 'Extent to which students find difficulty with the work of the class';
(4) *Satisfaction:* 'Extent of enjoyment of class work';
(5) *Competitiveness:* 'Emphasis on students competing with each other'.[63]

Ten further dimensions are added in the Learning Environment Inventory, designed for the secondary school level, but only one of these pertains directly to relationships among pupils:

(6) *Diversity:* 'Extent to which differences in students' interests exist and are provided for';
(7) *Formality:* 'Extent to which behaviour within the class is guided by formal use';
(8) *Speed:* 'Extent to which class work is covered quickly';
(9) *Material Environment:* 'Availability of adequate books, equipment, space and lighting';
(10) *Goal Direction:* 'Degree of goal clarity in the class';
(11) *Favouritism:* 'Extent to which the teacher treats certain students more favourably than others';
(12) *Apathy:* 'Extent to which the class feels no affinity with the class activities';
(13) *Democracy:* 'Extent to which students share equally in decision-making related to the class';
(14) *Cliqueness:* 'Extent to which students refuse to mix with the rest of the class';
(15) *Disorganization:* 'Extent to which classroom activities are confusing and poorly organized'.[64]

The LEI has been widely applied. It yields consistent results: Haertel *et al.* examined ten data sets from the United States, Canada, Australia and India; in all these, learning outcomes were positively correlated with Cohesiveness, Satisfaction, Task Difficulty, Formality, Goal Direction, Democracy, and Material Environment, and negatively correlated with Friction, Cliqueness, Apathy, Disorganization, and Favouritism.[65]

The MCI, LEI, and the other instruments described by Fraser have been developed more or less as 'general purpose' instruments, applicable to most inquiries in which it is necessary to obtain a measure of classroom subenvironments. Among these is the Classroom Environment Scale, designed by Moos for evaluating secondary schools:

(1) *Involvement*: 'Extent to which students have attentive interest, participate in discussion, do additional work and enjoy the class';

(2) *Affiliation*: 'Extent to which students help each other, get to know each other easily and enjoy working together';

(3) *Teacher Support*: 'Extent to which the teacher helps, befriends, trusts and is interested in students';

(4) *Task Orientation*: 'Extent to which it is important to complete activitites planned and to stay on the subject matter';

(5) *Competition*: 'Emphasis placed on students competing with each other for grades and recognition';

(6) *Order and Organization*: 'Emphasis on students behaving in an orderly, quiet and polite manner, and on the overall organization of classroom activities';

(7) *Rule Clarity*: 'Emphasis on clear rules, on students knowing the consequences for breaking rules, and on the teacher dealing consistently with students who break rules';

(8) *Teacher Control*: 'The number of rules, how strictly rules are enforced, and how severely rule infractions are punished';

(9) *Innovations*: 'Extent to which the teacher plans new, unusual and varying activities and techniques, and encourages students to contribute to classroom planning and to think creatively'.[66]

The CES, too, taps pupils' perceptions of the 'learning environment', not what school might mean to them personally.

However, Moos' conceptual model, to which we turn next, conveys his own interest in the interaction between person and environment.

A Social–Ecological Model

This chapter has concerned an elusive phenomenon, namely, school effects. Schools undeniably differ in outcomes, but intake characteristics account for most of the variance. We may assert that the presence of school effects, however small, nevertheless calls for an explanation. The research fields described in this chapter yield few answers. Evaluations of school organizations are often carried out with effective management and teaching in mind, and rarely probe directly the causal chain from the way a school is organized to its pupils' behaviour and development. Such issues have been investigated in other research fields, discussed elsewhere in this book.

Broadly, it is believed that the school organization influences behaviour in so far that people within it endorse or concede similar expectations about locational functioning. Prescriptions for action arise from the school's function, regime, and population. For example, school uniform means expectations about dress; a pupil's non-adherence to the uniform could lead to conflict with teachers, who may perceive the pupil as 'awkward', if not 'problematic'. But if the rules about uniform are relaxed, this aspect of 'pupil deviance' evaporates. In this way, a school's policy can determine teacher–pupil relationships. Expectations can arise from the unique combination of individuals who make up a school at a given time. For example, some teachers may be relatively strict, others more approachable, and pupils quickly learn who expects what. Certain expectations are permanent, arising from the school's function in society: it is expected that teachers will teach, and pupils will learn. The school organization thus influences the way that individuals' actions are interpreted by others in the school, and the individuals' construal of their own role and powers within the school. At least one crucial link in that complex causal chain, the effects of teacher expectations on

113

pupil performance, has been extensively investigated (a topic discussed in the next chapter).

Currently, not shortage of 'facts', but the want of an integrative conceptual framework is acutely felt. A major step towards conceptual integration is the model developed by Rudolf Moos, an American professor of psychiatry. Moos is well-known among researchers for his evaluative work in psychiatric hospitals, secondary schools and colleges. His work is certainly not new (his most relevant publications appeared in the 1970s). However, his theoretical premises, to do with the psychological interaction between people and institutions, have received little attention.

In a book entitled *Evaluating Educational Environments*, Moos outined a model which has several appealing features, not least the postulation of a dynamic, reciprocal interaction between environmental and personal variables.[67] Moos called his model 'social-ecological' in order to emphasize that social- and physical-environmental variables must be considered together. A main theme in Moos' work is the existence of both environmental and personal systems, which influence each other through selection factors, appraisal and activation or arousal. Moos identified four domains of the *environmental system*:

(1) *The physical setting*: architecture, use of the spatial environment, etc.

(2) *Organizational factors*: size, faculty–student ratio, average salary level, affluence or wealth, and student behaviour or attainment variables.

(3) *The human aggregate*: students' age, ability level, socioeconomic background, and other intake characteristics.

(4) *Social climate*: the emphasis on punctuality, neatness, etc., related to a sense of continuity and consistency which students infer from college events.

The *personal system* comprises the individual's expectations and cultural values, personality factors, and coping skills.

The environmental and personal systems interact through several interrelated mediating factors. The first mediating factor is *selection*: most environments admit new members selectively, and most people select the environment they wish to enter. The fact that in schools free selection might be limited, does not nullify Moos' assertion. Children do not choose their schools (or to go to school in the first place), but reluctant pupils, feeling themselves coerced into the educational setting, might select 'not to belong' there. Sociologists have shown that pupils' alienation, the sense of being an outsider, is often associated with low attainment and sometimes implicated in disaffected behaviour. Events in school could confirm or disconfirm a pupil's expectations, whether favourable or hostile towards the school. Likewise, a school assesses pupils' performance continuously, and a pupil's behaviour may confirm or disconfirm teachers' expectations.

Selection thus indicates *cognitive appraisal*, the second of Moos' mediating factors, and cognitive appraisal leads to *motivation* (which Moos equates with activation or arousal). He draws attention to the interplay between personal and environmental characteristics regarding motivation:

> a highly talented student is more likely to experience a lack of challenge in a classroom; some students are more easily motivated than others . . . challenging classrooms tend to be seen as competitive; some environments are more likely to motivate students than others.[68]

Motivation, in turn, leads to *efforts at adaptation* and *coping*, a further mediating variable. Adaptation and coping can also be influenced by personal and environmental characteristics.

Individuals' attitudes, motivation and coping skills change as a result of experience (the model has feedback loops). Therefore, the process of interaction between the personal and environmental systems culminates in stability or change of personal values and interests, aspiration and attainment levels, self-concept and health. Ultimately, then, we arrive at the *outcome* indices used in school effectiveness studies (among others) to show school effects. The way that the person–environment relationship can result in a certain self-concept is described by Moos with the example of a new student in a college with high academic standards. In such a college, the

115

student is exposed to 'classroom examinations, discussions among students about grades, studying, intellectual arguments among students, and debates between faculty and students'.[69] Consequently, the student might feel competitive, inferior, and anxious about possible academic failure; but presumably the same individual would have been affected differently if he or she attended a different college. As Moos notes,

> In terms of short-term behavioural effects, this student can devote more time to studying, spending less time in social activities, and perhaps increase his or her intellectual aggression; as a result, the student may have greater feelings of loneliness and isolation. Alterations in self-concept and changes in behaviour that could persist beyond college [might result].[70]

Moos' social-ecological model not only accommodates all the salient aspects of the child–school interface, but gives a clear statement about their interrelations. It is a-theoretical and content-free, in so far that it does not predict particular educational or psychological outcomes. It does not suggest how certain attitudes or coping strategies, or certain aspects of the environmental system, might determine outcomes. Rather, it is a way of organizing our approach to the evaluation of the impact of educational organizations on individuals.

Notes and References

1 Hargreaves, D. H. *Interpersonal Relations and Education.* London: Routledge and Kegan Paul, 1975, p. 45.

2 Cf. Nash, R. *Schooling in Rural Societies.* London: Methuen, 1980.

3 Barker, R. G. and Gump, P. *Big School, Small School.* Standford, CA: Stanford University Press, 1964.

4 Gump, P. V. 'Big schools, small schools'. In Barker, R. G. (ed.), *Habitats, Environments and Human Behaviour.* San Francisco: Jossey-Bass, pp. 245–257, 1978.

5 Ibid., p. 246.

6 Ibid., p. 249.

7 Ibid., pp. 250ff.

8 Ibid., p. 253.

9 Wicker, A. W. *An Introduction to Ecological Psychology.* Cambridge: Cambridge University Press, 1984.

10 David, 1976, reviewed in Nash, 1980, op. cit.

11 Finn, J. D. and Achilles, C. M. 'Answers and questions about class size: a state-wide experiment'. *American Educational Research Journal,* **27**, 557–577, 1990; cf. Mortimore, P. and Blatchford, P. *The Issue of Class Size.* Briefing No. 12. London: The National Commission on Education, 1993.

12 Mortimore, P., Sammons, P., Stoll, L., Lewis, D. and Ecob, R. *School Matters: The Junior Years.* Somerset: Open Books, 1988.

13 Mortimore, P. and Blatchford, P., 1993, op. cit.

14 Ibid., p. 4.

15 Ingram, J. and Worrall, N. 'Children's self-allocation and use of classroom curricular time'. *British Journal of Educational Psychology,* **62**, 45–55, 1992.

16 Mortimore, P. and Blatchford, P., 1993, op. cit.

17 Ibid., p. 4; their italics.

18 Ibid., p. 4.

19 See contributions in Reynolds, D. and Cuttance, P. (eds), *School Effectiveness: Research, Policy and Practice.* London: Cassell, 1992; Reynolds, D. (ed.), *Studying School Effectiveness.* London: The Falmer Press, 1985.

20 Cf. Reynolds, D., 1985, op. cit.

21 Reynolds, D. 'School effectiveness and school improvements: an updated review of the British literature'. In Reynolds, D. and Cuttance, P. (eds), *School Effectiveness: Research, Policy and Pratice.* London: Cassell, pp. 1–24, 1992.

22 Mortimore, P. *et al.*, 1988, op. cit.

23 Ibid., pp 250ff.

24 Reynolds, D. and Parker, A. 'School effectiveness and school improvements in the 1990s'. In Reynolds, D. and Cuttance, P. (eds), *School Effectiveness: Research, Policy and Practice.* London: Cassell, pp. 171–188, 1992.

25 Reynolds, D. 'Introduction: ten years on – a decade of school effectiveness research reviewed'. In Reynolds, D. (ed.), *Studying School Effectiveness.* London: The Falmer Press, 1985, p. 195; his italics.

26 Mortimore, P. *et al.*, 1988, op. cit.

27 Reynolds, D., 1992, op. cit., p. 10.

28 Cuttance, P. 'Frameworks for research on the effectiveness of schooling'. In Reynolds, D. (ed.), *Studying School Effectiveness.* London: The Falmer Press, 1985, pp. 13–14; his italics.

29 Reynolds, D. and Parker, A., 1992, op. cit., p. 178.
30 Weinstein, C. S. and Woolfolk, A. E. 'The classroom setting as a source of expectations about teachers and pupils'. *Journal of Environmental Psychology*, 1, 117–129, 1981.
31 Strivens, J. 'School climate: a review of a problematic concept'. In Reynolds, D. (ed.), *Studying School Effectiveness*. London: The Falmer Press, 1985, p. 50.
32 Ibid., p. 48.
33 Ibid., p. 49.
34 Finlayson, D. S. 'Measuring "school climate" '. *Trends in Education*, 30, 19–27, 1973.
35 Cf. Brown, R. *Social Psychology*, 2nd edn. New York: The Free Press, 1986.
36 Rutter, M., Maughan, B., Mortimore, P. and Ouston, J. *Fifteen Thouand Hours: Secondary Schools and Their Effects on Children*. London: Open Books, 1979.
37 Ibid., p. 179; their italics.
38 Ibid., p. 166; their italics.
39 Ibid., p. 179; their italics.
40 Ibid., p. 184.
41 Reynolds, D. (ed.), 1985, op. cit.
42 Reynolds, D. and Cuttance, P., 1992, op. cit.
43 Entwistle, N., Kozeki, B. and Tait, H. 'Pupils' perceptions of school and teachers: I – Identifying the underlying dimensions; II – Relationships with motivation and approaches to learning'. *British Journal of Educational Psychology*, 59, 326–350, 1989.
44 Ibid., p. 328.
45 Ibid., p. 327; their italics.
46 Fraser, B. J. *Classroom Environment*. London: Croom Helm, 1986, p. 1.
47 Haertel, G. D., Walberg, H. J. and Haertel, E. H. 'Socio-psychological environments and learning: a quantitative analysis'. *British Educational Research Journal*, 7, 27–36, 1981.
48 Hattie, J. and Watkins, D. 'Preferred classroom environment and approach to learning'. *British Journal of Educational Psychology*, 62, 345–349, 1988.
49 Ramsden, P., Martin, E. and Bowden, J. 'School environment and 6th form pupils' approaches to learning'. *British Journal of Educational Psychology*, 59, 129–142, 1989.
50 Entwistle, N. *et al.*, 1989, op. cit.
51 Marjoribanks, K. 'Ability and environmental correlates of

attitudes and aspirations: personality group differences'. *British Journal of Educational Psychology,* **56**, 322–331, 1986.

52 Lee, P. C., Statuto, C. M. and Kedar-Voivodas, G. 'Elementary school children's perceptions of their actual and ideal school experience: a developmental study'. *Journal of Educational Psychology,* **75**, 838–847, 1983.

53 Fraser, B. J. and Fisher, D. L. 'Use of actual and preferred classroom environmental scales in person-environment fit research'. *Journal of Educational Psychology,* **75**, 303–313, 1983.

54 Cited in Starbuck, W. H. 'Organizations and their environments'. In Dunette, M. D. (ed.), *Handbook of Industrial and Organizational Psychology.* Chicago: Rand McNally College Publishing, pp. 1069–1124, 1976.

55 Fraser, B. J., 1986, op. cit.

56 Ibid., Appendix A.

57 Ibid.

58 Finlayson, D. S., 1973, op. cit.

59 Entwistle, N. *et al.*, 1989, op. cit.

60 Ibid.

61 Lee, P. C., *et al.*, 1983, op. cit., p. 838.

62 Ibid., p. 840; their italics.

63 The scale descriptions are quoted from Fraser, B. J., 1986, op. cit., p.20.

64 The scale descriptions are quoted from Fraser, B. J., 1986, op. cit., pp. 18–19.

65 Haertel *et al.*, 1981, op. cit.

66 Moos, R. H. *Evaluating Educational Environments.* San Francisco: Jossey-Bass, 1979; descriptions are quoted from Fraser, B. J., 1986, op. cit., p. 19.

67 Moos, R. H., 1979, op. cit.

68 Ibid., p. 4.

69 Ibid., p. 9.

70 Ibid., p. 10.

CHAPTER 5
The Social Niche (1):
Teacher–Pupil Relationships

All children find at school an established order, a distinctly structured milieu, within which they must find their own niche. As Jackson pointed out, the 'highly stylized environment of the elementary classroom' is distinct not simply because of 'the paraphernalia of learning and teaching and the educational content of the dialogues that take place there', but because the child is faced with three facts of life: *crowd, evaluation,* and *power.*[1] Adapting to life in classrooms involves getting used to being a member of a crowd: most things done in school are done with others or in the presence of others. Furthermore, children must get used to the constant evaluation of their words and deeds by others. They also witness, and participate in, the evaluation of others. Third, divisions between the weak and the powerful are clearly drawn at school. In school, teachers are in a powerful position: 'Most students soon learn that rewards are granted to those who lead a good life. And in school the good life consists, principally, of doing what the teacher says.'[2] This calls for constant exploration on children's part:

> The children [in their accounts] reveal a complex knowledge of the rules of social interaction. . . . Furthermore, because they constantly explored the dimensions of the rules operating in any one situation, they were able to cope with a variety of teachers who had different conceptions of the rules of teacher–pupil interactions and of the educational process.[3]

School ethnographers documented the complexity and richness of social worlds in schools.[4] In particular, interactions between teachers and pupils have been exhaustively investigated.[5] Sociologists have highlighted the 'hidden curriculum': the subtle and not-so-subtle ways in which teachers reinforce gender stereotypes in the course of their interactions with pupils and in their classroom management, for instance.[6] In this chapter, only a few themes can be picked up, and those selected here draw attention to classroom ecology.

Teacher Expectations

One apparent consequence of teacher power is sometimes referred to as the *expectancy effect*, a correlation between teacher expectations and pupil performance. In explaining such correlations, writers allude to the fact that teacher classroom management shapes the learning environment as it exists for pupils. The likelihood that a teacher's low expectations of certain 'types' of pupils (e.g., socially disadvantaged) might be among the causes of the pupils' poor performance has troubled workers in education for a long time. The idea seemed plausible since R. K. Merton, in 1948, defined the self-fulfilling prophecy as a general mechanism of social behaviour. In a classic field experiment, *Pygmalion in the Classroom*, Rosenthal and Jacobson demonstrated a relation between teacher expectations and pupil performance.[7] They led elementary school teachers to believe that a new IQ test, administered at the beginning of the school year, indicated that certain children, 'bloomers', should show an increase in intellectual competence. In fact, label 'bloomer' was assigned at random by the psychologists. The startling result was that an IQ test administered at the end of the year did show significantly greater gains in IQ among the 'bloomers' than among peers. This seemed a clear case of a self-fulfilling prophecy.

In the wake of the Pygmalion study, ample evidence for expectancy effects has accumulated. Although Rosenthal and Jacobson's findings are controversial – partly because of methodological flaws of the original study, and because attempts to replicate it have yielded inconsistent results regarding IQ gains – correlations between teacher expectations and academic performance (such as measured in maths or reading tests) have been shown in hundreds of studies. At issue is how to interpret the statistical association between teacher expectancy and pupil performance. Until recently, the main

121

effort was to affirm the reality and strength of expectancy effects in educational settings, and to identify conditions which render the 'effect' most likely.[8] A rigorous research into the causal processes underlying the correlation took second place. It is perhaps time to reverse research priorities.

As is the case with most fields of educational research, the primary concern has been pragmatic. Ultimately, we wish to prevent undesirable effects of teachers' biases. It is therefore important to know that the self-fulfilling prophecy can happen in educational settings – but it is even more important to know how exactly, or when, it operates in the classroom. Given that a teacher, in his or her professional capacity, structures pupils' learning environments on the basis of assumptions about their needs and potential, we may need to look beyond what is going on between teacher and pupil. We may need to consider, for instance, both learning and self-esteem affordances of classroom environments for low- or high-expectancy pupils. A shift of perspective along these lines would (or should) generate inquiries that have been hitherto understated in research, such as inquiries about pupil perspectives.

THE EXPECTANCY EFFECT: EVIDENCE AND EXPLANATION

The expectancy effect hypothesis rests on the observation that a small percentage (5–10 per cent) of individual differences in attainment cannot be accounted for by differences in ability, motivation, or personal circumstances. Instead, the differences correspond to teachers' early assumptions about individual differences. However small, such 'effect' can make a substantial difference to a pupil's education or development. The questions initially posed in investigations of teacher expectancies reflect the origins of the research field in social psychology of the 1960s and 1970s. Especially in the United States, the social psychologist's main task was understood as the discovery of interpersonal mechanisms. Self-fulfilling prophecy effects were demonstrated in numerous field and laboratory experiments with adult subjects, usually entailing simulations of social encounters between strangers. In those, all the 'perceiver' knew about the 'target' person, prior to their brief interaction, would be phoney information planted by the experimenters. It has been commented that such artificial, if not arbitrary, settings hardly provide an adequate model of social behaviour. Nevertheless, self-fulfilling prophecy effects shown in the laboratory underline the fact that interpersonal interactions can be influenced by social stigma, labelling, and stereotypes.

Critics do not dispute that interpersonal expectations can, and sometimes do, have self-fulfilling prophecy effects. Nor do critics doubt that this sometimes happens between a teacher and a pupil in classroom settings. While teachers rarely interact with a new class without knowing something about at least some of the pupils, if only staff-room gossip, it is quite plausible that their initial interactions would be influenced by pervasive, and largely invalid, beliefs about how socioeconomic status, ethnicity, gender, 'personality', or indeed IQ, determine pupil behaviour and attainment. But this is not the only factor influencing teacher–pupil interactions, let alone pupil performance. Controversy surrounds the extent to which the correlation in naturalistic settings can be said to reflect a self-fulfilling prophecy.

Most of the evidence that expectancy effects in educational settings occur spontaneously (i.e., without researchers' manipulation) comes from longitudinal studies. In a typical design, a class about to start the year with a new teacher is selected. The teacher predicts the pupils' performance on the basis of early impressions, and these predictions are subsequently correlated with the pupils' actual attainment at the end of the year, or on interim occasions. Could the expectations generated by in-service teachers be accurate perceptions of the pupils in question?

> There is little doubt that teacher expectations are associated with later achievement, but this may be because in large measure teachers are accurate in their judgements of children's academic potential, and behave differently, and appropriately, toward children of different ability.[9]

In reality, teachers form and revise their opinions on the basis of ongoing interactions with pupils, whose own behaviour changes over time. The impact of phoney information, supplied to teachers in brief experiments, could be temporary. Attempts to isolate teachers' 'spontaneous' biases have relied mostly on pen and paper simulations, often involving hypothetical targets of expectations. Teachers may be given fictitious case histories, and asked to rate the protagonists' competence, motivation, or attainment. Such simulations bear scant resemblance to classroom interactions in real life, and arguably tap the respondents' cultural stereotypes, rather than their professional attitudes.

The social psychologists who looked for the self-fulfilling prophecy effects in interpersonal settings were chiefly interested in the issue of social stereotype. As a result, the research attention given to teacher biases is perhaps disproportionate, in view of other factors involved in classroom relationships, such as the teacher's custodian role towards children, the teaching philosophy and agenda that the teacher implements, and the fact that most of a teacher's interactions with any individual child take place in the presence of other children (whose expectations of the child may also influence his or her behaviour). The specifically educational implications of expectancy effects may have less to do with interpersonal processes than with how these processes relate to learning outcomes. That is, we may ask, not just how teacher biases influence pupil behaviour, but how this influence interacts with pupil ability, motivation, academic self-concept, or attitudes to school.

A further issue concerns the unpredictability of expectancy–behaviour causal relationship. In a critique of the wider 'expectancies' field, Miller and Turnbull proposed that self-disconfirming prophecies may be just as common as self-fulfilling ones (for instance, teachers might give extra attention and encouragement to a pupil whom they believe to be less capable, and so increase the pupil's chances).[10] But when self-disconfirming prophecy effects are found, the tendency is to view the findings as oddities, 'flukes' that can be accounted for by some special circumstances. Particularly problematic, in the conventional view, are the findings that similar beliefs sometimes lead to opposite behaviours, and contradictory beliefs sometimes lead to a similar behaviour. Such quandaries do not invalidate the empirical data, but query some of the conventional assumptions in the field.

Whether accurate or biased, teachers' beliefs can affect pupils' education in a concrete way: teachers are likely to modify the amount or style of teaching according to their perceptions of pupils' needs and potential. This applies on the macro level of educational provision, as well as on the micro level of a school class. A postgraduate in computer studies, writing to a daily newspaper, criticized the lack of academic pressure in the special school where she had been placed following an assessment of below-average IQ:

> Perhaps more damaging than the assessment was the low expectations of me and fellow pupils by our teachers and the system provided for us . . . They did not stretch us or encouraged us to succeed . . . Computing was the foundation for my self-confidence. It was something I was good at and could excel in. Yet they discouraged my talent.[11]

However, classroom observations reveal that not all teachers 'write off' low-expectancy pupils. On the contrary, some teachers put more effort into helping a pupil whose needs seem to be greater (although they might withhold material which they believe would be too advanced for the pupil).

Badad *et al.* both interviewed teachers about their pupils and observed the teachers in their classrooms.[12] Some of the teachers, when discussing low-expectancy pupils known to them, communicated negative affect accompanied with dogmatic behaviour; but when they interacted with those pupils in the classroom, they compensated with more active teaching. Badad *et al.* found expectancy effects in both conditions (interview and classroom). The discrepancy is not so puzzling when we consider that well-meaning, 'compensating' teachers nevertheless single out pupils as needing special attention.

Indirectly, differential treatment might affect performance by communicating the teacher's low opinion of the pupil's ability, even if the 'treatment' consists of positive attention and more actual help than is given to classmates whom the teacher regards as competent. It would be imprecise to suggest that prominent writers on classroom interactions have overlooked this point. Far from it. However, in much of the research literature, the main causal role is attributed to the pattern of teacher–pupil interactions, the assumption being that the pupil responds to cues in the teacher's behaviour. This can be taken further to propose that response patterns, which amount to increase or decrease in academic effort on the pupil's part, are reinforced by the system of rewards and controls used by the teacher. These operant conditioning principles have guided behaviour modification techniques used in special education.[13] McNamara *et al.* implemented an intervention package in a special classroom for disruptive pupils.[14] Their programme, designed to reinforce desirable conduct, entailed restructuring the classroom environment, (e.g., the seating arrangement was changed from tables to rows, the teacher systematically used extrinsic rewards). The 'package' thus boiled down to management strategies which experienced teachers might use anyway. If successful, we may conclude that the processes underlying its success are also involved in teachers' 'unaided' influence on pupil behaviour.

Somewhat to their dismay, McNamara *et al.* discovered that their programme changed not only the pupils' disruptive conduct, but also, 'unexpectedly', the teacher's regard for the pupils: as conduct improved, the teacher began to treat the pupils more positively. The psychologists felt that 'expectancy effects' confounded their results (i.e., the improvement in pupil conduct could not be attributed solely to the design of their behavioural programme). For our purposes, their observation provides a clear example of a feedback loop. The possibility that pupil behaviour can affect teacher behaviour is acknowledged in the early expectancy literature,[15] though understated in research. More pertinently, McNamara *et al.* seem to regard the 'expectancy effect' as separate from reinforcement mechanisms. By implication, 'reinforcement' is not enough to explain how teacher expectations influence pupil behaviour.

In the study mentioned earlier, Badad *et al.* explain their findings with the speculation that 'Very fine nuances in teacher behaviour – many of which are non-verbal, uncontrollable, and often undetected in natural observation – might have substantial, cumulating effects on students.'[16] It seems rather mysterious that children respond to behavioural nuances that are too subtle to be detected in natural observation. The increasing popularity of information-processing models makes it easier to acknowledge the primacy of pupils' cognitive processes. But what information do children process? There is evidence (discussed later) that children are not very good at interpreting their teachers' expectations about their ability from the teachers' behaviour towards them, though they can correctly link peers' ability levels to teacher treatment. Children compare themselves to peers – and 'streaming' is made obvious by the teacher's general strategies. Could children simply be responding to cues about their 'place' in the classroom environment, in addition to any explicit verbal and non-verbal communication that the teacher directs at them? A similar idea is expressed by Schultz:

> teachers start with information about students that sets up an expectancy. This expectancy affects the teacher's reactions, attitudes and so forth, which in turn affect the sociopsychological climate. *The entire process then leads to changes in student behavior and attitude.*[17]

It is not what the teacher 'does' to the child, but how the child adjusts to what the teacher does in general. Schultz does not depart radically from the conventional belief that teacher expectations are the initial condition for differential treatment which, in turn, initiates classroom processes culminating in expectancy effects. However, by drawing attention to a pupil's adaptation to the classroom social milieu, Schultz's statement implies that the initial conditions for expectancy effects are set up jointly by both teacher and pupil belief systems.

Pupils' perspectives on classroom interactions were rarely considered as a primary causal factor in the expectancy effects. If anything, pupils' perceptions are discussed as if those are interferences with the supposedly 'normal' causal chain.

When teacher expectations or differential treatment 'fail' to precipitate the anticipated effect, *intervening variables* are imagined. Jussim has developed a three-stage model, integrating the mainstream literature on the expectancy effect in education.[18] The stages are: teacher expectations, differential treatment, and student reactions. The whole process begins with teachers' initial expectations (based on stereotypes, reputation, standardized tests, early performance, or naive prediction process), followed by the maintenance or change of expectations (affected by confirmatory biases, flexibility of expectations, and the strength of disconfirming evidence). This 'feeds' into the second stage, differential treatment: psychological mediators (teacher perceptions of control, similarity, dissonance between own beliefs and behaviour, causal attributions of pupil/own actions, and affect) compound with situational mediators (e.g., ability grouping, grade level), and lead to teacher treatment of students (involving feedback given to students, emotional support, types of assignments, attention, opportunities to learn, amount and difficulty of material taught). In all, those teacher-initiated processes elicit the final stage, student reactions. In Jussim's model, students' ultimate reactions are behavioural (i.e., academic effort and persistence, classroom attention, participation, and co-operation), but can be influenced by psychological mediators: students' perceived control over educational outcomes, the value students attach to scholastic activities, their intrinsic interest in school, their self-concept and self-esteem.

One implication is that cognitive, affective and motivational factors on the pupil side prevent or distort the otherwise direct link from teacher expectancy to pupil performance. Are we to believe that pupils whose level of performance coincides with their teachers' expectations lack an 'inner life'? Of course not. An adequately phrased theory would run as follows: appraisal of one's classroom situation is always primary, but the behavioural consequences of individuals' cognitive appraisal would vary, either because their circumstances are different, or they interpret similar events differently. For instance, Jussim points out that according to social exchange theory, the more individual students value teachers' reactions, the more susceptible they may be to confirming the teacher's expectations: they will be more likely to behave in ways designed to evoke favourable reactions from the teacher than would peers who care less about teacher evaluations.[19] We may conclude, then, that the child's self-concept or self-esteem is as primary a factor as teacher's biases.

For the so-called self-fulfilling prophecy to happen, a pupil must be 'primed' to impute personal importance to teachers' messages, i.e., to be relatively sensitized to feedback from the teacher – easily encouraged or discouraged, as the case may be. This 'priming' takes place outside the dyadic teacher–pupil relationship. Parental attitudes to schooling, social values reinforced in peer groups in and out of school, and the child's experiences with other teachers, can all influence a child's reactions to the particular teacher.

RECIPROCAL EXPECTATIONS

Perhaps the incidence of self-fulfilling prophecies in classrooms has been exaggerated, but there is little doubt that it does occur. Why should the 'target' of a wrong expectancy behave as if to confirm it? Two traditions have guided the early literature, behaviourism and symbolic interactionism. Explanations centred on a notion of reinforcement mechanisms (e.g., social learning) or on personal gains for the child (e.g., social exchange) often feature in educational psychology. Sociologists of education, and some psychologists, referred to symbolic interactionist ideas, based on the work of the American psychologist G. H. Mead.[20] The central premise in this approach is that human reality is created in the manipulation of language and language-like symbols between people.

The nuances between behaviourist and symbolic-interactionist perspectives can be illustrated with the case of teacher praise. In a behaviourist framework, the positive effects of praise may be explained (or explained away) by pointing out that pupils work harder in order to get more praise. Why should praise be a powerful reward for a child? The global assumption is that humans are innately motivated to act in ways that maximize social acceptance or esteem. It follows that pupils are 'innately' inclined to adjust their behaviour in response to messages about themselves in teacher's reactions (though, of course, individual differences are to be expected).

If so, whatever passes between teacher and pupil is a crude form of communication, the kind of behavioural reciprocity that Mead called *the conversation of gestures*.[21] Mead illustrated this communicative process with an account of a dog fight: each dog adjusts and readjusts his posture in response to changes in the other dog's posture and vocal gestures (e.g., growl). Mead considered the conversation of gestures as fundamental also in human interaction. However, he distinguished between the conversation of gestures and language proper, which is based on *social acts*. Unlike the conversation of gestures, social acts are characterized by shared meanings, scaffolded by the use of symbols which are understood in similar ways by participants in an interaction. Recent work in remedial education provides an illustration: working with children who had learning difficulties in maths, Carske carried out an 'attributional retraining' programme which entailed verbal reinforcement of the children's positive self-references.[22] The children were encouraged to attribute the outcomes of their work to their own effort; academic improvement followed. Carske's programme differs from merely praising the children's effort: it guided the children into construing their own work in the same way that their teachers would.

In a symbolic-interactionist perspective, evidence for expectancy effects should trigger questions about pupils' interpretation of teachers' behaviour towards them. This was not the case in research practice.[23] With few exceptions, the *teacher's* part in the interaction has been singled out for rigorous investigation. The child's 'part' seemed limited to reciprocating teacher expectations with increased or decreased academic effort. As seen earlier, such reciprocation can only partially be attributed to actual learning opportunities created by the teacher, for classroom observations indicate that not all teachers put less effort into teaching low-expectancy pupils. Unfortunately, most studies do not assess the degree to which teachers merely react to existing differences among pupils, exacerbate or compensate for such differences. The issue is further compounded by possible age and individual differences in pupils' interpretations of teacher behaviour. Three studies, which highlight the different factors involved, are described below.

Weinstein *et al.*, in the United States, raised the long overdue question about children's ability to perceive and interpret the meaning of teacher differential treatment towards themselves and peers.[24] Using inventories, they found substantial age differences in children's awareness of their teachers' expectations and in the relation between such awareness and the children's self-expectations. Compared to younger children (first and third graders), self-descriptions among fifth graders more widely mirrored their teachers' expectations, irrespective of the pupils' awareness of the teachers' differential treatment in the classroom. This suggests that children, as they progress through the school years, internalize a consensus about their specific position in the ability hierarchy. The children's views of themselves are no longer (if they ever were) solely dependent on immediate classroom situations. Weinstein *et al.* also found that first and third graders were less accurate than fifth graders in predicting teacher expectations and reporting differential patterns in their own interactions with the teacher; but the differences in teacher behaviour towards high- and low achieving peers, as identified by the younger children, were congruent with the teachers' expectations.

Whether or not children are aware of their teachers' expectations, they hardly remain ignorant of their own academic status relative to peers. In Britain, Roy Nash asked junior school teachers to rank their pupils in order of ability in reading, writing and number; the rankings were not communicated to the children.[25] Separately, Nash asked some of the children to name classmates they considered better than themselves in each subject. Nash found a significant positive correlation between the teachers' and the children's responses. How do children find out their relative status? Nash carried out his observations in mixed ability classes. But he noticed that in most classrooms the setting arrangement reflected ability groups – and streaming by tables carries very clear messages to children about themselves. In Nash's study, one teacher attempted to mask the ability streams by dividing the class into colour groups which bore no relation to the seating arrangement. The children interviewed by Nash nevertheless were well aware of the order in which colours represented ability. Nash speculated that children 'may strive to maintain their relative status within the class for the sake of personal consistency', once they have accepted their positions.[26]

Worrall et al. found that not all children in the same primary school class interpret and reciprocate the teacher's expectations in the same way.[27] Their study followed three classes of 9- to 11-year-olds who started the year with new teachers (all female). On Day 1 and three further occasions, spread over the school year, the researchers collected and compared the teachers' ratings of the children's classroom demeanour, the children's interpretations of their teachers' evaluations, and the children's ratings of the teachers' classroom management. Worral et al. discovered that over the year, high-achieving boys and girls increasingly mirrored the teachers' expectations; low-achieving girls showed an 'unexpected' pattern consistent with striving to maintain a favourable self-image, whereas low-achieving boys were, in the authors' phrase, 'generally out of touch', as if the teacher's expectations made no difference to them.

The study by Worral et al. shows teacher-to-child causality, as opposed to mere correspondence between teacher and child perceptions. Particularly striking was the increased differentiation, over the year, of boys' and girls' return evaluation of their teachers. On Day 1, the teachers seemed to favour girls, but the girls indicated no awareness of this, nor were they more inclined than boys to favour the teacher. By Day 93, the teachers' continuing favouring of girls was mirrored in the girls' better ratings of their teachers. However, when the sample was divided into high- and low-achievers, it seemed that teachers' early impressions regarding ability were mostly accurate. The teachers' initial judgements presumably guided their classroom management, to the effect of maintaining or constraining what the child could achieve over the year. Worral et al. note that while 10-year-olds are quite capable of responding to gender-tagged messages, they are less responsive to ability-tagged messages. Previous research, mentioned by Worral *et al.*, indicates that children tend to confuse 'ability' with 'effort'. This may explain the response pattern among the low-achieving girls. Given the teachers' early favouring of girls in general, the low-achieving girls may have responded to ability-tagged messages from the teacher with increased effort: they were 'striving to hold on to something they sense as slipping away after the first term of the new class'.[28]

Taken together, evidence for age and individual differences indicate a complex interplay between teacher social skills, classroom management, the sociometric composition of the pupil group, and the development of children's academic self-concepts. Whatever the impact of a teacher's expectations on the pupil's performance, it should be explained as arising from such interplay. The 'expectancy effect' may be understood in terms of the evolution of interacting dynamic systems within the general structure of the educational setting.

Just before the explosion of expectancy effect research, Jackson commented that while pupils are confronted with permanent prospects of praise and reproof, the teacher is not the only one who passes judgement: 'classmates frequently join in the act'.[29] Furthermore, judgements are not confined to academic competence: social evaluation in non-academic respects is just as powerful (if not more).

Jackson pointed out:

> The dynamics of classroom evaluations are difficult to describe, principally because they are so complex. Evaluations derive from more than one *source*, the *conditions of their communication* may vary in several different ways, they may have one or more of several *referents*, and they may range in *quality* from the intensely positive to intensely negative. Moreover, these variations refer only to objective, or impersonal features of evaluation. When the subjective or personal meanings of these events are considered, the picture becomes even more complex.[30]

The natural complexity of classroom systems does not make

it impossible to identify effects of teacher attitudes or behaviour, but it prompts a rethinking of their causal role.

Role and Negotiation

Classroom communication extends beyond discourse, beyond what teachers and pupils say to each other or how they say it. Communication implies getting a message across. Messages are not necessarily directed by a teacher at a particular pupil, although this happens, of course. Classroom situations define individuals' positions in that social setting, and thus 'tell' pupils something about themselves.

A teacher who regularly ignores a pupil's work is 'sending' a message that pupils quickly pick up. As one low-stream secondary school boy told Hargreaves 'I don't think they [teachers] bother about us here. They can't do 'cos they don't mark our books.'[31] Hargreaves tells also of a teacher who, in order to prevent theft, kept all the equipment locked up in the cupboard, even during lessons:

> If a boy required a new pencil or rubber, the teacher would go through the process of locking and unlocking the cupboard. Occasionally the boys would ask needlessly for materials simply to watch the master performing this extensive ritual. The boys were thus given no responsibility – he even sharpened their pencils himself.[32]

The message was clear: 'You just can't afford to trust that lot,' as the teacher himself told Hargreaves.[33] His fears were not groundless, for theft was reportedly common in that school. To communicate trust and treat pupils as responsible persons is commendable in principle, but pupils might regard a well-meaning, liberal-minded teacher as 'soft' if they construe the teacher role as that of an authoritarian.

Pupils are far from passive recipients of signals. On their side, there is an active process of selective attention and decoding according to their personal frames of reference. They 'suss out' and 'size up' the teacher.[34] Nash noticed how 12-year-old boys' expectations about teacher behaviour related to their classroom interactions with two student teachers: they seemed to 'test out' the student teachers' ability to control the class.[35] Beynon and Delamont similarly concluded, on the basis of their observations, that school violence should be understood as hypothesis-testing on the behalf of pupils and teachers.[36]

This leads to the twin themes of role and negotiation: some conflicts between teachers and pupils may boil down to mismatched expectations about what each is supposed to do at school, i.e., their respective roles; their interactions would therefore consist of trying to establish where exactly they stand in relation to each other, i.e., negotiating their respective positions. The idea that an individual is 'manoeuvred' by collective consensus into a particular position within a group is encapsulated in the sociological concept of *role*. More recently, theorists have put the accent on individuals' own *negotiation* of their positions in the social world.

FROM 'ROLE' TO 'POSITION'

The macro structure of the school determines the allocation of tasks and authority among pupils and teachers. This gives rise to a set of criteria by which to evaluate individuals: 'A *role* is a set of activities and relations expected of a person occupying a particular position in society, and of others in relation to that person.'[37] Bronfenbrenner has stressed that the pupil role is definable not only by what children do or are supposed to do at school, but also by *who* they do it with, what is 'done' to them, and how these interpersonal interactions relate to educational aims: 'when a teacher explains, the pupil is expected to pay attention'.[38] In keeping with G. H. Mead's model of the social genesis of the self, Bronfenbrenner proposed a dynamic and person-centred concept of roles as *contexts for human development*.

As a developmental psychologist, Bronfenbrenner's perspective differed somewhat from the conventional approach at the time. Generally in the early sociological literature, a role implied culture-specific structures, or sets of obligations. The emphasis was on individuals *enacting* social roles. The traditional frame of reference would address issues such as: What do children do, and what are they expected to do, at school? What factors determine whether individuals conform or rebel? Even then, however, it was felt that simply mapping the social world in terms of roles did not fully explain the richness and dynamics of human behaviour.[39] How do children construe what is, and is not, acceptable behaviour at school? How do they interpret their own actions? How do they go about fitting in at school? Although the role concept generated insights that are as pertinent now as they were over thirty years ago, when Goffman first described how people present themselves to others in everyday settings,[40] certain emphases have changed over the years. The direction of the change brings current thinking in line with Bronfenbrenner's perspective.

Current theories expand on the idea that the social group creates the context in which individuals define their own identities or selves. A role implies more than a 'job description', i.e., more than a statement of the tasks and authority that go with a particular position. There are also tacit expectations about how 'types' of individuals perform the tasks that go with certain positions or social situations. For instance, Delamont discovered in her classroom observations that girls were often treated by teachers as if they, the girls, were less likely than boys to be competent in maths and sciences.[41]

It is a relevant comment that stereotypes such as the 'non-mathematical girl' may well have changed, or could change. Roles are designated by a consensus reflecting a particular culture or subculture. As Calvert noted in her comprehensive description of the pupil role, 'this consensus is far from perfect. The expectations for pupil behaviour will vary somewhat depending on whether we consult teachers, parents, the pupils themselves, or some other group.'[42] By implication, there is no absolute Pupil Role. Furthermore, although a particular role (within a specified group) may be described in terms of normative behaviours, the role description neither explains nor predicts individuals' actual performance. People do not slot into structure which exist transcendentally, as if independent of their own actions and understandings. In an influential book, *The Explanation of Social Behaviour*, Harré and Secord urged the replacement of role enactment with rule-following.[43]

They pointed out that knowledge of a role means knowing the *rules* for certain kinds of actions in the proper order and appropriate circumstances. It follows that the psychological process of learning rules for social behaviour is universal, though the rules themselves may differ widely across social contexts.

In general, group norms and expectations, irrespective of 'content', create a *context*, a niche into which individuals grow. Whether individual children accept or reject the pupil role (as defined in their environment) depends on their own interpretation of the consequences of their actions either way. Goffman's concept of *role distance* points to occasions when being seen by others as not conforming to normative expectations serves a personal purposes.[44] If doing well at school is highly valued by parents and other influential people in the child's life, the child may be motivated to appear as a competent pupil. If challenging school authority brings status among peers, or is congruent with attitudes expressed by people whom the individual emulates (i.e., role models), role distance is likely. 'Pupils will form their own groups with their own distinctive values and standards . . . which may be in keeping with the values of the school or in opposition to them.'[45] Therefore, to understand individuals' social behaviour, we must consider the social contexts, or frames of reference, in which they themselves construe the implications of their actions.

Although role theorists did not agree on fine detail, the process they all described pivots on the idea of a person perceiving other people and being perceived by others. Reciprocal expectations and perceptions are communicated in many subtle ways among members of a group, ways which are rarely rationalized or reflected upon by the individuals involved, but nevertheless disclose their intentions, plans, biases, etc. In any social situation, we essentially react to others' verbal and nonverbal behaviour on the basis of what their actions, and their reactions to ours, mean to us. Thus our relative *positions* are defined in the course of interpersonal interactions.

An insight into the process in operation is provided in

Hargreaves' account of his research in a secondary modern school for boys.[46] Hargreaves tells of an occasion when he asked to send a boy across the road to the post office; the teacher agreed, and Hargreaves asked one of the boys, Derek. The rest is best told in Hargreaves' words:

> The teacher turned to me and said, 'You don't want to send him if you want to get those stamps today,' and asked another boy to run the errand. Derek, who seemed both surprised and pleased by my request, now began to scowl. When I insisted that Derek should go for me, Derek looked at me and said, 'Are you sure?'[47]

The teacher's attitude had nothing to do with Derek as a pupil, but with Derek as a person – and Derek 'grew' into the social niche reinforced by the teacher.

Since the early 1970s, Rom Harré and his associates have explored the ways in which individuals acquire personal powers to carve niches for themselves in the social world. Social niches cannot be mapped out adequately in terms of 'fixed' roles. A junior school pupil once told me about an incident in which he physically hurt a teacher, explaining that it was a bad thing to do because the teacher was a woman. By evoking gender, the 10-year-old boy unwittingly *positioned* himself (in our chat) as the 'powerful' one, thus reversing the asymmetry inherent in the teacher–pupil roles, whereby the teacher is more powerful.

In recent papers, Harré and co-writers propose the replacement of the static concept of role with the dynamic concept of *position* or *positioning*, to do with the discursive production of selves.[48] Exploration of this concept has just begun, and it may be a while before its precise utility in educational psychology can be evaluated. However, it captures the idea that people seldom fit the templates of definable roles. Instead, people negotiate their position in any given situation, according to their own evolving story-lines, their own continuously revised understanding of the social world.

The concept of positioning elaborates an idea that is already well established in sociology and social psychology; namely, the development of selfhood through interpersonal transactions.[49] Attending school involves the child or young person in discursive interactions with others, and those interactions are inevitably implicated in the shaping of his or her concept of self. But 'social agency' can mean a power to intimidate classmates or to outwit teachers. Moreover, it is naive to expect that children's natural curiosity would motivate them to explore curricular topics. During one of my informal visits to a junior school class, the teacher set the pupils the task of writing about something which had made the strongest impression on them during a recent educational trip to a local castle. I conversationally posed the essay question to one boy, who replied enthusiastically that the 'best thing' was a pond outside the castle. He and two friends, exploring outside the 'official' route, discovered the pond, and one of them slipped into the water. The boy could not tell me much about the castle. Whatever he learned, it was not what the teacher had intended.

There seems to be a mismatch between what sociologists or social psychologists have in mind when they speak of social agency, autonomy or personal powers, on the one hand, and what educators have in mind when they envisage pupils as autonomous learners, on the other. A pivotal theme in modern educational ideology is that pupil control over the learning environment plays a crucial part in education. The child-centred approach emphasizes enquiry and discussion in place of a didactic method. It is believed, not without good reason, that educational aims are best met when children assume responsibility for their own learning, and when they are steered towards problem-solving instead of rote-learning. Cognately, the teacher's role is redefined. In this view, the teacher's fundamental duty is to facilitate the child's 'learning to learn' (as opposed to mere transmission of information), and the teacher–pupil relationship is envisaged as a collaboration between social agents. When advocating the implementation of this philosophy, however, it is crucial to consider children's readiness for this new 'pupil role'.

Ingram and Worrall followed the transition of a small junior school class (twelve pupils) through a succession of learning environments.[50] The class was first observed during the last five weeks before the summer break. Their teacher at the time practised what Ingram and Worrall call a *traditional directive* style: the children were seated in fixed, teacher-allocated positions facing a central blackboard; most activities were based on given textbooks and worksheets, set by the teacher; teacher–pupil interaction was initiated via raised hands, and children's movement or interactions among themselves were discouraged; rewards and controls were extrinsic (praise and criticism, ticks or written comments). When the class returned after the summer, a different teacher implemented a negotiative teaching style. The class was observed during the initial five-week period of adjustment (the *transitional negotiative* environment) and again after two terms in which the children had control over their use of curricular time (the *established negotiative* environment).

In the traditional negotiative period, the children chose their own seating and arrangement of desks, and the arrangement was activity-oriented. The children had a greater say in their use of textbooks and work topics, although the teacher still directed the general curriculum. Teacher–child interactions did not depend on hand-raising, and child–child interactions were openly encouraged. Intrinsic rewards (satisfaction with work) were emphasized, and extrinsic controls were kept to a minimum. Later, in the established negotiative classroom, resource areas were set up for language, art, maths, science and computing. The children chose their own seating in each area. The teacher acted as a consultant, and did not direct the children in favour of a particular curricular area. Each morning and afternoon began with a class meeting during which all activities were negotiated and planned. Free movement and interaction were encouraged.

Classroom observations and the pupils' self-reports revealed clear differences. In the established negotiative classroom, pupils on average spent equal time on most curricular areas, and individuals showed a preference for longer activity periods than they had been allowed in the traditional directive regime (in which curricular imbalance was greater). Ingram and Worrall conclude, 'While the curricular diet of the traditional classroom was dominated by the 3Rs, the negotiative diet seems more balanced across the curriculum as a whole – indeed a more "wholesome" diet.'[51]

The results of Ingram and Worrall's study are promising. However, when an educational innovation is implemented on a wide scale, as a matter of government policy, not all teachers are keen on the change, or able to implement it effectively; pupils are less likely to feel themselves privileged, as would participants in a special scheme. The transposition of an educational environment from the 'experimental' context to the mainstream is more than a matter of copying a promising programme many times: as the environment of the programme changes, the programme itself inevitably becomes something else, sometimes less effective. There might be management problems not encountered in the original project. The issue of class size must be taken into account: Ingram and Worrall observed a class of twelve pupils; in 1991, the average class size in England was 26.8 at the primary school level.[52] It is doubtful whether 30 children can be guided into autonomous classroom activities as effectively as twelve children.

The structuring of curricular time in the primary school is conventionally considered to be the responsibility of the teacher; it makes sense in a large class (but whether large classes are beneficial is debatable). The older among us recall the primary school day being punctuated with the sound of a buzzer, controlled from the office, when books would be packed away and the books for the next lesson be taken out. Even as primary education shifted towards 'integrated' timetabling, in common practices the teacher remained responsible for allocating tasks and supervising their completion within his or her schedule. Although the 'integrated day' is designed with something like Ingram and Worrall's negotiative environment in mind, in reality most classrooms are closer to what they call a traditional directive environment. The partial implementation of child-centred education puts children in a somewhat confusing situation, as the following studies suggest.

Ingram and Worrall report two studies in which they investigated how junior school children cope (or cop out) in directive settings.[53] In the first study, for which they selected a small class of 9- and 10-year-olds, the psychologists compared the teacher's planned timetable for certain days, his record of the curriculum areas actually covered during those sessions, and the children's records of what they were doing. A poor fit between the teacher's and the children's records was discovered, and this discrepancy increased during the term: the children recorded fewer lessons than the teacher did. Moreover, there were large variations in the records of different pupils, and inconsistencies in the records of the same pupils over different periods of the study.

Therefore, in the second study, Ingram and Worrall looked at how individual children experienced the curriculum. The psychologists interviewed 53 children aged 7 to 11, from four directive classrooms, about the perceived pace and difficulty lessons, the strategies they used when finding themselves not in step with the lesson, and their emotional reactions to being ahead or behind the rest of the class. The interviews revealed two 'kinds' of children: those who thought that the pace of the curriculum was very easy, whom Ingram and Worrall dubbed 'frontrunners'; and those who thought it was very hard, dubbed 'backmarkers'. None of the children interviewed by the psychologists thought that the pace was 'just right'.

The frontrunners found themselves finishing the set work too soon, and had to fill up the time by doing more of the same activity, by reading or some other acceptable activities. However, the majority of children (77 per cent of the sample) saw themselves as backmarkers. They found it difficult to keep up with the teacher, and were generally behind in their lessons. Unable to finish set work within the prescribed time, some children would typically continue after the teacher directed the class as a whole to begin a different subject. The backlog accumulated over the day, even over several days. Some children would leave work unfinished. Consequently, backmarkers experienced less curricular activities than the teacher was providing. Yet their teachers, also interviewed by the psychologists, maintained that the 'paper timetable' accurately represented curricular exposure.

As Ingram and Worrall comment, the children saw themselves as never in step with the timetable, but the teachers 'were not sensitive to anything other than the sporadic and inevitable variations for particular children'.[54] Summing up, Ingram and Worrall reflect:

> Although on the face of it the child in the traditional-directive classroom ought to have little scope of constructing his or her own curriculum, in a curious way it turned out that this responsibility was thrust upon the child, if the child wished to maintain an appearance of contact with the classroom enterprise. It was a responsibility that any primary-school child might find daunting to carry.[55]

Predictably, most backmarkers expressed negative feelings about themselves when asked how they felt when they could not finish the work to the teacher's schedule. Thus a teacher's classroom strategies inadvertently created situations in which children experienced themselves as incompetent, with obvious implications for self-esteem.

COMMONALITY OR COMMUNICATION?

In Ingram and Worrall's negotiative classroom, described earlier, the children and teacher acted as collaborators in the education enterprise.[56] Given the chance, children may approach the management of curricular time slightly differently than would teachers. This is partly because different tasks face a learner and a tutor in any group situation. In a negotiative classroom environment, learners choose their own activities, and co-ordinate their plans with the plans of their peers. The tutor, in any type of classroom, plans to provide all learners with access to the curriculum, and must modify plans in view of immediate constraints or prevailing conditions (e.g., time, availability of resources, the class's characteristics), considerations which rarely enter the learner's planning. Second, it is worth noting that in Ingram and Worrall's study, by the time the children settled into the established negotiative environment, they were older and wiser. The learner's age and educational background can be important determinants of the degree to which learner and tutor hold similar views of their shared enterprise. Finally, when commenting on learning methods, pupils refer to what has made an impact on their own learning, whereas teachers refer to what they have found (or believe) to make a positive impact on most pupils.

Children are not competent critics of pedagogy, but given several years at school, they certainly have first-hand knowledge of what 'works' for them. 'Pupils often offer clearer and more detailed accounts than their teachers of how particular teaching strategies interact with their learning processes.'[57] In their qualitative study, Cooper and McIntyre compared Year 7 pupils' and teachers' perceptions of effective classroom learning in English and history. Teachers and pupils perceived similar classroom situations as conducive to learning and understanding. However, whereas the teachers took a contextualized view, evaluating the utility of a given method in the context of the topic being taught and classroom conditions, many pupils considered certain methods as intrinsically powerful learning aids.

The nature of the pupils' preference is revealing. They favoured methods such as drama/role play, visual aids, and use of stimuli relating to pop-culture – all of which are to some extent multi-sensory, interactive, and fun. The methods towards which the pupils did not show a particular preference were comparatively more teacher-led and 'intellectual' in nature: the teacher making explicit the agenda for the lesson, recapping, using texts or worksheets, etc. In Cooper and McIntyre's study, then, the pupils felt that methods which created satisfying emotional states had the most impact on their learning. The teachers too were aware of the importance of pupils' affective states, not only as means to educational ends. Pupils and teachers alike perceived certain classroom states or events, broadly definable as social climate, as desirable *outcomes* (whereas, as Cooper and McIntyre point out, outsiders tend to construe the social climate as a 'process' leading to learning effectiveness).

It is encouraging that teachers and pupils agree on many points, but this in itself does not necessarily disclose a high degree of teacher–pupil communication. A commonality between teacher and pupil perspectives means that their expectations are collateral (parallel) or compatible. The fact that both teachers and pupils enjoy working in a friendly atmosphere reflects a common denominator as humans, i.e., collateral expectations. Compatible expectations arise from different lines of reasoning which lead to similar conclusions. For instance, Cooper and Mcintyre found that although there was a high degree of commonality in the ways teachers and pupils spoke about specific tasks in English lessons (e.g., filling out passport forms), the pupils were less likely to evaluate those tasks as increasing language competence, but believed that the tasks were designed to train them in practical skills which they imagined they would need in adult life.

Shades of meanings separate co-operation from collaboration. Co-operation implies that teachers and pupils work jointly towards set goals (e.g., 'covering' a curricular topic); pupils co-operate with the teacher in a disciplined traditional classroom. Collaboration means that the goals themselves are defined jointly. Therefore, the learner and tutor must share the same frame of reference from the outset. Making children see their schooling from our adult viewpoint is intrinsic in formal education. It is generally held that the school ought to instil positive regard to literacy, numeracy, and other skills which constitute basic competence in our culture. *Tutor–learner* collaboration may not be feasible before the child has internalized such educational values.

However, *adult–child* collaboration at school can, and does, begin much earlier. It begins with the shared interest in *the child as a person* (as distinguished from the interest in the acquisition of knowledge or a formal qualification). The importance of pupils' perception of their teachers as responsive to their personal needs crops up time and again in research. As mentioned in the previous chapter, Finlayson discovered that the degree to which pupils perceived their teachers as sensitive to pupil personal needs ('teacher concern') was an important determinant of a school's climate, with implications for school effectiveness.[58] Children's adjustment at school, a pre-condition for internalizing educational values, may depend greatly on their belief that the teacher cares about them – and the onus is on the teacher to communicate to the child that such belief is well founded.

The Class as an Ecosystem

The chapter began with a discussion of evidence and explanation for the effects of teacher expectations. The need for reworking the applicability of the self-fulfilling prophecy thesis to educational settings has been identified. It was suggested that the traditional explanations of expectancy effects may be unduly restricted in their focus on what goes on between a teacher and a pupil. The narrow focus on one-to-one inter-actions misses some essential features of school reality. Attention was drawn to the likelihood that expectancy effects could be mediated by what teacher differential treatment means to the child's perceived position among peers and self-esteem. The presentation of self in a social group and the impact of collective expectations on the individual are embodied in the sociological concept of role, also outlined in this chapter. In the literature on social behaviour, dissatisfaction with the static conception of role has led to the dynamic concept of *positioning*, which underlines discursive negotiations between social agents. A similar theme has been expanded here with reference to children's negotiations of the learning environment.

In all, this leads to the ideas of the classroom group as a molar system, a complex organization comprised of individuals and their interactions. The word *system*, applied in the present context, embodies the premise that the dynamics of the classroom group are not identical with the sum total of individuals' activities in isolation, due to the cumulative effect that any individual's activity may have on the activities of others.

The idea of a school class as a system is hardly new. Getzels and Thelen proposed a conceptual framework for the study of the classroom group as a social system.[59] Their model essentially organizes our thinking about classroom processes, and does not purport to predict or explain those events: it identifies relationships between dimensions of the topic (e.g., how we may relate organism-centred processes to institutional ethos), not between the people who make up the classroom group. In contrast, workers in special education such as Upton and Cooper in Britain,[60] and others in the United States, have more recently expounded what they call the ecosystemic perspective. By focusing on teacher–pupil communication, the later concept of the class as a system (or ecosystem) pertains to relationships between real people.

In the ecosystemic perspective, behaviour problems are explained in view of what teachers and pupils actually say to each other or do in response to each other's utterances. In special education, the focus on a single dimension – the interpersonal – is justifiable in so far that pupil behaviours which teachers find problematic are often associated with interpersonal conflict, reified in discourse. The basic concepts are extrapolated from psychiatric systems theory, associated with family therapy, with acknowledgement of some obvious dissimilarities between clinical and classroom settings.[61] In the United States, Molnar and Lindquist were perhaps the first to introduce the term *ecosystem* in educational psychology.[62] In their view, the school class constitutes an ecosystem in that everyone in the classroom influences and is influenced by the behaviour of everyone else. Thus, a pupil's disruptive behaviour is not merely symptomatic of some 'problem' (conduct disorder) of that individual, nor is it just a 'problem' for the teacher, but it affects the state of the whole system.

Proponents of systems theory in psychiatry and educational psychology often state their indebtedness to von Bertalanffy's General Systems Theory, a mathematical model that predicts complex dynamic interactions in natural systems.[63] Following the theoretical definition of a system, educational psychologists highlight the following propositions as their tenets:

(1) Problem behaviour does not originate from within the child who displays it but from within the interaction between that child and other people in the classroom.

(2) The cause of any instance of problem behaviour is part of a

cyclical chain of actions and reactions between the participants.

(3) Interactional patterns may be conceptualized as limited to an immediate context (the classroom) or implicating wider social influences (e.g., home and wider-community influences on the participants' expectations from other people in the classroom).[64]

The same can be said about non-problematic behaviour. Research on leadership, for example, describes how the behaviour of one person can influence group dynamics. The focus on problem behaviour reflects the applied framework in which educational psychologists work. In this framework, the most important tenet is the pragmatic corollary:

(4) when behaviour problems occur in the classroom, the disturbed interpersonal relationship (not the 'disturbing' child) should be diagnosed and treated.

The call is to identify response patterns which exacerbate, if not trigger, teacher–pupil conflict. Such ecosystem analysis is seen as a preliminary to intervention based on changing interactional patterns in the classroom.

The ecosystemic approach allows for the possibility that a child who is problematic in one teacher's view (i.e., in one interpersonal system) may be regarded as 'no problem' by another teacher or adults outside school. Also, a disruptive pupil causes problems for teachers, but could be well-liked among classmates.[65] In principle, an ecosystemic analysis can be used to compare school classes and to identify features of 'healthy' v. 'disturbed' classroom systems. Ecosystemic thinking sidesteps gratuitous generalizations, such as the assumption that middle-class teachers must have low expectations of working-class children. On the other hand, a holistic focus on interactional patterns runs the risk of overlooking precisely those individual-specific factors which can cause classroom hostility or discord (such as a teacher's biased beliefs about working-class pupils).

Compelling as the idea of the school-class ecosystem may

be, we need to consider carefully whether it satisfies von Bertal-anffy's definition of a system as 'a complex of interacting elements'.[66] Something that responds as a system reacts to an outside influence as one unit, an indivisible whole (more or less). Since, according to the definition of 'whole', all the elements within the system are interconnected, a change in any element (itself a complex of interacting elements, i.e., a subsystem) will ultimately affect the rest to some degree, and this may result in a structural change in the system as a whole. Over time, reactions to both external influences and internally generated changes accumulate in a patterned way, governed by natural laws (e.g., equilibrium), so that the system is seen to evolve as a unified whole. Hence, holistic complexity, cyclical causality, and self-regulation or self-construction, are distinctive properties of a system. An organism is the best example.

Drawing an analogy between a classroom group and an organism may be putting it too strongly, but is not entirely off the mark. In the classroom, an outside influence such as the temporary presence of a student teacher will affect the class's activities in direct and indirect ways. Pupils may receive more help than they would otherwise; some may be distracted from their work, or impelled to 'show off'; the class teacher may organize activities differently, taking into account the student; and so on. The impact of the student's stay on classroom ecology is thus holistic and complex. The fact that individuals in the classroom group react separately to an outsider, their reactions reflecting their own beliefs, feelings, 'positioning', etc., is consistent with the idea of a system as composed of subsystems which are qualitatively different from the molar system. However, when imagining the school class as a system, a whole in which pupils and teacher are 'mere' subsystems, we must not lose sight of the fact that an ecosystem is an abstraction, a theoretical invention, arguably useful for reinforcing the argument that behaviour can be understood only in its relevant context. The only real entities here are people.

Notes and References

1 Jackson, P. W. *Life in the Classrooms*. New York: Holt, Rinehart and Winston, 1968, p. 9.

2 Ibid,., p. 26.

3 Davies, B. 'An analysis of primary school children's accounts of classroom interaction'. *British Journal of Sociology of Education*, 1, 1980, p. 257.

4 E.g., Davies, B. *Life in the Classroom and Playground: The Accounts of Primary School Children*. London: Routledge and Kegan Paul, 1982.

5 E.g., Hargreaves, D. H. *Interpersonal Relations and Education*. London: Routledge and Kegan Paul, 1975; Brophy, J. E. and Good, T. *Teacher–Student Relationships: Causes and Consequences*. New York: Holt, Rinehart and Winston, 1974; Nash, R. *Classrooms Observed*. London: Routledge and Kegan Paul, 1973; Delamont, S. *Interaction in the Classroom*, 2nd edn. London: Methuen, 1983.

6 E.g., Delamont, S. *Sex Roles and the School*. London: Methuen, 1980.

7 Rosenthal, R. and Jacobson, L. *Pygmalion in the Classroom: Teacher Expectation and Pupils' Intellectual Development*. New York: Holt, Rinehart and Winston, 1968.

8 See review by Brophy, J. E. 'Research on the self-fulfilling prophecy and teacher expectations'. *Journal of Educational Psychology*, **75**, 631–661, 1983.

9 Blatchford, P., Burke, J., Farquhar, C. and Tizard, B. 'Teacher expectations in infant school: associations with attainment and progress, curriculum coverage and classroom interaction'. *British Journal of Educational Psychology*, **59**, 1989, p. 20.

10 Miller, D. T. and Turnbull, W. T. 'Expectancies and interpersonal processes'. *Annual Review of Psychology*, **37**, 233–256, 1986.

11 'Viewpoint' column, *The Independent*, 11 April 1991.

12 Badad, E., Bernieri, F. and Rosenthal, R. 'When less information is more informative: diagnostic teacher expectations from brief samples of behaviour'. *British Journal of Educational Psychology*, **59**, 281–295, 1989.

13 Cf. Upton, G. (ed), *Educating Children with Behaviour Problems*. Cardiff: Faculty of Education, University College Cardiff, 1983.

14 McNamara, E., Evans, M. and Hill, W. 'The reduction of disruptive behaviour in two secondary school classes'. *British Journal of Educational Psychology*, **56**, 209–215, 1986.

15 E.g., Rosenthal, R. and Jacobson, L., 1968, op. cit.
16 Badad, E. *et al*, 1989, op. cit., p. 282.
17 Schultz, R. A. 'Sociopsychological climates and teacher-bias expectancy: a possible mediating mechanism'. *Journal of Educational Psychology*, **75**, 1983, p. 167; my italics.
18 Jussim, L. 'Self-fulfilling prophecies: a theoretical and integrative review'. *Psychological Review*, **93**, 429–445, 1986.
19 Ibid.
20 Mead, G. H. *Mind, Self and Society*. Chicago: University of Chicago Press, 1934.
21 Ibid.
22 Carske, M. L. 'Learned helplessness, self-worth motivation and attribution retraining for primary school children'. *British Journal of Educational Psychology*, **58**, 152–164, 1988.
23 Nash, R., 1973, op. cit.
24 Weinstein, R. S., Marshall, H. H., Sharp, L. and Botkin, M. 'Pygmalion and the student: age and classroom differences in children's awareness of teacher expectations'. *Child Development*, **58**, pp. 1079–1093, 1987.
25 Nash, R., 1973, op. cit.
26 Ibid., p. 18.
27 Worrall, N., Worrall, C. and Meldrum, C. 'Children reciprocations of teacher evaluations'. *British Journal of Educational Psychology*, **58**, 78–88, 1988.
28 Ibid., p. 86.
29 Jackson, P. W., 1968, op. cit., p. 20
30 Ibid., p. 20; his italics.
31 Hargreaves, D. H. *Social Relations in a Secondary School*. London: Routledge and Kegan Paul, 1967, p. 102.
32 Ibid., p. 99.
33 Ibid., p. 99.
34 Delamont, S., 1983, op. cit.
35 Nash, R. 'Pupils' expectations for their teachers'. *Research in Education*, **12**, 47–61, 1974.
36 Beynon, J. and Delamont, S. 'The sound and the fury: pupil perceptions of school violence'. In Frude, N. and Gault, H. (eds), *Disruptive Behaviour in Schools*. London: John Wiley and Sons, pp. 137–151, 1984.
37 Bronfenbrenner, U. *The Ecology of Human Development*. Cambridge, MA: Harvard University Press, 1979, p. 85; his italics.
38 Ibid., p. 85.

39 Cf. Hargreaves, D. H., 1975, op. cit.; Calvert, B. *The Role of the Pupil.* London: Routledge and Kegan Paul, 1975.

40 Goffman, E. *The Presentation of Self in Everyday Life.* Garden City, NY: Doubleday, 1959.

41 Delamont, S., 1980, op. cit.

42 Calvert, B., 1975, op. cit., p. 60.

43 Harré, R. and Secord, P. F. *The Explanation of Social Behaviour.* Oxford: Blackwell, 1972.

44 E.g., Hargreaves, D. H., 1975, op. cit.

45 Rutter, M., Maughan, B., Mortimore, P. and Ouston, J. *Fifteen Thousand Hours: Secondary Schools and Their Effects on Children.* London: Open Books, 1979, p. 194.

46 Hargreaves, D. H., 1967, op. cit.

47 Ibid., p. 107.

48 Davies, B. and Harré, R. 'Positioning: the discursive production of selves'. *Journal for the Theory of Social Behaviour,* **20**, 43–64, 1990; Harré, R. and Van Lagenhove, L. 'Varieties of positioning'. *Journal for the Theory of Social Behaviour,* **21**, 392–408, 1991.

49 See Shotter, J. *Social Accountability and Selfhood.* Oxford: Blackwell, 1984; Harré, R. *Personal Being: A Theory for Individual Psychology.* Oxford: Blackwell, 1983.

50 Ingram, J. and Worrall, N. 'Children's self-allocation and use of classroom curricular time'. *British Journal of Educational Psychology,* **62**, 45–55, 1992.

51 Ibid., p. 54.

52 Mortimore, P. and Blatchford, P. *The Issue of Class Size.* Briefing No. 12. London: The National Commission on Education, 1993.

53 Ingram, J. and Worrall, N. 'Varieties of curricular experience: backmarkers and frontrunners in the primary school'. *British Journal of Educational Psychology,* **60**, 37–51, 1990.

54 Ibid., p. 60.

55 Ibid., p. 62

56 Ingram, J. and Worrall, N., 1992, op. cit.

57 Cooper, P. and McIntyre, D. 'Commonality in teachers' and pupils' perceptions of effective classroom learning'. *British Journal of Educational Psychology,* **63**, 1993, p. 397.

58 Finlayson, D. S. 'Measuring "school climate".' *Trends in Education,* **30**, 19–27, 1973.

59 Getzels, J. W. and Thelen, H. A. 'The classroom group as a unique social system'. In Nelson, B. H. (ed.), *The Dynamics of Instructional Groups,* 59th Yearbook of the National Society for the Study of Education, Part 2, pp. 53–82, 1960.

60 Upton, G. and Cooper, P. 'A new perspective on behaviour problems in schools: the ecosystemic approach'. *Maladjustment and Therapeutic Education*, **8**, 3–18, 1990.

61 Speed, B. 'Systemic family therapy and disturbing behaviour'. In Upton, G. (ed.), *Educating Children with Behaviour Problems*. Cardiff: Faculty of Education, University College Cardiff, pp. 168–185, 1983.

62 Molnar, A. and Lindquist, B. *Changing Problem Behavior in Schools*. San Francisco: Jossey-Bass, 1986.

63 Von Bertalanffy, L. *General Systems Theory: Foundations, Development, Applications*. New York: Braziller, 1968.

64 Adapted from Upton, G. and Cooper, P., 1990, op. cit.

65 Cf. Delamont, S., 1983, op. cit.

66 Von Bertalanffy, L., 1968, op. cit., p. 55.

CHAPTER 6
The Social Niche (2): Pupil–Pupil Relationships

The humanist psychologist and educator Carl Rogers expounded the idea that there is more to learning than intellectual performance. Rogers distinguished between conventional school learning, which 'involves the mind only . . . does not involve feelings or personal meanings [and] has no relevance for the whole person', and 'a significant, meaningful, experiential learning'.[1] Schools, in Rogers' view, ought to facilitate the latter kind of learning. Whatever the teaching ideology, nobody would seriously deny that the impact of the learning environment on the child is first and foremost 'experiential' – and that peers have a special role in the child's experiential environment. Just in what ways peer relations are special in education is a current issue in developmental psychology. Peer relations may conflate with school learning on three levels: incidental, instrumental, and intrinsic. First, being bullied, ridiculed or rejected by schoolmates leads to stress, anxiety, and ultimately school avoidance, all of which underlie the child's learning. Second, academic motivation can be powerfully influenced, in either direction, by peer group norms: being a 'swot' might be perceived as a status handicap; being 'brainy' could gain esteem. Third, what children learn from and with other children can have a more profound effect than what they learn from a teacher.

Discussing issues concerning social competence, Erickson and Shultz suggested that in ordinary perception, 'contexts are constituted by what people are doing where and when they are doing it'; moreover, the people who interact within a location at a given time 'become environments for each other'.[2] This chapter concerns the conditions for peer relations created by the school, ways in which schoolmates constitute a child's environment, and educational implications of peer relations. Two 'applied' research areas are rapidly expanding: peer tutoring, co-operation and collaboration;[3] and, separately, playground behaviour, with special attention to bullying.[4]

Learning in a Social Context

The view that much of children's socialization and education should be carried out in age-graded institutions is a characteristic of industrialized societies, reflecting 'mass production' or 'assembly line' thinking. Contrary to the age stratification imposed by the traditional educational system, cross-cultural and historical evidence indicates that children's peer relations evolved under conditions which favour small mixed-age groups.[5] Since the late 1970s, the idea that cognitive development occurs primarily among individuals of mixed abilities has become a central issue, culminating in the now well-established field of social cognition.[6] This has led to an interest in children's ability to teach other children, or work jointly towards a solution of problems.

Peer teaching or collaboration is usually advocated on grounds that it brings intellectual gains; the likelihood that it is more fun, pleasant, or emotionally fulfilling for children to work together than alone or with adults is seen as a fringe benefit. I shall argue that, on the contrary, affect comes before intellect.

COGNITION IN CONTEXT

As children grow older, from the preschool throughout the primary school years, their peer interactions change 'from simple organisation to complex hierarchies, from loosely differentiated interchanges to differentiated interaction'.[7] Nursery school children behave like an aggregate of individuals, although they do take an interest in each other, engage in mimicry and turn taking, and share play materials. Older children display reciprocal social relations, and peers become increasingly 'significant others'. The developmental perspective on children's friendships is reviewed later in this chapter. For the moment, suffice it to note that friends first operate on the same world, and in later childhood explain it together.

Among young children, peer interactions tend to be object-focused (friends play with the same toys, share food, like to be 'on' the same reading book). Discourse among 10- and 11-year-olds discloses deliberate efforts to come to a shared understanding about the world within the school.[8]

Such evidence was interpreted by some as indicating that the child first learns that other people can perceive the world differently, and eventually acquires the 'knack' of co-ordinating his or her perspective with others. Psychologists working in the Piagetian frame of reference have highlighted the central role of *perspective taking*, or the 'co-ordination of perspective', in peer relations.[9] Piaget, whose theory of cognitive development has had the most profound impact on contemporary developmental psychology and primary education, proposed that young children are *egocentric*. That is, they cannot yet imagine a viewpoint that differs from their own. A child at this stage would presumably be unable to empathize with other children (let alone adults) in school, at home, in the street – or when asked by a psychologist to solve a problem which demands imagining another person's viewpoint. According to Piaget, social development involves a cognitive process of decentring, which manifests itself in the growing child's increased ability to imagine others' points of view.

Critics of Piaget have demonstrated that whether young children appear egocentric or not depends very much on the children's perception of the situation that makes it necessary for them to 'guess' another person's viewpoint. They may find it difficult to describe what a mountain looks like from the other side, as in Piaget's famous 'three mountains' task, but can correctly infer whether a policeman can or cannot see a hiding thief.[10] If young children's thinking is more concrete than that of older children and adults, their social cognition might well be more context-dependent, and their interpersonal judgements be more strongly influenced by their feelings and beliefs about the other person.

If child–child interactions are oriented towards improved 'perspective taking', then children may be sensitive to alternative perspectives evident in peers' behaviour or talk. Young children readily pick up from each other new things to do with a toy, for instance. Relatively recently, psychologists have begun exploring educational applications. However, the implications of children's prosociality for their cognitive development were realized long ago by the Russian psychologist Lev Vygotsky, whose pioneering work was discovered in the West several decades after his death. Vygotsky proposed that a child's integration into a social world prepares the ground for the development of thought and language – and not the other way around. He regarded an affective-social relationship as a necessary condition for any 'intellectual' progress.

The impact of Vygotskian ideas on contemporary Western psychology has amounted to a paradigm shift, given the earlier dominance of Piagetian theory. Piaget acknowledged that social interaction is necessary for the development of a child's thought, especially moral understanding, but considered the progress of what he called 'social logic' and 'individual logic' as 'two inseparable aspects of a single reality, at once social and individual'.[11] Until the late 1970s, his followers, based in Geneva, concerned themselves almost exclusively with the development of cognitive structures through the child's interactions with the non-social environment.

Contrary to Piaget, Vygotsky suggested that the true direction of the development of thinking is from the interpersonal to the individual: 'what the child can do in co-operation today he can do alone tomorrow'.[12] Doise and other workers in the Piagetian school have set out to substantiate Vygotsky's basic thesis that 'social interaction exercises a causal effect on cognitive development'.[13] Their experiments resulted in considerable evidence that, after working on a task with another child who presents a different approach to the problem, children often use more advanced cognitive strategies than they did previously. Doise and Mackie compared three explanations for this improvement: *social learning*, Piagetian *cognitive conflict* theory, and the Vygotskian viewpoint, which they call the *sociocognitive conflict* approach.

According to the social learning approach, children imitate the superior strategy, or model their behaviour on others. The theory of cognitive conflict elaborates Piaget's concept of cognitive equilibrium: children settle on certain ways (schemas) of operating on the world until their strategies are found inadequate; challenges presented by the real world cause perturbations which induce the reorganization and restructuring of the child's schema on a more advanced level of equilibrium. In keeping with this view, cognitive conflict theory states that when children become aware of a solution to a problem which is discrepant from their own, the resultant conflict may be sufficient to initiate such reorganization. Both social learning and cognitive conflict theories assume that the individual operates as a solitary agent, though their respective adherents differ regarding the locus of development. Piagetians assume that development occurs 'inside' the child's mind; social learning theorists, subscribing to the behaviourist viewpoint, feel that there is no reason to look for anything other than the observed changes in the response pattern. Moreover, both approaches reduce participants in an interaction to mere producers of either cognitive conflict or correct response models, as the case may be.

The socio-cognitive conflict approach asserts the essentially social nature of interactions. Doise and Mackie point out that

> in true interaction, as distinct from nominal interaction such as working side by side or observing someone else, participants are generally required to agree on a single or joint answer requiring co-operation and co-ordination. Whether real co-ordination rather than compliance or the passive acceptance of another solution results from the interaction depends largely on the social behaviour of participants.[14]

Both the social learning approach and the traditional cognitive conflict theory assume that progress takes place when the child is confronted with superior solutions. According to socio-cognitive conflict theory, cognitive gains can result from confrontation with solutions which are equally or less advanced than the child's own: 'The criterion for progress is that conflict or opposition should be socially present, not that presented solutions be superior to that of the subject.'[15]

The thesis of socio-cognitive conflict in a sense reinforces Piaget's contention, cited earlier, that social and individual factors constitute a single reality; but this reality comprises an intricate process:

> By co-ordinating their actions with the actions of other individuals, children progress cognitively and are able to participate in even more complex interactions which allow yet more progress to be made. The play of causality between social interaction and cognition is thus reciprocal; the two develop in a causal spiral constituted by social interactions and cognitions of increasing complexity.[16]

However, as discussed presently, this developmental spiral must be viewed in the broader context of the social-affective relationship.

PEERS AS TEACHERS

Social cognition research supports the idea that children can scaffold each other's progress, and may do so in three ways: as tutors, co-operators and collaborators. It is customary to distinguish between (1) *peer tutoring*, the didactic transmission from one child to another, (2) *co-operative learning*, which refers to classroom situations in which children contribute jointly to a project or a task, and (3) *peer collaboration*, in which children work together on a task which neither of them is capable of doing separately.[17] As teaching methods, these may have different strengths: the acquisition of mechanical and specific skills seem to benefit more from peer tutoring, whereas collaboration seems to enhance best the mastery of abstract concepts.

Although fine details are not yet resolved,[18] there is a consensus that learning improves when pupils are organized to work together on curricular tasks. Another dimension is added by Sharan, who investigated the effects of teaching methods based on joint work in multi-ethnic Israeli classrooms.[19] Sharan envisages increased integration as a result of co-operative learning. He comments on the disparity between the 'empty' administrative act of desegregation and classroom reality, in which pupils keep to their separate groups: 'traditional whole-class instruction is certainly not the teaching method to be preferred in desegregated classrooms'.[20] Sharan thus puts the 'peer teaching' topic in wider social and societal contexts, and alludes to social-psychological (as distinct from educational or cognitive) implications:

> School claim to be the major setting outside the family for the socialization of the young. Yet the instructional methods practised in most classrooms today foster behaviour that is predominantly competitive and individualistic, not at all oriented toward pro-social and cooperative modes of behaviour with peers. Pupils are told to be helpful and considerate of others, but classroom practices do not cultivate cooperation, and pupils are reprimanded for cheating or copying when they share their school work with their classmates.[21]

Enhancing social relations through peer teaching can potentially lead to increased effectiveness of peer teaching as a means for education. Friends interact differently from non-friends (let alone classmates among whom there is racial tension). Hartup reviews a few studies which examined peer collaboration with friends and nonfriends:[22] with friends, children explored a given problem more extensively, their conversation was more vigorous and connected, and afterwards they remembered more about the task. Hartup concludes that 'friends should be uncommonly good teachers and collaborators, better than nonfriends', but to date 'Tutoring effects have never been studied in relation to the attraction existing between tutor and tutee.'[23]

Interpersonal interactions are influenced by the status of the participants, their affective relationship, the setting in which the interaction takes place, and similar factors. Doise and Mackie asserted that the combination of these factors mediates 'cognitive conflict':

> Where interaction is dominated by one member, the situation may resemble a passive modelling situation for the non-dominant partner, while in other situations, the social relations between participants may result in a heightened probability that solutions will be truly integrated.[24]

The importance of status differences between partners is

clearly seen in a study carried out in the 1960s by Greenfield and Bruner:[25] African children presented with classic conservation problems by adult white experimenters could justify apparent inconsistencies or contradictions in their own judgements by attributing special powers to the experimenters; no cognitive conflict ensued. When the same children worked on similar tasks with peers, many progressed to making more advanced judgements.

The next step is the realization that not all peers are of equal social status. In a recent study, Tudge found that working on a mathematical task with a more competent partner was indeed likely to result in cognitive improvement, but regression was just as likely.[26] In his study, 'competence' was measured by the kind of rule that the child applied to the problem. To an adult, which rule is more advanced may be obvious, but it is not so to a child. Since Tudge prompted the partners to discuss among themselves their proposed solutions, sometimes the more competent partner (who used more advanced rules in a pretest) was persuaded by the other to apply the lesser rule. Tudge suggests that in previous studies the improvement following collaborative problem-solving might reflect the fact that more competent children are probably more confident.

THE SOCIAL-AFFECTIVE CONTEXT OF PEER TEACHING

Investigating communication among children, Streeck observed groups of children involved in peer tutoring experiments.[27] His study was conducted in a mixed-grade class in an elementary school in the poorest neighbourhood of San Diego, California, and the children (7- to 9-year-olds) were Black and Mexican-American. Streeck videotaped work groups within the classroom, and analysed their talk, their respective roles within their joint activities, and nonverbal gestures indicative of affiliations and disaffiliation (e.g., patterns of gazing at peers). Streeck concluded that the assignment of a 'peer-teacher' role to a single child presented problems for the others, requiring 'the shifting of established attention patterns' and introducing 'a formal status and an element of power into a network of interpersonal relations'.[28] A major feature of the work group's interactions was 'gender politics':

> boys and girls form two small huddles on opposite sides of the table with a wide gap in between. Channels of communications are restricted accordingly: gaze and talk are overwhelmingly directed at co-members of the same category... There is occasional talk between boys and girls during their joint activity, but it is antagonistic. These are insult and argument sequences.[29]

However, Streeck detected what he describes as 'silent cooperation across the border': 'a number of barely noticeable supportive interchanges' between Regina, the youngest child who found the task difficult, and the boy Wallace, who was on some occasions the peer-tutor, despite the fact that the two never spoke to each other.

Generally, the importance of social-affective factors is discussed in terms of 'climate' or 'ethos', a good working atmosphere, which may facilitate effective instruction due to teachers' management and leadership skills, and may be conducive to learning by default: in a friendly class, the absence of stress-inducing factors or distracting influences frees the learner for the intellectual endeavour. Research on the social-affective aspect of peer teaching, scant as it is, evidences that a positive social context for learning is more than an interference-free or well-managed environment. It indicates that *relating to others* generally comes before task performance. Just being with others has special significance to the human organism. Early social psychologists documented 'social facilitation' phenomena: the presence of others can lead to arousal which in turn increases the rate of performance on a well-practised solitary task. Observations of peer interactions among young children reveal a rudimentary process of co-ordinating own behaviour, mood and attitudes with others, very early in childhood.

Piaget assumed that the young child is initially egocentric, and becomes more prosocial as sensitivity to others' perspectives increases as a result of interpersonal interactions, especially with peers. The theories of cognitive conflict and socio-cognitive conflict followed more or less from this premise of increasing empathy on the child's part. To what extent does young children's prosocial behaviour reflect empathy?

Birch and Billman investigated social-contextual factors that influence preschoolers to share food with friends and acquaintances during snack times.[30] They found that offering food was more likely if on a previous occasion the child received food from another. This finding contradicted the hypothesis that exposure to 'distress-producing' situations (i.e., not being offered food by others) would foster sensitivity to the needs of others. Birch and Billman conclude that social learning, rather than empathy, is involved: young children model their behaviour on the behaviour of others in similar past situations rather than reflecting on their own experiences. It may be further speculated that exposure to 'pleasure-producing' situations, such as receiving food, reinforces the action (sharing) associated with the happy state. Lennon and Eisenberg examined the relation between preschoolers' emotional states and their peer interactions.[31] The researchers videotaped triads of $2^1/_2$- to 4-year-olds playing with a single toy. They looked at how often the toy was shared, and inferred the benefactors' and recipients' mood from their facial expressions. Increased sharing was linked to positive affect, rather than to negative affect. Other studies, cited by Lennon and Eisenberg, indicate that young children are less likely to respond with prosocial behaviour to peers' display of anger or sadness. These and many similar studies indicate how children, from a young age, create mutual worlds they enjoy and understand. Individual differences in the 'knack' of initiating such mutual worlds is a main factor underlying children's social isolation or popularity.[32]

The Two Worlds of Childhood

'Children fight, compete and insult each other, but they keep travelling in packs, passing, as it were, through territories that are under adult control.'[33] At school, childhood culture is subordinate to adult rules regarding where, when and how children may interact within school boundaries. The school sets the stage for peer relationships in some obvious ways. By grouping children, the school determines the crowd from which individuals may draw their friends, Meyenn looked at how boys and girls in a Midlands middle school organize their social life.[34] Meyenn observed groups of 11- to 13-year olds 'in class, in the playground, coming and going home from school, in the corridors, at the weekly lunch-time disco, at sporting events, and in the dining hall'.[35] One of the most striking features of these pupils' peer networks, noted by Meyenn, was that they were formed largely within class-group boundaries.

Social relations may be influenced by the way the school system categorizes individuals (e.g., top- vs. low-stream). Class or 'house' loyalties are reinforced in school competitions; teachers often address a class as an entity. Does the structured world of school reinforce an 'us and them' view of the world in general? Traditionally, social psychologists have seen in children's group behaviours an analogue of adult social behaviour.[36] In one famous American study, known as the Robbers Cave experiment, Sheriff and his colleagues studied how competition between two summer-camp groups escalated to animosity and camp 'warfare'; the conflict dissipated when the groups had to co-operate in emergencies, such as problems with the water supply and vehicle breakdown. Since the Robbers Cave experiment was reported, in 1961, it has been widely held as an exemplar of intergroup conflict and co-operation. Similarly, the classical laboratory experiments on the minimal conditions for in-group favouritism, carried out by Henry Tajfel, involved teenage pupils – but have been replicated with adults many times. Many of the group processes discovered in experiments involving children and adolescents are evident also in adult social behaviour, but discontinuities between peer relations in childhood and adulthood come to light when children's friendships are examined.

AN INSIDER VIEW

The unique importance of peers for a child is apparent in children's accounts and expectations about school. In a study of girls' attitudes to school, Lomax concluded that peers are the most important feature of a child's school experience, irrespective of whether the child likes or dislikes school, is happy or unhappy there.[37] In my study of pupils' perspectives, carried out in the early 1990s in junior schools in poor areas of Cardiff, most children made by far more references to peer interactions than to teachers, conduct or work matters, when they described school environments. However, their descriptions reveal a reality in which the activities underlying the construction and maintenance of friendships are perceived as irrelevant, if not contrary, to educational goals.

A 'good' educational environment is conventionally associated with restricted peer interaction. Although classroom activities are done alongside, sometimes with other children, spontaneous interactions often mean neglect of work, trouble, or sheer 'naughtiness'. This was reflected in the distribution and quantity of the children's responses, especially to the School Apperception Story Procedure (SASP), one of the three tasks devised for the study reported here. In the SASP, the children selected from a set of fifteen line-drawings those pictures they felt represented six imaginary schools (three pictures per 'school'): a good school, a happy school, a liked school ('the kind of school you'd like to go to'); and the converse, i.e., bad, sad, and disliked schools. The children then explained their choices by telling how the pictures showed the given type of school. The pictures show a pupil alone, with peers, or with a teacher, in classroom, corridor and playground situations; the faces are blanked out, so mood is inferred by the children according to their interpretations of what is happening in the picture.

Bearing in mind that the children were describing specified types of school, reponses may reveal a child's perception of how salient are peer interactions in that environment. When children selected pictures of groups in a classroom to represent good, happy, or liked schools, they mentioned mostly activities which do not involve interactions among pupils (e.g., 'they are working'). Comments by one third-year boy, 'Chris', illustrate: classroom activities described in the plural are not social in nature; any elaboration focuses on individuals. A picture in which the teacher is sitting on top of the desk, an open book in her lap, and the class are gathered informally in front of her, shows a 'good school' because

> They're being good while the teacher's reading a book. One boy is doing a musical instrument [*points to boy in front of the picture, who seems preoccupied with something not clear in the picture*]. Two boys are sitting on a table, teacher's sitting on a chair. It looks a good school because they're quiet.

The child's observation that the teacher is sitting on a chair (contrary to what the drawing shows) does not necessarily reflect the ambiguity of the SASP pictures. It suggests that the child projected his own expectations about the classroom situations he was imagining; therefore his descriptions often depart from the pictures. Incidentally, this tendency was more common among children who were regarded as well-adjusted by their teachers (as Chris was), children with behaviour problems tended to stick closely to the pictures. Chris later used the same picture to describe the 'liked school':

> They're in a choir and they like playing music. All the rest had to do the song and he is doing an instrument, he is showing the teacher how to do it. The teacher and them are really happy.

(Incidentally, music activities are not actually shown, and Chris's interpretation was unique, possibly reflecting his own interests.)

All but one of Chris's more explicit references to peer interactions (a reference to playing a game) evoke rejection and conflict, or playing in the classroom, presumably construed as misconduct. In his view certain pictures clearly show bad, sad or disliked schools:

> She [*a girl*] won't give him a crayon, he tried to nick one so she smacked him, now the teacher [*not in the picture*] comes. They [*boys at the back*] are playing a game. The teacher will take her to the headteacher and she will get told off.

And another picture:

He's [*boy seated at a front desk, apparently crying*] done something wrong, they're all making fun of him, then he starts to cry and get angry with them. He stopped crying and started doing his work, all the children stopped laughing.

These three people are picking on the boy and he's crying – the teacher [*not in the picture*] tells him to tell her next time and she'll send them outside.

In their response to the SASP, 36 children (48 per cent of the sample) mentioned peer interactions mostly when describing bad, sad and disliked schools; 27 children (36 per cent) made the most references to peers when describing good, happy or liked schools; a further 12 children (16 per cent) mentioned peers equally in both 'positive' and 'negative' types of school. The gloomy aspect was perhaps easier to pick up in the pictures, even in some not showing group situations. A picture of a solitary child, head on the table as if crying, was selected 131 times by 73 children, solely with negative implications. Children listed possibilities: 'Maybe someone has been punching him playtime, or he fell over and everyone was laughing at him,' one boy suggested. The SASP set does not contain pictures which have unambiguous positive implications regarding peer interactions. A picture of a small group in the playground was selected by 57 children as representing a positive interaction (e.g., 'they're playing together', 'they are friends'; one boy commented on the fact that the picture shows boys and girls together!) – but 16 children selected the same picture with negative suggestions ('they're fighting'). Given the imbalance in the set, it is remarkable that nearly half of the total references to peer relations were made in association with good, happy and liked schools. However, despite their quantity, most comments were laconic, referring to a global state ('friends') or activity ('playing together'). Further descriptions such as 'playing together nicely' and 'they are not fighting' put the accent on appropriate conduct, rather than on peer relations *per se*.

A second task devised for the study, the School Rating Grid (SRG), pin-pointed further the children's notions about the differences between positive and negative aspects of the school environment. In an initial phase of the SRG, the children were asked to state one characteristic of each of the six imaginary schools. The answers are predictable, but the prominence of particular answers in the sample is revealing. In the children's view, the following typify good, happy and liked schools:

- friends (59 per cent of references to peer interactions in a 'positive' school);
- the absence of bullying or mockery (18 per cent);
- playing together, 'getting on with each other' (14 per cent);
- the presence of likeable peers (9 per cent);
- helpfulness (7 per cent).

Bad, sad and disliked schools were characterized by the following:

- bullying or mockery (78 per cent of the references to peer interactions in a 'negative' school);
- having no friends (11 per cent);
- the presence of dislikeable peers (6 per cent);
- disrupting games or work, telling tales and getting others in trouble (5 per cent).

In sum, most children evaluated schools in terms of *friends vs. bullies* (rather than in terms of presence/absence of either friends or bullies). Their construing of peer relations at school thus highlights situations in which individuals are either happily together (friends) or against each other (bullying).

To what degree does having friends, being punched or ridiculed, discriminate between desirable and undesirable school environments in a child's view? Individuals might differ. Two children may say that 'having friends' is a characteristic of a good, happy or liked school (in fact, 59 per cent of the sample said that). But in the view of one child, having friends depends more on the person than on the school, and tells less about the kind of environment a school is than do other factors, such as the standards of work or teacher behaviour; the other child might construe having friends as determined by the kind of environment a school is. To find out how predictive certain factors mentioned by the children are for the individuals who mentioned them, the SRG involved a second phase, a personalized scale. In this phase, the children rated the characteristics of particular school types they previously suggested across all six schools types and their actual school. A child in whose view having friends depends mainly on the school would arguably rate 'having friends' as always (or most times) present in good, happy and liked schools, and never (or almost never) in bad, sad and disliked schools. The child for whom having friends depends on the person, would rate 'having friends' as happening to more or less the same degree across the contrasting school types.

For most children (87 per cent of the sample), bullying, having no friends, and similar aspects of peer relations were high predictors of bad, sad or disliked schools. For 60 per cent of the sample, having friends, the absence of bullying, helpfulness among children, and similar aspects were likewise strong predictors of good, happy or liked schools. More specifically, 63 per cent of the references to *bullying* were highly predictive; only 41 per cent of the references to *friends* discriminated between the types of school to a similar degree. For most children, then, the incidence of bullying is a stronger indicator of what a school is like than is the presence of friends.

The disconcerting implication of the above finding is that the children's implicit view of bullying as endemic to school life (whereas friendships are relatively independent of school) might be accurate. The Opies remarked that in school playgrounds, children's play seems markedly more aggressive than when the children play in the street or 'wild places'.[38] On the positive side, if schools exacerbate bullying, schools can ameliorate the problem. In the study reported here, no differences related to age, gender or behaviour problems were found in the extent to which 'bullying' seemed to matter. However, there were school differences. Although the children in all schools said much the same things, those attending School A (described in Chapter 2: it is the one with the isolated playground) were more 'reserved' when judging a

school by the incidence of bullying and other negative interactions. In School A, less children than can be expected by
chance variations between samples regarded such interactions
as highly predictive of school type; in the other three schools,
more children than expected regarded negative interactions
as high predictors. The difference is statistically significant,
though in itself it cannot tell us why School A was more
successful in that respect. There are several possibilities. The
size and layout of the playground could have helped reduce
conflict. Teachers in School A might have handled problems
among pupils differently than did their counterparts in the
other schools (though I have no evidence in support of this
conjecture). Another plausibility relates to the fact that School
A pupils were interviewed in the spring term, whereas the rest
of the schools were visited after the summer half-term. As
work pressures were relaxed towards the end of the school
year, children might have attributed a greater salience to peer
relations as a characteristic of school life than they did earlier
in the year. The ecology of children's responses has to be
taken into consideration.

Generally, the children's responses consistently point to
'situation appropriateness' of peer relations. This may be due
to the nature of the above tasks: the children were, after all,
asked to describe 'schools'. To what extent do children regard
peer interactions (appropriate or inappropriate) as under participants' control? Following Piaget's theory of moral development, Keasey and Sales provide some empirical support to the
possibility that most children under 7 years of age are aware
of the difference between accidental and intentional damage,
though children's understanding of intentionally in criminal
situations continues to improve with age.[39] There are implications for behaviour problems at school. More broadly, the
findings reported below suggest that intentionality enters all
social interactions: from the children's perspective, far from
passive compliance with school rules, their social situations at
school are construed as created by themselves and peers.

In a third task devised for my study, the School Behaviour
Game (SBG), the children were asked directly about pupils'
behaviour and activities in school. In the course of a board

game (described in Chapter 7), the children were asked to state something they might do that makes other children happy, things that friendly children and (separately) bullies do, and things other children do that made them, the respondents, happy or sad. In response to the 'positive' questions, the children mentioned:

- playing together (46 per cent of the answers);
- helping with work or personal problems (19 per cent);
- sharing crisps or sweets, and lending toys or stationery (11 per cent);
- telling jokes or clowning to make others happy (11 per cent);
- being friends (9 per cent);
- miscellanea; e.g., paying compliments, scoring a goal for the team (5 per cent).

The following answers were given in response to the request to name 'something that other children do that makes you sad':

- bullying, including physical harm, victimization, and mockery (73 per cent of the answers);
- rejection and 'betrayal' ('my friend's playing with children I don't like') (12 per cent);
- disturbing one's play or work (11 per cent);
- miscellanea; e.g., 'not doing what I want them to do' (4 per cent).

In sum, on the positive side, children decide to play together, share things, and joke to create a good atmosphere; to a lesser extent, the answers allude to moral obligations (helping) or interpersonal alliance ('be friends with you'). On the negative side, other children create unpleasant, even painful, situations.

The majority of the SBG answers imply *situations initiated by children*. Although these situations occur within the educational setting (and might be appropriate or inappropriate in that context), the interactional networks which constitute those situations are fairly independent of the 'official' system.

Many writers have commented on the 'double life' of children, their concurrent memberships in adult and peer societies. Childhood culture is portrayed as inaccessible to adults: a culture with its own intricate lore and language, traditions and taboos, rules and rituals, such as documented by the Opies.[40] Children seem to operate differently when interacting with adults than when interacting with peers: 'The knowledge children bring to adult–child interactions is different from that brought to their shared culture', wrote Bronwyn Davies,[41] who noticed that the children she listened to were switching codes when they spoke to her and among themselves. Youniss has pointed out that when children interact with adults, they are newcomers into an established order:

> Within the child–adult relation, children discover that there is a social system into which they and adults fit. The system is known to adults, and it is the children's task to find out what this system is.[42]

When interacting with other children, they are part of a different kind of system: 'When children turn to peers, however, they . . . learn that a system can be created with other persons. The system works functionally, is open to modification, and gives a sense of mutual meaning.[43]

Children seem to conciliate their concurrent memberships in adult–child and child–child systems by finding out the range of appropriate and inappropriate behaviours for particular situations. Davies concluded from her conversations with Aboriginal Australian 10- to 11-year-old pupils that children tend to construe behaviour as role-dependent more than person-dependent: 'They are less concerned with consistency of action from individuals than they are with consistency within given situations.'[44] As seen earlier, an emphasis on the 'situation appropriateness' of peer interactions has emerged from the responses of Welsh children in my study.

The children interviewed by Davies seemed aware of two cultures with parallel agendas, sometimes of mutual benefit and sometimes conflicting: '*Alongside* the teacher's agenda, they quite busily pursued their own agendas... Mucking around, and having fun and intereacting with each other were as much, if not more, part of the school day as learning lessons.'[45] For children, the boundaries between the two worlds might become blurred when a teacher hands over what they are accustomed to regard as the teacher's responsibility. For this reason, children can find the transition to an 'open classroom' confusing, as Davies has observed in her study.

Children's confusion about classroom responsibilities indicates their prior integration into a social order in which teacher and pupil roles are sharply demarcated. Further, the 'open' or so-called 'child-centred' classroom ultimately reflects an adult agenda. It is believed that learning is enhanced when children take the initiative about curricular activities – but it is expected that they will occupy themselves with teacher-approved activities, not follow their own whims.[46] Pupil culture remains 'an illegitimate "underlife" in the classroom.'[47]

British sociologists of education have described the conflict between (secondary school) pupils and teachers as a power struggle, a 'battle of wits'.[48] Sarah Delamont puts her finger on the potential quandary for a member of the two conflicting worlds:

> The pupil's status in the classroom has two aspects: status with peers and with teachers... the pupil who is too popular with the staff may be disliked by all the other pupils... In classrooms where the predominant perspective is anti-authority, anti-teacher, anti-school, high status in the peer group will guarantee unpopularity with the staff.[49]

Early in their school life, children learn to 'stick together', not to tell tales, not to become a 'teacher's pet'. Delamont further points out that in classes comprising mixed batches in terms of pupils' race, gender, and ability, 'complex variations in pupil–pupil and pupil–teacher relationships will be found'.[50] A clash of memberships is not an inevitable state of affairs: 'In the hard-working top stream the reverse will be the case, and the successful scholar and captain of football are likely to have friends and be well thought of by the staff.'.[51]

173

Delamont's statement implies that a conciliation is contingent on the extent to which the pupil culture conforms to teacher values. One insinuation is that, in teachers' conventional view, leaving children to their own devices would result in a 'Lord of the Flies' syndrome.

Sociologists describe children's and (predominantly) adolescents' peer groups as factions engaged in a power struggle with teachers, and pupil solidarity as engendered by school regimes. Bronfenbrenner expressed concern that the school establishment institutionalizes the separation of children from the adult community: (American) schools are socially and physically 'insulated from the life of the community, neighbourhood and families the schools purport to serve as well as for the life they are supposedly preparing the children',[52] and are increasingly structured and situated to the effect of alienating youth from society. Consequently, the transmission of social values and mores across the generations suffers; a psychological 'vacuum' is created, and filled by peers.

PLAYGROUND BEHAVIOUR: BULLIES AND FRIENDS

To the observer, the playground at breaktime seems to contain a microcosm created by the children themselves, a world in which their own creativity and social needs find expression. The romantic view, pioneered by Iona and Peter Opie in their anthropological observations of British children, has focused on children's games and folklore.[53] In that view, the importance of school breaktimes stems from the developmental function of free play. On the basis of his observations in Oxford primary schools, Sluckin concludes that in the school playground, 'They learn how to join in a game, how to choose and avoid roles, how to deal with people who cheat or make trouble, and above all else how to manipulate situations to their own advantage.'[54] School breaktimes provide almost unique opportunities for acquiring social competence. As Blatchford says: 'The school playground is important because for some children it may be the *only* setting within which they can play with other children.'[55] This is a fact of life.

Blatchford goes on to discuss the kinds of social relations observable in the playground: name-calling and teasing, fighting, friendships, rejected children, power and status, and fair play. To what extent are those necessary aspects of social development, as distinguished from situational effects? In reality, the so-called 'free play' that is feasible and safe in the typical playground does not necessarily represent the activities that children would ideally choose. Nor are children left there entirely on their own. As Fell pointed out, there are the 'dinner ladies': 'untrained, low paid women . . . responsible for children between a fifth and a quarter of the school day'.[56] Fell's account of the SALVE project, which aims to train school lunchtime organizers, brings home how neglected this side of the school life has been. Fell hopes that such training will reduce the overall level of violence in schools; implicit in this hope is the assumption that breaktime settings breed violence.

School playgrounds have held a particular attraction for researchers interested in child behaviour. There, children are left very much to their activities, yet being confined to a defined area for a finite period, their behaviour can be easily observed: 'Few settings are likely to show so naturally the ways in which children behave in one another's company . . . relatively free from adult constraints and direction', as Blatchford asserts.[57] For a psychologist, the school playground is a naturalistic setting in so far that behaviour is not manipulated by research design; but it is not a natural setting, and the typical playground is arguably not the best environment for child development.[58] Playground behaviour can reveal general age and gender differences in play, interactional patterns, aggression, and so on,[59] but the possible effects of being allowed only a short period for social interaction in a crowded and barren area must be considered.

In the romantic view, life in the playground, with its ups and downs, was seen as a training camp for the 'real world'. Problems such as bullying and victimization were seen as 'character-building' or 'inoculation' experiences. In my experience, some children not only survive a phase of victimization, but indeed seem to emerge wiser and stronger later on. Others suffer lasting emotional harm, and cases of suicide have been reported.[60] The same can be said about any negative life event: some individuals cope successfully, others succumb. Nobody advocates that children ought to be exposed to family break-down, bereavement, or other traumas and hassles by way of character-building.

In his review of British research on playground behaviour, Blatchford contrasts the 'romantic' view with the 'problem' view.[61] Since the late 1980s, researchers have been taking a closer look at playground behaviour in the context of problematic social relations. Bullying, victimization and related problems are not confined to playgrounds, but seem to occur mostly at school and between schoolmates. In her analysis of telephone calls to the Childline, La Fontaine has found that over three-quarters of the bullying reported by children took place at school.[62] The fact that these issues commonly come under the title 'playground behaviour' implies that the problems are believed to have little to do with the learning environment, with what the school institution is for, but are aspects of the environment that children create for themselves within the school boundaries.

It is seldom asked to what extent the playground setting itself influences children's behaviour there. The Opies commented in passing on differences between children's behaviour in school playgrounds and elsewhere, but little rigorous research has been done towards identifying such differences. Regarding the quality of breaktime play, Blatchford has sensed a pervasive view among teachers that 'there is a good deal of unnecessary aggressive and anti-social behaviour' in playgrounds:

> Much of children's play is seen to be physical squabbling, with much low-level physical play involving chasing and fleeing, jumping on backs, and fighting. Much of this is in turn attributed to acting out scenes from television programmes and films on video.[63]

If any teachers subscribe to that view, they overlook at least three underlying factors: relations between classroom and playground behaviour; the distinction between violence and rough-and-tumble; and the importance of 'folklore' for children's socialization.

Outdoor play was originally introduced in school curricula

on the basis of the nineteenth-century belief that children needed to release surplus energy that accumulates during confinement. Although that belief has no scientific credibility, recent experimental evidence indicates that children, especially boys, tend to become increasingly restless and inattentive as time spent in sedentary seat work increases.[64] Perhaps a new look at the classroom environment is called for, before passing judgement on playground behaviour.

Second, there is a world of difference between aggressive behaviour and rough-and-tumble. Boulton suspects that adults supervising children during breaktimes sometimes intervene in friendly horseplay, and yet fail to recognize less overt forms of violence which can do psychological harm.[65] Boulton proposes an evolutionary basis for rough-and-tumble play (though the same can be said about violence); my contention is that physical play is not necessarily 'low-level' in quality. It may be necessary to stop children's play for safety reasons, but it is mistaken to punish or disapprove of the participants as if they were culprits in a misdemeanour. Similarly, parents may realize children's needs for outdoor play, but forbid them to play on the road.

Third, the observation that children model their behaviour on aggression seen on television and in films discloses essentially positive psychological mechanisms implicated in children's integration into the cultural world. A related and very serious point is that children acquire the idea that aggressiveness is acceptable. However, the observation is a comment on society and the media, not on what playground activities mean to the child. When I was collecting data for my research on children's perceptions of school, American wrestling was a popular television programme. Several boys named 'pretend wrestling' as the activity they do or prefer to do in the playground (some added that it was banned at school). It was as much a part of their folklore and repertoire as the traditional games of bulldog, tag, and others. None of the children in my study mentioned any of those activities when asked to name something that a bully does in the playground. Children are well aware that bullying implies malice, and is directed at the psychological self: 'bullying is premeditated and calculated rather than thoughtless and accidental'.[66]

In Britain, the need to determine if and how the conditions provided in playgrounds exacerbate social problems has become tragically topical following the murder of an Asian boy in a Manchester school.[67] The likelihood that the murder was racially motivated drives home the fact that the playground world is embedded in a wider social context. However, although race may be used against a child by bullies, so can any 'peculiarities'. Victims of bullying calling the Childline attributed 'reasons' for bullying to themselves: they said they were bullied because they were fat, small, had ginger hair . . . 'the list was varied. It appears that any feature that makes one child different from the others may be used in bullying.'[68] La Fontaine adds that it is not clear whether those are the causes of bully/victim relationships.

So far, research has centred chiefly on determining the extent of problems, their nature, devising practical programmes to ameliorate them, assessing psychological consequences of bully/victim experiences and establishing contexts for counselling children involved in such relationships.[69] As Tattum summarizes, bullying can vary in nature (physical/psychological), intensity and duration, intentionality, number of children involved, and motivation.[70] The underlying factors include the size of the school or class, teachers' attitudes, the 'social climate', external characteristics of victims/bullies, and their respective attitudes to violence, aggression, self-esteem, and other psychological and behavioural characteristics. Roland, reviewing Scandinavian research, draws attention to gender differences: for boys, bullying seems to relate mainly to personal power; for girls, it seems more often a means of achieving group solidarity, as the victim is excluded and scapegoated.[71] These differences 'make sense' in view of what is generally known about the differentiation in children's socialization into gender roles,[72] which implies that bullying is at bottom ordinary social behaviour gone tragically wrong (rather than a 'fault' in bully/victim personalities).

Moreover, the gender differences may lie in the overt behaviour, more than in the psychological implications of bullying. The views of victims calling the Childline are instructive here:

> While in the literature on bullying it is common to find bullying linked with aggressiveness, that is with the bullies' expression of feelings, many of these children also seemed to perceive it as an act conveying a message: one of rejection and hostility. Bullying may serve to demonstrate to the victim that (s)he has no friends, while the instigator of the bullying can mobilise a group of supporters. The bullied child then feels isolated and lonely.[73]

To understand bullying, then, we should consider what friendships mean in childhood.

The Opies commented on the unpredictable nature of children's friendships: children 'make and break friends with a rapidity disconcerting to the adult spectator'.[74] Youniss, describing 'natural histories' of friendships, concluded that the here-and-now perspective shown by 6- to 7-year-olds reflects, first, 'the precedence of procedure over person', and second, 'the interchangeability of peers':

> Young children say that whomever they play or share with is their friend . . . The implication is that procedures are constant, but the people in them and the relations are not . . . A peer who plays today is a friend. If this peer does not play tomorrow, he or she is not a friend. That peer is replaced by another who does play.[75]

Youniss expressed the conventional view that 'friendship becomes a relation proper sometime in the middle of the school-age period'.[76] This may be the case only if by 'relation proper' we mean our adult expectations from friendship.

At odds with the adult assumption that friendship arises primarily from mutual attraction or a complementarity of personal attributes, children's selection of friends arises basically from proximity, from being together: 'A friend is a girl or boy that plays with you', wrote one of the children in Davies' study.[77] The child's view is pragmatic: 'If I dident [sic] have a friend, I would have nobody to play with', wrote another child.[78] From an adult perspective, this might be seen as a low-level friendship, the kind of relationship we may have with people we class as acquaintances, colleagues, and so on. A higher level of friendship 'hinges upon subjectively determined personal characteristics of the other ("niceness", kindness, trustworthiness and so on)'.[79] Davies queries the implicit assumption that children's peer relations are inferior to adult relationships.

Friends serve several functions, the prominence of which varies, as reflected in the way children's friendship patterns and concepts change over the years. Friendships among pre-school and infant school children centre on common pursuits and concrete reciprocation; older children define friendships in terms of mutual understanding, loyalty, and trust.[80] But far from being shallow or arbitrary, children's friendships fulfil crucial developmental functions, relevant to the child's situation, which is inherently different from the adult's situation. Davies has proposed that the breaking and making of childhood friendships serves to explore the dynamics of interpersonal relationships and to maintain the orderliness of the children's world. Davies noticed that children (10- to–11-year-olds) have 'contingency friends', to whom they turn when their friend is absent or offends them: 'If they withdraw to their contingency friends their bargaining power over their "best friend" is quite high.'[81]

Second, Davies points out, making sense of school is a task that children engage in together:

> The teachers may spell out the rules for classroom behaviour, but the sense to be made of it all is something adults cannot really provide. Friends are the source of meaning and therefore the source of identity... Their particular mode of viewing the world with its accompanying language, taboos, rituals and sanctions which function to maintain this meaning world, are developed in interaction with each other... the playing, the fighting, the making and breaking of friendships are necessary ingredients for the development and maintenance of the children's shared world.[82]

Davies' description echoes Hartup's assertion, regarding peer teaching, that 'friendships are unique contexts for transmitting information'[83] with implications for peer teaching, as discussed earlier.

Hartup considers four main functions of children's friendships. First, friendship relationships are contexts in which basic social competence is acquired and elaborated (e.g., communication, co-operation, and group-entry skills). Second, friends are sources of information about self, others and the world in general. Third, they are part of the child's social support network, providing emotional and cognitive resources both for 'having fun' and adapting to stress. Finally, children's friendships are forerunners of subsequent relationships by 'modelling the mutual regulation and intimacy that most close relationships require'.[84]

If children rely on peers to make sense of the world (perhaps to a greater extent than adults do), it follows that requirements for friendships are *proximity, intersubjectivity,* and *negotiation:* friends experience the same events, interpret them together, and agree on what those mean. For most children in Western society, the school is the major (if not the only) setting in which they meet other children, and their friendships often follow from the imposed proximity. There is, however, a profound qualitative difference between proximity in a small group and in a crowd. The former nurtures empathy and intimacy through collaboration and mutual sense-making. The latter breeds problems, because the natural inclination is to form small groups: the crowd splits into cliques which achieve cohesion by establishing social boundaries, all too often through ostracizing, scapegoating, and intimidating 'outsiders'.

Notes and References

1 Rogers, C. R. *Freedom to Learn for the 80's.* Ohio: Charles and Merrill, 1982, p. 19.
2 Erickson, F. and Shultz, J. 'When is a context? Some issues and methods in the analysis of social competence'. In Green, J. L. and Wallat, C. (eds), *Ethnography and Language in Educational Settings.* New Jersey: Ablex, 1981, p. 148.

3 E.g., contributions in Foot, H. C., Morgan, M. J. and Shute, R. H. (eds), *Children Helping Children*. Chichester: John Wiley and Sons, 1990.

4 E.g., Blatchford, P. *Playtime in the Primary School: Problems and Improvements*. Windsor: NFER-Nelson, 1989; contributions in Blatchford, P. and Sharp, S. (eds). *Breaktime and the School: Understanding and Changing Playground Behaviour*. London: Routledge, 1994.

5 Hartup, W. W. 'Children and their friends'. In McGurk, H. (ed.), *Issues in Childhood Social Development*. London: Methuen, pp. 130–170, 1978.

6 See contributions in Forgas, J. P. (ed.), *Social Cognition: Perspectives on Everyday Understanding*. London: Academic Press, 1981 and in Serafica, F. C. (ed.), *Social-cognitive Development in Context*. New York: Methuen, 1982.

7 Hartup, W. W., 1978, op. cit., p. 147.

8 Davies, B. *Life in the Classroom and Playground: The Accounts of Primary School Children*. London: Routledge and Kegan Paul, 1982.

9 Serafica, F. C. 'Conceptions of friendships and interaction between friends: an organismic-developmental perspective'. In Serafica, F. C. (ed.), *Social-cognitive Development in Context*. New York: Methuen, pp. 100–132, 1982.

10 Donaldson, M. *Children's Minds*. London: Fontana, 1978.

11 Piaget, 1965, quoted by Doise, W. and Mackie, D. 'On the social nature of cognition'. In Forgas, J. P. (ed.), *Social Cognition: Perspectives on Everyday Understanding*. London: Academic Press, 1981, p. 55.

12 Vygotsky, L. *Thought and Language*, trans. A. Kozulin. Cambridge, MA: The MIT Press, 1986, p. 188.

13 Doise, W. and Mackie, D., 1981, op. cit., p. 56.

14 Ibid., p. 61.

15 Ibid., p. 61.

16 Ibid., p. 78.

17 Damon, W. and Phelps, W. 'Strategic use of peer learning in children's education'. In Berndt, T. J. and Ladd, G. W. (eds), *Peer Relationships in Child Development*. New York: Wiley, pp. 135–157, 1989.

18 Topping, K. 'Cooperative learning and peer tutoring: an overview (with peer commentaries)'. *The Psychologist*, **5**, 151–161, 1992.

19 Sharan, S. 'Cooperative learning and helping behaviour in the

multi-ethnic classroom'. In Foot, H. C., Morgan, M. J. and Shute, R. H. (eds), *Children Helping Children*. Chichester: John Wiley and Sons, pp. 151–177, 1990.

20 Ibid., p. 172.

21 Ibid., p. 152.

22 Hartup, W. W. 'Friendships and their developmental significance'. In McGurk, H. (ed.), *Childhood Social Development: Contemporary Perspectives*. Hove: Lawrence Erlbaum Associates, pp. 175–205, 1992.

23 Ibid., p. 187.

24 Doise, W. and Mackie, D., 1981, op. cit., p. 61.

25 Reviewed by Doise, W. and Mackie, D., 1981, op. cit.

26 Tudge, J. R. H. 'Processes and consequences of peer collaboration: a Vygotskian analysis'. *Child Development*, **63**, 1364–1379, 1992.

27 Streeck, J. 'Towards reciprocity: politics, rank and gender in the interaction of a group of schoolchildren.' In Cook-Gumprez, J., Corsaro, W. A., and Streeck, J. (eds), *Children's Worlds and Children's Language*. Berlin: Mouton de Gruyter, pp. 295–326, 1986.

28 Ibid., p. 296.

29 Ibid., p. 305.

30 Birch, L. L. and Billman, J. 'Preschool children's food sharing with friends and acquaintances'. *Child Development*, **57**, 387–395, 1986.

31 Lennon, R. and Eisenberg, N. 'Emotional displays associated with preschoolers' prosocial behaviour'. *Child Development*, **58**, 992–1000, 1987.

32 Rubin, Z. 'The skills of friendship'. In Donaldson, M., Grieve, R. and Pratt, C. (eds), *Early Childhood Development and Education: Readings in Psychology*. Oxford: Blackwell, pp. 25–33, 1983.

33 Streeck, J., 1986, op. cit., p. 322.

34 Meyenn, R. J. 'Peer networks among middle school pupils'. In Hargreaves, A. and Tickle, L. (eds), *Middle Schools: Origins, Ideology and Practice*. London: Harper and Row, pp. 247–276, 1980.

35 Ibid., p. 249.

36 E.g., Brown, R. *Social Psychology*, 2nd edn. New York: The Free Press, 1986.

37 Lomax, P. 'The attitudes of girls with varying degrees of school adjustment to different aspects of their school experience'. *Educational Review*, **30**, 117–124, 1978.

38 Opie, I. and P. *Children's Games in Street and Playground.* London: Oxford University Press, 1969.

39 Keasey, C. B. and Sales, B. D. 'An empirical investigation of young children's awareness and usage of intentionality in criminal situations.' *Law and Human Behaviour,* 1, 45–61, 1977.

40 Opie, I. and P. *The Lore and Language of Schoolchildren.* London: Paladin, 1959; Opie, I. and P., op. cit.

41 Davies, B., 1982, op. cit., p. 3.

42 Youniss, J. *Parents and Peers in Social Development: A Sullivan-Piaget Perspective.* Chicago: University of Chicago Press, 1980, p. 13.

43 Ibid., p. 19.

44 Davies, B., 1982, op. cit., p. 112.

45 Ibid., p. 115; her italics.

46 Cf. Sharp, R. and Green, A. *Education and Social Control.* London: Routledge and Kegan Paul, 1975.

47 Davies, B., 1982, op. cit., p. 115.

48 E.g., Delamont, S. *Interaction in the Classroom,* 2nd edn. London: Methuen, 1983; Beynon, J. and Delamont, S. 'The sound and the fury: pupil perceptions of school violence'. In Frude, N. and Gault, H. (eds), *Disruptive Behaviour in Schools.* London: John Wiley and Sons, pp. 137–151, 1984.

49 Delamont, S., 1983, op. cit., pp. 81–82.

50 Ibid., p. 82.

51 Ibid., p. 82.

52 Bronfenbrenner, U. *The Ecology of Human Development.* Cambridge, MA: Harvard University Press, 1979, p. 230.

53 Opie, I. and P., 1959 and 1969, op. cit.

54 Sluckin, A. *Growing Up in the Playground.* London: Routledge and Kegan Paul, 1981, p. 119.

55 Blatchford, P. 'Research on children's school playground behaviour in the United Kingdom'. In Blatchford, P. and Sharp, S. (eds), *Breaktime and the School: Understanding and Changing Playground Behaviour.* London: Routledge, 1994, p. 24; his italics.

56 Fell, G. 'You're only a dinner lady! A case study of the SALVE lunchtime organiser project'. In Blatchford, P. and Sharp, S. (eds), *Breaktime and the School: Understanding and Changing Playground Behaviour.* London: Routledge, 1994, p. 134.

57 Blatchford, P., 1994, op. cit., p. 24.

58 Cf. Blatchford, P., 1989, op. cit.

59 Smith, P. K. 'What children learn from playtime, and what adults can learn from it'. In Blatchford, P. and Sharp, S. (eds),

Breaktime and the School: Understanding and Changing Playground Behaviour. London: Routledge, pp. 36–48, 1994.

60 Smith, P. K. 'The silent nightmare: bullying and victimisation in school peer groups'. *The Psychologist,* **4**, 243–248, 1991.

61 Blatchford, P., 1994, op. cit.

62 La Fontaine, J. *Bullying: The Child's View.* London: Calouste Gulbenkian, 1991.

63 Blatchford, P., 1989, op. cit., p. 10.

64 Pellegrini, A. D. and Davies, P. D. 'Relations between children's playground and classroom behaviour'. *British Journal of Educational Psychology,* **63**, 88–95, 1993.

65 Boulton, M. J. 'Playful and aggressive fighting in the middle-school playground'. In Blatchford, P. and Sharp, S. (eds), *Breaktime and the School: Understanding and Changing Playground Behaviour.* London: Routledge, pp. 49–62, 1994.

66 Tattum, D. P. 'Violence and aggression in schools'. In Tattum, D. P. and Lane, D. A. (eds), *Bullying in Schools.* Stoke-on-Trent: Trentham Books, 1989, p. 11.

67 Cf. Macdonald, B. *Murder in the Playground* (The Burnage Inquiry). London: Longsight Press, 1989.

68 La Fontaine, J., 1991, op. cit., p. 13.

69 See Besag, V. E. *Bullies and Victims in Schools.* Milton Keynes: Open University Press, 1989, for a detailed review.

70 Tattum, D. P., 1989, op. cit.

71 Roland, E. 'Bullying: the Scandinavian research tradition'. In Tattum, D. P. and Lane, D. A. (eds), *Bullying in Schools.* Stoke-on-Trent: Trentham Books, pp. 21–32, 1989.

72 Cf. Archer, J. 'Childhood gender roles: social context and organisation'. In McGurk, H. (ed.), *Childhood Social Development: Contemporary Perspectives.* Hove: Lawrence Erlbaum Associates, pp. 31–62, 1992.

73 La Fontaine, J., 1991, op. cit., p. 12.

74 Opie, I. and P., 1959, op. cit., p. 324.

75 Youniss, J., 1980, op. cit., p. 205.

76 Ibid., p. 208.

77 Davies, B., 1982, op. cit., p. 69.

78 Ibid., p. 68.

79 Damon, 1977, quoted in ibid., p. 69.

80 Hartup, W. W., 1992, op. cit.

81 Davies, B., 1982, op. cit., p. 70.

82 Ibid., p. 70.
83 Hartup, W. W., 1992, op. cit., p. 187.
84 Ibid., p. 184.

CHAPTER 7
A Child at School

The ecology of human development is the scientific study of the progressive, mutual accommodation, *throughout the life course,* between an active, growing human being, and the changing properties of the immediate settings in which the developing person lives, as this process is affected by the relations between these settings, and by the larger contexts in which the settings are embedded.[1]

Exponents of ecosystemic thinking have called for models which acknowledge the natural complexity and diversity of environments. Foremost among those is the American psychologist Urie Bronfembrenner, who, in 1979, presented a powerful critique of developmental psychology, urging the study of human development in real-life settings.[2] Less than a decade later, Bronfenbrenner noticed a very different state of affairs: 'In place of too much research on development "out of context", we now have a surfeit of studies on 'context without development".'[3] Moreover, looking back at his 1979 monograph, Bronfenbrenner admits that 'it has much more to say about the nature and developmental contribution of the environment than of the organism itself'.[4] In his 1992 revision, he underlines the term *developmentally-instigative,* which denotes personal attributes most likely to shape the course of development: 'the modes of behavior or belief that reflect an active, selective, structuring orientation toward the environment and/or tend to provoke reactions from the environment'.[5]

A book dedicated to school environments is likely to suffer a similar imbalance. Issues concerning the child's contribution to the child–school interface remain understated due to limitations of space. This chapter indicates some of the ways in which such issues may be approached in keeping with an ecosystemic perspective.

What does the child bring to the child–school interface? In the first instance, individuals interact with their school environments as they understand these environments. The following section looks at ways in which psychologists probe children's perceptions of school; the theme is picked up again in the final section, in a review of personal construct theory. Second, pupils' perspectives reflect developmental tasks associated with certain age groups,[6] but the school is only one of the social settings which scaffold child development. Bronfenbrenner's ecological systems approach, described later in the chapter, offers a framework in which to describe the conflation of school, home, and wider-community influences on development. Third, individual differences in attitudes, motivation, ability, temperament, coping strategies, and so on (not reviewed here), mean that children differ in their responses to school situations.

The new orthodoxy in developmental psychology casts doubts on the view that the relation of individual differences to schooling is simply 'survival of the fittest' in the sense that children possessing certain characteristics stand a better chance of fitting in. If interactions with the environment shape the person, then the very traits associated with thriving or failing in school are in part a product of that environment. Given the diversity of school environments, 'individual differences' research should embody the question: Which personal attributes are selected by which type of school/classroom environment?

Lisening to Children

Investigations of pupils' perspectives are unequivocally driven by a wish to further our knowledge of the world within the school gates, coupled with the belief that pupils' accounts may disclose something otherwise inaccessible, or at least something fresh and thought-provoking: 'listening to children makes us reconsider some of the habits we have taken for granted'.[7]

Plainly, that which pupils are uniquely qualified to offer is an insider's view of school. But research into children's perspectives of school is always more than collecting and sorting first-hand reports; it is channelled by researchers' interests which exist outside the child's world. Psychologists face the task of inferring children's belief systems from what they say, and describing a process linking children's beliefs to both environment and behaviour. Ultimately, we read behind what the child tells us.

THE CHILD AS 'INFORMANT' AND 'SUBJECT'

Pupils' and ex-pupils' views on educational settings occasionally find expression in literary reminiscences and in the media. For example, entries to a competition by the *Observer*, subsequently published in a book edited by Blishen,[8] offer a lively glimpse into the secondary school of the late 1960s. Additionally, pupils' viewpoints are sometimes made public, in a case-study style, in the writings of teachers moved by their classroom experiences: Holt's observations of children's academic failure are well-known;[9] Pye's account of withdrawn pupils is also noteworthy.[10] On the one hand, the scientific shortcomings of such anecdotal material are offset by the authenticity, poignancy and emotive force of its message; on the other hand, anecdotal evidence demonstrates the need for rigorous inquiry.

Some researchers have been aware of the need to listen to children and adolescents in order to find out what the school means to them. Fisher *et al.* investigated the effects of being temporarily transferred to a boarding school on 11- to 16-year-olds from the pupils' viewpoint, using a diary method.[11] Madge and Fassam looked at how physically handicapped pupils view their own social status, compared to that of able-bodied peers, in a book aptly titled *Ask the Children*.[12] But there is a twist. Madge and Fassam's systematic elicitation of children's perspectives (using semi-structured interviews in conjunction with thematic pictures) stemmed from the researchers' concern with the disabled child's social integration. While this is an important issue, to a child 'integration' could mean more than social acceptance. The pride of achievement I saw in a 10-

year-old brain-damaged girl upon managing a basic counting exercise (her level of maths) drove home to me that school can be about 'work' for the mentally disabled as well as for the able child.

Pupils' accounts of life at school may be taken at face value, or as an unwitting testimony for the effects of a particular educational system. These views need not be mutually exclusive: both the content of what children say, and how they say it, are viable topics for psychological investigation. Representing the position that children ought to be taken seriously as informants, Cullingford stresses that children's views 'deserve to be taken into account because they know, better than anyone, which teaching styles are successful, which techniques of learning bring the best out of them, and what the ethos of the school consists of'.[13] Jackson called for research into pupils' perceptions of school, concerned with the consistent proportion of pupils who expressed a dislike of school in American surveys, and the likelihood that children who said that they liked school might also be dissatisfied with some of its aspects and disgruntled at school some of the time: 'The most obvious reason for desiring to probe more deeply is that the proportion of students who claim to dislike school comprise a significant number.'[14] Discontent among pupils indicates a failure of the school system. Listening to children, then, must be followed with action.

Generally in a psychological framework, children's perspectives are looked into with the expectation that the data will enable an explanation of their behaviour or development. A call to listen to children rests on the premise that children can adequately communicate their feelings and impressions. Research into the young child's perceptions of school necessarily involves a greater reliance on researchers' inferences than might be the case in research with older children or adolescents. Beveridge and Brierley inferred children's constructs of the nursery school from their classroom talk during ordinary activities.[15] Not only children's communication skills improve as they grow older, but the yardsticks by which they evaluate school change. Lee *et al.* discovered that as children progressed through the elementary school grades, so the gap widened between their notions of an ideal school and their ratings of their actual school.[16] By the time children reached the upper grades, most had formulated a 'theory' of what school ought to be like, and judged their actual school accordingly; younger children could not go beyond their impressions of their actual school.

CHILDREN DESCRIBING SCHOOL IN RESEARCH

There are many ways of asking children about their school, and the ways the question are posed can affect the children's answers.

In the 1940s, Tenenbaum used a questionnaire and an essay question to ask New York 6th and 7th grade pupils whether or not they liked their school, and were they happy there.[17] Tenenbaum observed that many responses were stereotypical, followed 'conventional patterns', and had 'an adult character' about them:

> [the children] did not look at school as a place of joy or pleasure. There is no exuberant enthusiasm displayed. There is no zestful approach to the school situation. The children attend school with consciousness that it will help them out in later life.[18]

British schoolchildren in the 1990s may be very different from Tenenbaum's respondents, but it seems likely that almost any inquiry which involves an adult asking children about their school, especially when the adult is a visiting researcher introduced by the class teacher or headteacher, would similarly elicit normative responses. Children seem to participate in an adult-approved 'script': school is important, even if it is boring. The most influential adults in the child's life have probably reiterated exhaustively the importance of school. To the visitor, the child demonstrates that he or she has acquired this adult wisdom. In Jackson's words, 'Children, for the most part, like to please adults, and adults, for the most part, like to hear that children are enjoying school.'[19]

Children do not necessarily offer a hypocritical view: they simply respond as they justifiably feel is appropriate for the occasion. In order to minimize situation-specific biases,

Tenenbaum had his respondents answer the questionnaire and write their essays anonymously, in the absence of teachers or supervisors. A contrasting instance may be of interest. During a period of classroom observations at a junior school in a South Wales valley, I asked several children to write an essay 'all about school'. Since I wanted to collect samples of children's writing, the conventions of scientific impartiality which prescribed Tenenbaum's set-up did not apply.

The request, ostensibly for information about the school, was almost invariably interpreted by the children as an invitation to tell me about themselves (spelling mistakes corrected in the following extracts):

> School is nice because I can play with my friends. And I like working and sports and I like picking daisies and buttercups. And I like doing pictures and doing about spiders and worms and woodlice. And slugs and snails and about water and all water insects. And we go on the field and find insects. And I like the discos and trips and every time we do good work we have stars or team points or well done. And I like playing with [names of two girls]. And my sister and her friend and I like Mrs Jones [this author] and Mrs [the class teacher] and sums and reading books and I like stories and I like doing pretty stuff and I like [names of other two girls]. And I like playing in the playground and on the tumps. (A girl, age 7)

Knowing the classroom context in which the essays were elicited gives a further dimension to the children's description. A boy (age 8) wrote:

> In school I am on maths group A. On Maths group A it is fun. Because now we are on peak plus. On peak plus we do things like maths games, puzzles, and all sorts of fun things to do in maths. I am on language patterns group 1 as well. In school some work is easy but some is hard. Sometimes it is noisy in the classroom but sometimes it is quiet. I can remember when I was in the infants in middle class when we went up Caerphilly Railway Society to have a ride on a steam locomotive.

His reminiscence provided him with an excuse to look up

reference books about steam engines. Presumably he was keen on the subject, but it also happened that his teacher at the time was keen to implement the topical emphasis on 'investigation'; and this boy had a reputation of being top-of-the-class to maintain.

Self-report seems an inevitable element in the children's description of school. Perhaps the most dispassionate essay came from an older girl (age 9) whose disaffected behaviour greatly concerned her teacher, but even she found it necessary to report her own position:

> In school on a Wednesday we have to go to lines. Then we come in and go straight to class. Sir calls our names to see if we are here and after he calls our names the buzzer goes for us to go down to the hall and say our prayers and sing hymns. Then we come back to class and get out our mathematics books. Me [punctuation added] and [a boy] do different maths to the other people since we are not good at maths.

Her statement of her low-attaining in maths contrasts her otherwise impersonal account of the Wednesday morning.

Exploring children's perceptions of school presents the problem of making their private worlds public. Indirect or disguised inquiries are designed not necessarily to prevent 'faking' the answers, but to tease out the tacit criteria that children employ to make sense of life at school. Cullingford asked children in their final year of the primary school and children in their first year of the secondary school to compare the two schools.[20] The younger children described how their future school might differ from their present one, and the older children reminiscenced about their previous school, comparing it to their present one. The children's comparisons revealed how they thought about school in general. Indirect inquiries are prompted also by the intuition that in the social world of childhood, among the children themselves, school might mean other things than what children think adults want to hear. Davies, having based herself in the library of an Australian primary school to record unstructured conversations with groups of children, discovered that the best school in the children's opinion was the one which allowed ice-cream on the premises![21]

In questionnaire or interviews, researchers' questions – direct or indirect – might bias the responses. Projective techniques offer an alternative. These techniques range widely in format, materials and procedures, but all entail presenting the person with some material, usually nonverbal, which the person interprets or manipulates.[22] In one of the most concrete applications of this rationale, Ruth Pickford asked French, American, Scottish, English and Welsh schoolchildren (7 to 11 years old) to play out a lesson using a set of toy pupils, teacher, and classroom furniture.[23] The children's play scenarios provided her 'much spontaneous data on socialization goals, methods and values of different communities, as they are reflected in the experiences of their children',[24] ranging from evidence for cross-cultural diversity in emphasis on academic discipline, attitudes to teachers, and similar domains, to factual information, such as the American custom of beginning the school day with Allegiance to the Flag. More conventional methods are derivatives of the Thematic Apperception Test, in which children are asked to make stories based on pictures depicting school situations;[25] a similar technique, the School Apperception Story Procedure, has been described in the previous chapter.

The Mesosystem

Children are aware that events at home can affect their moods at school. When, as part of my research, children described a 'sad school,' most talked about having no friends at school, being unable to cope with the work, not liking the children, and so on – but a few speculated that children might be sad at school because their pet had died. Sometimes classroom behaviour clearly reflects influences which originate elsewhere. In a recent study, Turner looked at relations between the quality of the child–mother attachment relationship, the sex of the child, and the child's interactions with adults in the preschool.[26] The child's attachment style (secure, insecure) was assessed in a laboratory procedure, on the basis of the child's reactions to the mother after a brief period of separation. Turner's observations of the children's interactions with preschool staff revealed differences related to the quality off the children's attachment to their mothers, as seen in the laboratory. For example, in the preschool, insecure children sought more help than did secure children (although, interestingly, the secure children were more successful in eliciting help from adults).

Unless an ecological approach to the child–school interface is limited to the interplay between human organisms and physical surroundings, the fact that children have a life outside school must be acknowledged. This did not escape the proponents of the ecosystemic approach to classroom behaviour problems, Upton and Cooper:

> While some behaviours may be explicable in terms of classroom and school ecosystems, many others can only be fully understood if we consider the family and social systems of which pupils and teacher are a part, membership of which influence, and in turn are influenced by, events in school.[27]

Upton and Cooper suggest a distinction between 'simple' and 'complex' classroom systems, respectively. The distinction is consistent with the idea that behaviour is best understood in view of a *relevant context*; the relevant context is not necessarily the classroom setting. When a child is focused upon, the *child–school interface* (not school *per se*) is envisaged as a 'field' of convergent influences – influences originating in the child's family, school, and other settings. Bronfenbrenner has labelled this field a mesosystem (full definition below).[28]

Bronfenbrenner's mesosystem, or Upton and Cooper's 'complex' system, are not the objects and people with whom the child interacts, but influences mediated by the child. Another way of looking at it was forwarded by Moos, whose social-ecological model[29] has been described in Chapter 4. Moos described a dynamic relationship between an *environmental system* (e.g. school) and a *personal system*, a relationship characterized by mutual apraisal and adjustment. Moos' model highlights the fact that it is the child who 'carries' into school situations any attitudes and expectations, habits and coping strategies, which are generated or reinforced out of school, as well as in it.

Bronfenbrenner's *ecological systems* model is not a 'theory' in the strict scientific sense (it does not tell us why certain influences occur, nor predict outcomes of particular relations); it is a framework for integrating existing knowledge and for generating new inquiries about factors underlying human development. Bronfenbrenner urged a realistic view of the developing person as embedded in concentric nested systems which comprise the social and personal influences implicated in development.[30] He proposed the following hierarchy of systems:

(1) A *microsystem* is a pattern of activities, roles, and interpersonal relations experienced by the developing person in a given face-to-face setting with particular physical and material features, and containing other persons with distinctive characteristics of temperament, personality, and systems of belief. Examples are home, school, peer group, a workplace.

(2) The *mesosystem* comprises the linkages and processes taking place between two or more settings containing the developing person (e.g., the relations between home and school, college and workplace). In other words, a mesosystem is a system of microsystems.

(3) The *exosystem* encompasses the linkage and processes taking place between two or more settings, at least one of which does not ordinarily contain the developing person, but in which events occur that influence processes within the immediate setting that does contain that person. For instance, for a child, the relation between the home and a parent's workplace.

(4) The *macrosystem* consists of the overarching pattern of micro-, meso-, and exosystems characteristic of a given culture, subculture, or other broader social context, with particular reference to the developmentally-instigative belief systems, resources, hazards, lifestyles, opportunity structures, life-course options, and patterns of social interchange that are embedded in each of these systems. The macrosystem may be thought of as a societal blueprint for a particular culture, subculture, or other broader social context.[31]

The utility of this hierarchy can be illustrated as follows. For a girl in a maths class, the microsystem comprises curricular tasks, her interactions with the teacher and peers, influences due to time of day, noise, and so on; in other words, all the people, objects and ambient conditions present. Delamont described how teachers, in their daily classroom routines and incidental comments, can reinforce the stereotype of females as inept in maths;[32] thus, the girl's progress could be influenced by *microsystemic* processes. Irrespective of classroom processes, the girl might suspend her efforts to learn maths because of her identification with a 'non-mathematical' mother[33] – or, conversely, increase her efforts because of special encouragement at home. According to Bronfenbrenner's model, home influences bearing on the girl's behaviour in the maths class signify *mesosystemic* processes. Further, parental attitudes or the teacher's methods may be traced to settings to which the girl has no access, such as the environment in which the 'non-mathematical' mother was raised or the teacher's training. When these are taken into account, *exosystemic* processes are at issue. Finally, *macrosystemic* processes include, among other things, the professional opportunities available to girls; a limited scope can affect the girl's performance via her belief that maths is irrelevant to her future life.[34] Individuals' beliefs and ambitions must be considered in a historical and societal context: a mathematically inclined girl today might perceive different prospects than did her mother or her grandmother.

It is important to note that Bronfenbrenner's classification depends solely on distal relations to the individual in focus. The following example may elucidate. In British education, the policy whereby a statement must be made specifying a child's special educational needs, and how those are to be met, has affected the lives of children on a national scale since its implementation about a decade ago. For a disabled child in contemporary Britain, the prescribed practice is a feature of his *macrosystem*. When put into operation, the statementing process becomes a feature of the child's *exosystem*, for people with whom the child interacts – parents, teachers, an educational psychologist, a social worker – confer to determine his educational environment, but do so in settings to which the child has no access. Finally, when the recommended provision is made, it structures the child's *meso–* and *microsystems*, comprising the processes directly experienced by him. For the people involved in the statementing, however, processes which are exosystemic for the child characterize their own micro- and mesosystems. Likewise, for the policy-makers, processes which are macrosystemic for children, are micro- and mesosystemic.

The ecological systems model represents one response, among several, to conceptual problems regarding human development. As Baltes *et al.* pointed out, 'because of the apparent dynamic relationship between a developing individual and a changing society, it has become a widespread belief that intraorganismic, personological explanations of life-span developments are insufficient'.[35] Baltes and his colleagues recognized the same problems noted by Bronfenbrenner in his 1979 monograph, but arrived at a somewhat different solution, an approach known as life-span developmental psychology. Baltes *et al.* envisage development as a product of the interplay between three sets of influences. The first set, normative age-graded influences, refers to what used to be considered as the major factors underlying child development: biological and environmental determinants which have a strong relationship with chronological age, in so far that their timing and duration are highly similar for most, if not all, individuals in a given culture or subculture: 'biological maturation and age-graded socialization events, including many aspects of the family life cycle, education, and occupation'.[36] The second set, normative history-graded influences, relates members of a given generation (cohort) to historical times. Economic depressions, wars, or events leading to changes in the demographic and occupational structure of a given society potentially affect all people living through those times, although the impact of the events may differ for different age groups. The third set, non-normative life events, refers to circumstances which are not age- or history-related, but have a significant impact on the individual's development (e.g., the birth of a sibling, relocation, divorce, medical problems, accidents).

The threefold paradigm can be applied to any domain of development (Baltes *et al.* use memory and intelligence as cases in point). To paraphrase an earlier illustration, a girl's progress in maths is an interplay between her developing competences and widening potential, compared to most children of her age and educational background (normative age-graded), societal opportunities, social attitudes, and educational innovations which differentiate her generation from other generations (normative history-graded), and personal circumstances, such as her own flair for the subject, her teacher's personality, her parents' attitudes, and 'peer group pressure'. A life-span model directs attention to the meshed determinants of the girl's progress, whereas Bronfenbrenner's ecological systems model, as outlined earlier, pertains to environmental conditions. The distinction is subtle, but facilitates divergent inquiries.

The ecological systems and life-span approaches complement each other in several respects. Bronfenbrenner has prompted a view of the individual as 'a growing, dynamic entity that progressively moves into and restructures the milieu in which it resides';[37] and since the environment also exerts an influence, 'the interaction between person and environment is . . . characterized by reciprocity'.[38] Life-span psychologists have used the metaphor of a river to convey a similar notion: like the flow of a river, so personal development both follows the contours of the land and alters the landscape.[39] However, life-span psychology can be said to describe the hydrodynamics, the characteristics of the flow: 'The life-span orientation is about the community of life events that jointly determine the future condition of the organism.'[40] By comparison, the ecological systems model looks at the metaphorical river banks, the interface between stream and land in a given section.

While the life-span model concerns interactions between various determinants of development, the ecological systems model is directly about person-environment interactions. The latter brings to the fore at least two points: the changing significance of ostensibly similar factors, and the role of the person's self-perceptions in person–environment relations. The impact of school–environmental factors on children or young people depends on how they experience them – and individuals' perceptions and anticipations, belief systems and attitudes, change over the years. Factors such as teacher differential treatment, seating location, and other aspects of classroom ecology might vary across the age groups. It is a matter for empirical research to find out whether this is the case, and in what ways person–environment relations change over time.

A System in Motion

The American clinical psychologist George Kelly described personality as 'a system in motion'.[41] His approach, personal construct theory, highlights the meaning-seeking and meaning-giving nature of human inner life, and asserts the uniqueness of individuals. Kelly applied his approach only to personality study, especially in therapeutic settings. Since the 1950s, others have greatly expanded its range.[42] The potential of personal construct psychology has been recognized by many psychologists working in the world of education.[43]

Extrapolating a theory and methods from one field to another often calls for modification. Salmon, distinguishing between the educational and clinical frameworks, has commented that unlike clients in psychotherapy, pupils do not choose to come to school, and may perceive the curriculum as largely irrelevant to their life.[44] It is, of course, debatable to what extent *child clients* have a choice about coming to the clinic. The crucial difference lies in the fact that for a child, as for an adult client, the clinical microsystem – i.e., interactions with the therapist, diagnostic and intervention activities as experienced by the client – is centred explicitly on him or her. Education may be called 'child–centred', but an individual child is expected to fit in the established order, and is one of a crowd. Not only does the quality of therapist–client transactions differ from teacher–pupil transactions, but the ecology of clinical and educational settings diverge in some fundamental way. It may be queried, then, as Yorke has in his extensive critique of personal construct theory, 'whether widening the aperture of the theory has restricted its depth of focus and led to greater conceptual and empirical fuzziness'.[45] This is, on Yorke's part, a constructive criticism: he has endeavoured to elucidate and strengthen personal construct psychology.

Educational and clinical settings are structured with different aims in mind, but in a global sense both are environments designed to change individuals' behaviour with specific goals in mind. The successful extrapolation of personal construct theory may depend on the extent to which it explains human behaviour in general.

THE PERSONAL CONSTRUCT SYSTEM

According to Kelly, 'Man looks at his world through transparent patterns or templates which he creates and then attempts to fit over the realities of which the world is composed.'[46] In other words, people construe (interpret) their environments via belief systems which they construct for themselves over time. The concept of *personal construing*, crucial in Kelly's thinking, pivots on future-oriented exploration of the world. The metaphor of the 'Intuitive Scientist' is often cited by Kelly and his followers: like a scientist, a person predicts the consequences of events on the basis of previously acquired knowledge and a theory about the nature of the world. As Kelly put it, 'a person is not a victim of his biography but . . . he may be enslaved by his interpretation of it.'[47] Kelly envisaged psychological existence as an ongoing activity of implicit hypothesis-testing: we negotiate situations according to what we expect to happen.

Kelly's approach was above all pragmatic, addressing a problem presented to a therapist or a counsellor: how can a person share other people's private ways of looking at the world, so to understand what troubles them and why they act as they do? A person is not simply the sum total of influences that determine his or her development. Knowing others' biographies tells us little about what their life events have meant to them; we may sympathize, but not empathize. Insight into other people's viewpoints requires that we follow their own reasoning and sense-making of events. Therefore, a method for tapping people's implicit theories about reality, however 'peculiar' that theory might be from our point of view, is required. With such sentiments, Kelly set out against the mainstream of his day, the psychoanalytic frame of reference.

His theory is formally stated in a Fundamental Postulate and eleven Corollaries. Suffice it to quote the Postulate: 'A person's processes are psychologically channelized by the ways he anticipates events.'[48] Kelly regarded the Postulates and Corollaries as assumptions for the sake of theory-building, assumption that can be held up to scrutiny. The theoretical scope of Kelly's propositions is perhaps limited by his emphasis on hypothesis-testing, the anticipatory aspect of person–environment relations. Yorke has felt that, ordinarily, people are not as explorative as Kelly assumed.[49] Hinkle interpreted Kelly's Fundamental Postulate as implying 'simply that a person's anticipations constitute a parameter in the description of his actions'.[50] Kelly's theorizing also understates the human faculty for creativity and humour, or 'lateral thinking'. However, bearing in mind Kelly's explicit goals, in the clinical context, the notion of a personal construct system has tremendous merit. What is meant by personal constructs is best introduced with a practical illustration, albeit fictitious (for simplicity's sake).

The gist of Kelly's rationale may be illustrated as follows. If pupils' perceptions of school curricula are to be investigated in a Kellyan framework, the pupils may be asked to compare and contrast maths, English, geography, and other subjects. The researcher would note which criteria they apply to the task. Some pupils may compare the subjects in terms of difficulty or demandingness; others may assess the interest that given subjects hold for them; yet other pupils might use relatively uncommon criteria, perhaps distinguishing between subjects taught in the morning and those taught in the afternoon. Undergraduate students, choosing their optional modules, have been known to base their selection on their opinions and feelings about the lecturers. Such criteria are not necessarily objective attributes of the things under comparison, but are features (constructs) of a personal way of dealing with those things: 'while much of this experimentation necessarily involves sense-data, . . . Kelly sees construct systems as involving hierarchical abstractions which may well be removed a considerable distance from the sense-data to which they relate'.[51] Above all, constructs indicate a subjective classification system, used by the individual to make sense of the world. Pupils who compare school subjects in terms of interest negotiate a somewhat different academic reality than do classmates who evaluate subjects according to demandingness. In an actual inquiry, several constructs would be elicited from any individual; correlations between the person's constructs may then be worked out. For example, some pupils may construe subjects that are more difficult, in their view, as also more interesting; for them the constructs *difficult* and *interesting* are positively correlated (and perhaps subordinate to the construct *challenging*). Other pupils may regard a subject's difficulty and interest as unrelated – or even negatively correlated (i.e., the less difficult it is, the more interesting; perhaps subordinate to '*I can understand it*').

Kelly's writings are somewhat fuzzy about the nature of constructs, and have led to disparate interpretations. The analogy of 'transparent patterns or templates', quoted earlier, suggests a mental structure, somehow in-built into the mind. He seems to ascribe to personal constructs the status of thing-like entities by stressing that they are 'real', can be manipulated, and are independent of their verbal labels: 'many of one's constructs have no symbols to be used as convenient word handles'.[52] Writers who class Kelly's approach as cognitive, in an 'information processing' sense, echo those emphases.

An alternative reading of Kelly shifts the emphasis away from regarding the construct system as a structure which filters sense data, towards viewing it as the *perceptual process* itself: 'A construct is a way in which some things are construed as being alike and yet different from others.'[53] To paraphrase an observation made by the eighteenth-century philosopher Kant, one apple and another apple could not be perceived as *two apples* without an intuitive notion of addition. Being added up is obviously not a property of apples, and does not change them in any way; *addition* is a property of human perception.

Likewise, distinguishing two apples from a pear is intrinsic to the process of perceiving the world as classifiable into categories of things. In a similar vein, Kelly devised a procedure called *triadic elicitation*, in which a person tells how two of three 'elements' are alike and different from the third. The elements may be people known to the client (the original application), the school subjects we list for our respondents in the earlier hypothetical illustration, situations, concrete objects, or any other array of things that lend themselves to comparison. As individuals work their way through a number of triads, their construing process may become apparent.

Personal constructs, then, may be best regarded as verb-like, regularities which are abstracted from a person's mental operations or inferred from interactions with things, and serve a function in maintaining a person–environment interface. For Kelly, anticipating or explaining events does not necessarily mean being able to talk about them. At no stage of life does Kelly regard the human as a blank slate upon which sense data make an impression. Even a baby lying in a cot is systematically exploring the world.

Kelly held that parts of construct systems can be communicated and shared, but emphasized the private nature of construing. His conception has much in common with Gibson's theory of *affordances*, discussed in Chapter 3, and with the role of *cognitive appraisal* in Lazarus' model of stress, mentioned in passing in that chapter. For instance, construing a situation as dangerous requires little reflection, let alone verbal articulation, but involves an implicit assessment of the situational demands and one's resources (Lazarus' cognitive appraisal), and picking up options for action (Gibson's affordances). Kelly would have been concerned with identifying what precisely the individual recognizes as a threat, and how this reading of the situation (on the individual's part) fits in with his or her preferred ways of relating to the world. In Kelly's view, *threat* means an awareness of an imminent comprehensive change in one's 'core structure'. For example, if being highly competent is the core of a person's implicit theory of self, a situation in which her expertise is likely to be inadequate can profoundly undermine that deep conviction which structures her interactions with the world. Such a threat can be as powerful as the awareness of an imminent change in life-threatening situations (and, as pointed out in Chapter 3, the physiological stress response is similar). However, it is clear why certain situations are construed by most organisms, human and non-human, as life-threatening; it is less clear why being 'exposed' as incompetent should be a threat – other than to a person whose self-concept hinges on being competent. The importance of being thought of as competent is related to that person's social accountability; it guides her *positioning* herself among other people (in Harré's sense of the term, introduced in Chapter 5).

In British social psychology of the 1970s onwards, social accountability and the discursive production of selves have become major topics for research and theorizing, using conversational material (discourse) as the 'raw data'. Yorke has integrated the personal construct framework and the discourse-centred perspective in his personal constructs hermeneutics.[54] Yorke heuristically replaced Kelly's maxim 'Man the Scientist' with 'Man the Historian', to emphasize the role of explanations in human experience. There is a qualitative difference between explanations and hypothetico-deductive procedures: explanations 'seek to identify the causal influences on an event that has already taken place, instead of testing the effect of selected variables believed to have a causal influence on the situation'.[55] That is, in the contemporary *Zeitgeist*, it is not expected that behaviour should always be explained, or explainable, by identifying and verifying 'determinants'. There are a host of other reasons to probe people's constructs. 'Man does not live by causal explanation alone!'[56]

In this frame of reference, personal constructs theory is very apt. For example, if children compare classroom situations in terms of 'working vs. misconduct' (as discovered in my research; cf. Chapter 4), we may surmise that, in their view, pupils work and misbehave at school, *but not simultaneously*. The construct does not inform about the conditions that make either activity more probable, but indicates that children who perceive classroom behaviour in these terms construe work as something that a pupil *ought to do*, by way of role enactment, rather than as something that is of intrinsic interest or personally significant. Furthermore, children who construe classroom work as appropriate conduct basically reiterate normative criteria, the do's-and-don'ts of school life.

As seen, several writers in the past three decades have drawn attention to the power of social forces to influence the construct system, an issue neglected by Kelly. Personal construct systems may not be wholly self-constructed, as Kelly assumed, but activated in a particular cultural context, the crucial factor being language. Leman suggested that Kelly's error was to speak in terms of *thought v. the world outside thought*, instead of in terms of *language v. the world represented in language*.[57] Such revisions and amendments lose Kelly's all-embracing pitch, exemplified in his speculations about infants' constructs, which are inevitably preverbal constructs. Language is not necessary for rudimentary constructs such as *edible* v. *inedible* and *pleasant* v. *painful* – but those are nevertheless ways in which an infant or an animal may anticipate events. The essence of Kelly's thesis is that phenomena have meanings only in so far that the individual (metaphorically) maps them on to an existing construct system; an actual event either corroborates a personal theory about the world, and thus reinforces it, or leads to modification and elaboration of the construct system. Infants learn, as they grow older, that there are more ways of making sense of the world than in terms of edibleness, pleasure or pain, and similar rudimentary constructs. Post-infancy, the elaboration of construct systems is increasingly mediated by 'significant others', and, cognately, is predominantly language-based. A focus on discourse is therefore justifiable. But if the integrity of Kelly's theory is to be maintained, his concept of the personal construct system should not be reduced to discursive processing.

FROM EXPLORING TO UNDERSTANDING PRIVATE WORLDS

Kelly's major and unique contribution to psychology lies in the grid-based methodology he developed to explore subjective realities. Grid techniques aim to make explicit a person's construct system, and have several advantages over other instruments used by psychologists.[58] Kelly's original procedure, the repertory (or 'rep') grid, is highly structured, rather elaborate, and time-consuming. Its administration entails triadic elicitation of constructs followed by the client's or respondent's checking each element against each construct; the subsequent analysis is statistical. Many exponents of personal construct theory, especially in Britain, have narrowed the range of Kelly's concept of constructs by regarding grid data as similar in kind to explanations given in ordinary conversations. If so, is the rep grid really necessary? Do the statistical inter-correlations of a person's constructs give a better insight into his or her construing than can be gained by a qualititative analysis of what the person says? For several personal-construct psychologists, the answers are in the negative.

A shift in attitudes to the rep grid as a research instrument became apparent during the late 1970s and 1980s. This can be seen in Nash's work (some of which was reviewed in other chapters in this book): in *Classroom Observed*, published in 1973, Nash used the grid to investigate the ways pupils construed their teachers;[59] in 1976 and 1978, he moved from the full procedure to a freer form, extracting teachers' constructs of pupils from tape-recorded conversations.[60] The techniques devised by Kelly, as Salmon notes, are 'essentially a categorization, or sorting task, in which a number of items are judged in terms of dimensions that can be applied to them' – but, Salmon contends, since the Kellyan approach is above all *conversational*, to do with the elicitation of personal meanings, a simple alternative to the rep grid may be 'truer to genuine conversation, [for] it does not force the person into making judgements which feel artificial, which do violence to natural ways of thinking'.[61]

It remains a matter of researcher judgement which method is best. A general point is that any verbal responses (including grid data) convey more than speakers' explanations or perceptions of the topic in focus. A construct elicitation, whether carried out formally in the rep grid or informally in conversation, involves more than labelling percepts. If we ask pupils to compare maths, English, geography, etc., we would in effect be asking them to put into words, perhaps for the first time, something that might 'feel' obvious to them. However informal and friendly the conversation, interviews with children hardly constitute social transactions among equals. Children are implicitly positioned as ones who are held responsible for their views, who might say the 'wrong thing'. The appeal that grid technique initially had for Salmon[62] has stemmed partly from the very humane, child-sensitive interactional format those techniques can create: there are no right or wrong answers; 'deception' is not necessary. We do not need to manoeuvre the conversation into getting pupils to disclose their feelings on school subjects, for instance, nor put them on the spot by interrogating them about their feelings.

The triadic elicitation method, mentioned earlier, is usually considered too complicated for children. In my experience, 7- and 8-year-olds had no difficulty when asked to sort pictures depicting school situations – telling which (and why) two pictures showed a 'good school' and the third showed a 'bad school' – but found the same procedure confusing when asked to sort school activities, referred to verbally. The difficulty seemed to stem not from the three-way sorting as such, but from the abstract, and sometimes bizarre, nature of the questioning in the second task. The triadic elicitation procedure can be successfully used with children when presented in a way that makes it legitimate to ask bizarre questions, namely, a game. In one of the tasks devised for my study of pupils' perceptions of school, the triadic elicitation method was transposed into a board game for two. The School Behaviour Game is played by the interviewer and interviewee. The child advances a piece on a board according to dice throws and, having 'landed' on a free space, picks up from a pile a card bearing a number. The number corresponds to one of 24 questions, requesting the child to name activities or behaviours that might occur in typical school situations or in interactions between teachers and pupils and among peers. Those are analogous to the elements in the Kellyan procedure. The child's answer is written down on the card, which is then placed on the board to cover the space; in subsequent rounds, the child skips those places. The interviewer also advances a piece by dice throws, but can land on the child's cards and steal them. The child wins back the cards three at a time, as they become available, by telling how two of the activities written on them are similar and different from the third.

A personal construct rationale is used with children for at least three reasons. First, in clinical applications, the method enhances therapist-client interactions, although the techniques are often modified for ease of administration with children.[63] Second, the fact that the method taps a perceptual process allows the relating of individuals' construing to behaviour, and the relating of individual differences in behaviour to construing differences; the technique has become a basic research tool across many fields of inquiry, to some extent independently of Kellyan philosophy. Third, the method lends itself remarkably well to exploring reciprocal perceptions among people, or how different people construe a given aspect of their shared world.

At the clinic, practitioners have felt that personal construct theory and methodology allow access into a child's inner world, a window without which effective treatment may be impossible. Butler asserts that without insight into the child's view, 'the clinician fails to construe the construction processes of the child, and in so doing fails in the search for an understanding of that child'.[64] Butler refers to Kelly's Sociality Corollary, which states that *one person can play a role in a social process involving another person, to the extent that the first construes the construction processes of the other.*

Although personal construct theory allows full expression for the uniqueness of individuals, Kelly's Commonality Corollary takes into account that people sometimes interpret experiences in similar ways. Personal construct methodology has been used as a basic research tool in order to discover both commonalities and differences of construing in given populations, usually associated with clinical, social or educational problems. For example, Stanley looked at alienation in young offenders;[65] Hicks and Nixon assessed self-concepts in children in local authority care;[66] Rekcr found differences in the way that emotionally disturbed boys, compared to controls, interpreted people's emotional states.[67] In the field of remedial education, Honess *et al.* looked at how children with learning problems construed reading.[68] Explanations facilitated by such comparative studies can be taken to support the convention that there is something 'wrong' with the child who gives cause for concern. This need not contradict the likelihood that the child's problem arose in a disturbed social system, though it plays it down somewhat. By comparison, ecosystemic and sociological perspectives highlight the social context in which individuals' problems originate.

For some workers in education, such as Salmon, personal construct theory goes hand in hand with ecosystemic principles.[69] The approach allows concurrent explorations of multiple viewpoints which conflate, conflict or converge in the classroom. Unlike the inventory-based comparisons of pupils' and teachers' perceptions of the learning environment, described in Chapter 4, personal construct psychology maintains the uniqueness of viewpoints on singular environments. The Salmon Line (a modified grid technique) was devised by her in order to compare pupils' and a teacher's construing of Design and Technology, in a field study into classroom collaboration.[70] On a wider scale, Phillips used a modified grid technique to find out how secondary school teachers perceived 'types' of pupils, and how pupils in those schools perceived teachers.[71]

Implications for clinical applications were explored most notably by the educational psychologist Ravenette, who asserted that applying a personal construct model in the clinic 'allows us to see behaviour in terms of interpersonal perceptions rather than as necessarily intra-psychic'.[72] Kelly's theory centres on the idea that people map out the world in terms of their own constructions. In Ravenette's view, the so-called 'disturbed' child is 'one who is minimally able to modify his map in the light of his experiences or, if he does, those modifications do not make much sense to other people'.[73] Ravenette described a case study involving a 6-year-old boy, referred to the clinic because of his disruptive behaviour in the classroom. The boy's self-concept and problems were explored through the medium of drawing. Separately, his teacher's and headteacher's constructs in relation to the boy were elicited. Ravenette concluded that the child and his teachers were each seeking something different in their daily interaction.

Ravenette has a message to teachers, with clear implications for the classroom ecosystem:

> When children and teachers continue to maintain their own constructions of each other, in the face of continued interpersonal difficulties, we see this as hostility in the classroom. When a teacher can abandon, if only for a limited time, his existing constructions of his problem children, he may provide room for growth for each of them and for himself.[74]

In principle, a personal construct framework can add depth to ecosystemic analyses of educational settings. Observations of classroom interactions, discordant or wholesome, can be supplemented with explorations of the participants' outlooks. But having opened a window on to people's private worlds, how can we then explain their behaviour? Personal constructs do not facilitate prediction of behaviour, but sense-making; the crucial distinction is between explanation and intelligibility.[75] Nevertheless, the ways in which people make their worlds intelligible can influence their behaviour.

Thinking in terms of construct systems (without necessarily resorting to Kellyan methods of construct elicitation) goes beyond explanations that people may give in conversation. In a sociological study, secondary school pupils explained their truancy in ways which boiled down to one of two reasons: some pupils said that they stayed away mainly because they anticipated conflict at school; others said that activities elsewhere were more appealing than being at school.[76] We may label those reasons 'school push' and 'community pull', respectively. Clearly, neither 'school push' on its own, nor 'community pull', explains the prevalence of truancy in a school population, because individual pupils continue to truant for different reasons. To concede that both factors are involved, to a varying degree, goes little beyond paraphrasing the findings reported in that study. A model in which an explanation for the prevalence of truancy can be structured should involve a statement that can hold true for all truants. For example, it may be speculated that persistent truants avoid school because when they do attend their experiences tend to confirm their negative 'theory of school'. Theories of school would vary across pupils (individuals experience school differently), but all pupils have some theory of school (they all experience school). To verify this assumption, we would seek a reciprocal causality between events at school and their construing. A pupil's theory of school as hostile is likely to be confirmed by a teacher's harsh response to a recent absence; subsequently, the pupil will anticipate conflict and stay away ('school push'). A theory of school as boring and irrelevant can be confirmed, for a pupil, when lessons become hard to follow due to previous absences (hence, 'community pull'). In such ways, personal constructs make certain behaviour more likely.

It is sometimes assumed, naively, that if only people's attitudes can be assessed reliably, their behaviour can be predicted with accuracy. The fallacy is the assumption of a simple attitude–behaviour consistency. If the person is a system in motion, the time that passes between stating an attitude and acting can hardly be of no consequence. Indeed, where attitude–behaviour consistency does occur, it could indicate a psychological need to maintain an image of oneself as a consistent person. Personal construct psychology pivots on the notion of *coherence*, and workers in this framework look for the stability and systematic change of constructs, rather than for near-identical responses. A young person I know was underachieving as a child, although she was happy in the junior school; 'school' at the time meant a place to play with friends. In the comprehensive school, she discovered an interest in science and has since obtained high grades in most subjects; 'school' now means something more than a place for socializing. On the whole, her experiences of the educational establishment have been positive, supporting an implicit theory of school as a place where one's interests can usually be pursued, however those interests might change.

Notes and References

1 Bronfenbrenner, U. 'Ecological systems theory'. In Vasta, R. (ed.), *Six Theories of Child Development*. London: Jessica Kingsley, 1992, p. 188; his italics.

2 Bronfenbrenner, U. *The Ecology of Human Development.* Cambridge, MA: Harvard University Press, 1979.

3 Bronfenbrenner, U., 1986, quoted in Bronfenbrenner, U., 1992, op. cit., p. 188.

4 Ibid., p. 188.

5 Ibid., p. 223.

6 Lee, P. C., Statuto, C. M. and Kedar-Voivodas, G. 'Elementary school children's perceptions of their actual and ideal school experience: a developmental study'. *Journal of Educational Psychology,* **75**, 838–847, 1983.

7 Cullingford, C. *The Inner World of the School,* London: Cassell, 1991, p. 2.

8 Blishen, E. (ed.), *The School That I'd Like.* Harmondsworth: Penguin, 1969.

9 Holt, J. *How Children Fail.* Harmondsworth: Penguin, 1969.

10 Pye, J. *Invisible Children: Who are the Real Losers at School?* Oxford: Oxford University Press, 1989.

11 Fisher, S., Frazer, N. and Murray, K. 'The transition from home to boarding school: a diary-style analysis of the problems and worries of boarding school pupils'. *Journal of Environmental Psychology,* **4**, 211–221, 1984.

12 Madge, N. and Fassam, M. *Ask the Children: Experiences of Physical Disability in the School Years.* London: Batsford Academic and Educational, 1982.

13 Cullingford, C., 1991, op. cit., p. 2.

14 Jackson, P. W. *Life in the Classrooms,* New York: Holt, Rinehart and Winston, 1968, p. 54.

15 Beveridge, M. and Brierley, C. 'Classroom constructs: an interpretive approach to young children's language'. In Beveridge, M. (ed.), *Children Thinking Through Language.* London: Edward Arnold, pp. 156–195, 1982.

16 Lee, P. C., *et al.,* 1983, op. cit.

17 Reviewed by Jackson, P. W., 1968, op. cit.

18 Tenenbaum, 1940, quoted in Jackson, P. W., 1968, op. cit., p. 48.

19 Jackson, P. W., 1968, op. cit., p. 54.

20 Cullingford, C., 1991, op. cit.

21 Davies, B. *Life in the Classroom and Playground: The Accounts of Primary School Children.* London: Routledge and Kegan Paul, 1982.

22 See Semeonoff, B. *Projective Techniques.* London: John Wiley and Sons, 1976.

23 Pickford, R. 'A method for the comparative study of cultures

through children's representation of school in play'. *Projective Psychology*, **2**, 18–21, 1982.

24 Ibid., p. 20.

25 E.g., Solomon, I. L. and Starr, B. D. *School Apperception Method.* New York: Springer, 1968; Malpass, L. F. 'Some relationships between students' perceptions of school and their achievement'. *Journal of Educational Psychology*, **44**, 475–485, 1953.

26 Turner, P. J. 'Attachment to mother and behaviour with adults in preschool'. *British Journal of Developmental Psychology*, **11**, pp. 75–90, 1993.

27 Upton, G. and Cooper, P. 'A new perspective on behaviour problems in schools: the ecosystemic approach'. *Maladjustment and Therapeutic Education*, **8**, 1990, p. 9.

28 Bronfenbrenner, U., 1979, op. cit.

29 Moos, R. H. *Evaluating Educational Environments.* San Francisco: Jossey-Bass, 1979.

30 Bronfenbrenner, U., 1979, op. cit.

31 The definitions paraphrase those in Bronfenbrenner, U., 1992, op. cit., pp. 226–228.

32 Delamont, S. *Sex Roles and the School.* London: Methuen, 1980.

33 Stamp, P. 'Girls and mathematics: parental variables'. *British Journal of Educational Psychology*, **49**, 39–50, 1979.

34 Maccoby, E. E. 'Sex differences in intellectual functioning'. In Maccoby, E. E. (ed.), *The Development of Sex Differences.* London: Tavistock Publications, pp. 25–55, 1967.

35 Baltes, P. B., Reese, H. W. and Lipsitt, L. P. 'Life-span developmental psychology'. *Annual Review of Psychology*, **31**, 1980, p. 74.

36 Ibid., p. 75.

37 Bronfenbrenner, U., 1979, op. cit., p. 21.

38 Ibid., p. 22.

39 Cf. Sugarman, L. *Life-Span Development: Concepts, Theories, and Interventions.* London: Methuen, 1986.

40 Baltes, P. B. *et al.*, 1980, op. cit., p. 94.

41 Kelly, G. A. *The Psychology of Personal Constructs*, Vol. 1. New York: Norton, 1955.

42 Cf. Bannister, D. and Fransella, F. *Inquiring Man: The Psychology of Personal Constructs*, 3rd edn. London: Croom Helm, 1986.

43 See. e.g., Pope, M. and Keen, T. R. *Personal Construct Psychology and Education.* London: Academic Press, 1981; Salmon, P. *Psychology for Teachers: An Alternative Approach.* London: Hutchinson, 1988.

44 Salmon, P., 1988, op. cit.

45 Yorke, D. M. *The Repertory Grid: A Critical Appraisal.* Unpublished PhD thesis, University of Nottingham, 1983, p. 24.

46 Kelly, G. A., 1955, op. cit., p. 7.

47 Ibid., p. 144.

48 Ibid., p. 32.

49 Yorke, D. M., 1983, op. cit.

50 Hinkle, D. N. 'The game of Personal Constructs'. In Bannister, D. (ed.), *Perspectives in Personal Construct Theory.* London: Academic Press, 1970, p. 103.

51 Yorke, D. M., 1983, op. cit., p. 23.

52 Kelly, G. A., 1955, op. cit., p. 77.

53 Ibid., p. 74.

54 Yorke, D. M., 1983, op. cit.

55 Ibid., p. 54.

56 Hinkle, D. N., 1970, op. cit., p. 97.

57 Leman, G. 'Words and worlds'. In Bannister, D. (ed.), *Perspectives in Personal Construct Theory.* London: Academic Press, pp. 133–156, 1970.

58 Salmon, P. 'Grid measures with child subjects'. In Slater, P. (ed.), *Explorations of Interpersonal Space.* London: John Wiley and Sons, pp. 15–46, 1976.

59 Nash, R. *Classrooms Observed.* London: Routledge and Kegan Paul, 1973.

60 Cf. Yorke, D. M., 1983, op. cit.

61 Salmon, P., 1988, op. cit., p. 24.

62 Salmon, P., 1976, op. cit.

63 Cf. Ravenette, A. T. 'Grid techniques for children'. *Journal of Child Psychology and Psychiatry,* **16**, 79–83, 1975.

64 Butler, R. J. 'Towards an understanding of childhood difficulties'. In Beail, N. (ed.), *Repertory Grid Techniques and Personal Constructs: Applications in Clinical and Educational Settings.* London: Croom Helm, 1985, p. 27.

65 Stanley, B. 'Alienation in young offenders'. In Beail, N. (ed.), *Repertory Grid Techniques and Personal Constructs: Applications in Clinical and Educational Settings.* London: Croom Helm, pp. 47–60, 1985.

66 Hicks, C. and Nixon, S. 'The use of modified repertory grid technique for assessing the self-concept of children in local authority care'. *British Journal of Social Work,* **19**, 203–216, 1989.

67 Reker, G. T. 'Interpersonal conceptual structures of emotionally

disturbed and normal boys'. *Journal of Abnormal Psychology*, **83**, 380–386, 1974.

68 Honess, T., Murphy, C. and Tann, R. 'Reading problems and the child's identity: a Personal Construct Theory analysis of infant school boys and male adolescents'. *Human Learning*, **2**, 187–208, 1983.

69 Salmon, P., 1988, op. cit.

70 Salmon, P. and Claire, H. *Classroom Collaboration*. London: Routledge and Kegan Paul, 1984.

71 Phillips, D. D. *Reciprocal personal constructs of teachers and pupils in secondary schools.* Unpublished PhD thesis, University of Wales, Cardiff, 1986.

72 Ravenette, A. T. *Maladjustment: Clinical Concept or Adminstrative Convenience: Psychologists, Teachers and Children – How Many Ways to Understand?* Annual conference of the Association of Educational Psychologists, 1972, p. 3.

73 Ibid., p. 2.

74 Ravenette, A. T. 'Personal constructs theory: an approach to the psychological investigation of children and young people'. In Bannister, D. (ed.), *New Perspectives in Personal Construct Theory*. London: Academic Press, 1977, p. 280.

75 Hinkle, D. N., 1970, op. cit.

76 Bird, C., Chessam, R., Furlong, J. and Johnson, E. *Disaffected Pupils: A Report to the Department of Education and Science by the Educational Studies Unit.* Uxbridge: Brunel University, 1980.

CHAPTER 8
Problems of Adjustment

The philosopher Martin Heidegger reflected that a broken hammer makes us acutely aware of what hammers are for. Similarly, a child who fails to fit in at school makes us realize our own expectations about pupils. Certain conduct is unacceptable in school, in so far as it disrupts activities, troubles pupils and staff, damages property, and so on. Some behaviour patterns interfere with the child's daily life and education. This chapter looks at the way problems of adjustment are conceptualized in the educational context.

A child's integration into a school is a complex, many-layered and ongoing process. This complexity comes to light when we are confronted with 'failures'. Interestingly, there is no agreement about the definition of *positive* adjustment. In pragmatic terms, adjustment means the absence of problems which require professional intervention. However, the fact that about 80 per cent of pupils do not give their teachers cause for serious concern[1] does not necessarily mean that all those pupils are well-adjusted. Once a pupil's conduct is 'corrected' to the school's satisfaction, usually the interest in psychological adjustment is abated. Looking at problems of adjustment brings to light how little is known about determinants of ideal personal development.

The 'maladjustment' controversy in British special education, in the late 1970s and 1980s, has been instrumental in drawing attention to school-environmental influences on pupil behaviour. The controversy centred on the medical model, so called because it attributed problems of adjustment at school to individual pathology; critics blamed the school environment. Criticisms of the medical model echoed contemporary trends in the social and behavioural sciences: ecologically-oriented psychologists proposed that human behaviour can be understood only in relation to its real-life context; some social

217

psychologists began expounding the thesis that everything we do, down to our sense of self, is constructed in social contexts. However, at the time, these ideas were perhaps too novel to enter the educational debate.

Theories about the aetiology of maladjustment diverged in the relative importance attached to individual-specific or school-endemic factors. Somewhat later, the *reciprocal causality* between the two sets of variables became more explicit, e.g., in the ecosystemic approach to behaviour problems.[2] Thus, problems of adjustment simply indicate discordant relationships, not individuals 'unfit' for school or schools hostile to certain individuals. The focus on the 'health' of a classroom system pre-empts a notion of child/school dissonance, and has implications for the integration of children with emotional and behavioural difficulties in the mainstream classroom.

Looking at Problems

To behave well at school means following the normative code. 'Most students soon learn that rewards are granted to those who lead a good life. And in school the good life consists, principally, of doing what the teacher says.'[3] Many apparent failures to 'adjust' to the classroom environment may boil down to an incompatibility between what the teacher expects pupils to do and what the 'troublesome' individual is inclined to do.[4] For instance, there is nothing problematic, let alone pathological, about children's construing of peer relations as more important than school work; there is nothing remiss about teachers' insistence that pupils should apply themselves to work. But we can imagine conflict escalating when children persist in 'socializing' in class instead of working, and teachers, on their side, have low tolerance for what they regard as laziness or disruptiveness.

In education, it makes sense to talk about 'maladjustment' as a general condition of the child–school interface, *not of the child.* Strong objections (reviewed later in this chapter) have been raised against the assumption that being a 'nuisance' at school must be symptomatic of individual pathology. The recent conceptual dissociation of the *disturbing pupil* from the *disturbed child* in British education is evident in a spate of publications which focus on disruptive behaviour as an issue in itself.[5] Disruptive behaviour sometimes reflects individuals' discontent or dissatisfaction with the school; to stigmatize such individuals as 'ill' would be an injustice, since in some cases the school is remiss in meeting personal needs. However, a generalization in the opposite direction is equally misguided. In the case of some children, disruptive behaviour can signify hyperactivity, a conduct disorder which has an organic basis and can be treated, or it can signify maladaptive social learning, which needs remedying. Compulsive classroom 'clowns' might have an emotional problem. An assumption that individual pathology is never implicated in problems at school is not only incorrect, but carries the danger that children would be denied the help they need.

FROM SYMPTOM TO CAUSE

Problems of adjustment are customarily classified according to their symptoms, following either a rough distinction between emotional and behaviour difficulties, or some recognized psychiatric categories (e.g., mood disorders, conduct disorders). In any case, symptoms fall into two broad categories. The dichotomy is ubiquitous. Achenbach and Edlebrock discovered that many studies, despite a great diversity in instruments, subjects, raters, and statistical methods, had consistently reported childhood and adolescence problems which reflected either excesses or deficits of behaviour: individuals are either aggressive, hyperactive, and so on (*undercontrolled*), or depressed, withdrawn, and so on (*overcontrolled*).[6] The same tacit polarization emerged even in the responses of primary school children interviewed by me, who commented that if children are very sad in school (for whatever reason), they are not likely to misbehave.

Several writers propose that the dichotomy hinges on whether the behaviour creates problems for other people, or is indicative of a primarily personal problem. A boy who fights in school presents different problems than does a social isolate. Disruptive pupils create more problems for teachers than do withdrawn pupils. Fighting and classroom disruptions call for prompt reactions from teachers, whereas withdrawn pupils can (unfortunately) be ignored. There is no question who are the more 'problematic' pupils – but who are the least *adjusted?* Needless to say, the answer depends on the individual child and the circumstances, as much as on the nature of the 'symptom'.

The dichotomy mentioned above hinges not only on how the child's behaviour affects other people, but also on the extent to which its subjective meaning is accessible to other people. A disparity between children's views of their situations and others' views has been found to exist even when those others are the closest adults to the child. In their meta-analysis, Achenbach *et al.* found that children's self-ratings correlated poorly with the reports of teachers, parents, and child workers.[7] Similarly, Landau *et al.* noticed that predictors of hyperactivity in children's self-reports are not those typically considered the hallmark indicators of this disorder in diagnostic manuals.[8] Humphrey's observations of children's self-control in the classroom related more consistently to teachers' ratings of the same children than to the children's self-ratings.[9] A partial explanation is that parents, teachers, and others draw their inferences on the basis of limited data – they observe the child only in specific settings – whereas self-reports are based on respondents' global knowledge of their own behaviour. However, Achenbach *et al.* found a correlation of 0.22 between children's self-ratings and the adults' reports, whereas there was a correlation of 0.60 between the reports of the various adult informants.[10] This suggests that the self-reporter is not simply a better-informed respondent. There is a *qualitative* difference. Adults are generally more accurate in their description of children's *behaviour* problems, whereas children are better at describing their own *emotional* problems.[11] This divergence is not due to differences between adult and child, but indicates the private nature of emotional problems as opposed to the public nature of behaviour problems.

The global categorization of problems according to excesses versus deficits of behaviour seems to suggest a fundamental difference in the nature of the underlying causes. However, the reactions of different individuals to an environment perceived as uncontrollable, unpredictable or unfriendly can vary widely: some express anger and hostility; others, outwardly compliant, become withdrawn and depressed. Individuals' coping strategies differ, but the cause of their problems – a stress-inducing situation – is the same. Conversely, a similar behaviour might have a different significance in the case of different children: stealing might indicate variously a material need, social learning, a plea for attention, or a combination of any of those. 'Knowing the symptoms does not provide the key to the underlying causes; nor does knowing the underlying causes make it possible to predict likely symptoms.'[12]

Certainly in the classroom, there are few indicators that a problematic or worrying behaviour pattern is or is not school-specific, transient, or even warrants the concern. The apparently withdrawn child might be unhappy in school, suffer abuse at home (or both), or simply be 'slow to warm up' by temperament. Sometimes a psychologist's assessment is indispensible for corroborating teachers' suspicions and pin-pointing a problem and its cause. However, fashions in educational and clinical psychology have yielded divergent interpretations of classroom problems. Since behaviours which teachers find problematic or worrying seem to manifest on the *child* side of the interface, the tendency has been to look beyond them 'into' the child, in terms of personal disturbance, developmental deficits or biographical factors. Individual pathology, deficits, or unfortunate home circumstances precipitate problems at school, but not all classroom problems can be attributed to such causes. Since the detection of 'maladjustment' depends on teachers' definitions of situations at school, some workers in special education have sought causes in the *school* side of the interface. Teachers' biased expectations and personal thresholds of tolerance, leading to perceptions of deviance and self-fulfilling prophecies, do indeed explain some 'problematic' cases, but not all. Looking at classroom disturbances in terms of their relative severity, persistence and context-specificity, as proposed below, is an alternative to a symptom-based classification.

HIERARCHY OF PROBLEMS

Certain behaviours are unacceptable in school, seen as inappropriate for the child's age, or indicate unhappiness. These draw attention, and elicit teacher reactions, but the behaviours may or may not be symptoms of enduring conflicts or personal disturbance. *Focal problems* are pupils' behaviour patterns which raise teachers' concern or call for intervention. *Contextual problems* are interactional patterns which precipitate relatively enduring focal problems. *Residual problems* are characteristics of either the individual or the school, which prime the individual or the school to appraise the other unfavourably. An unfavourable appraisal gives rise to contextual problems, which manifest as focal problems in specific situations. Not all focal problems, however, are contextual. Similarly, not all contextual problems are indicative of residual problems.

For example, fighting in school is a focal problem: it is unacceptable, and elicits reactions from staff. But in the case of a particular boy, it could be an isolated incident. Recurrent fighting would suggest that the boy has an ongoing conflict which he seeks to resolve in a manner unacceptable in school (a contextual problem) or that aggression is his way of dealing with social situations (a residual problem).

Should we seek causes of problems beyond the problematic behaviour? The radical behaviourist B. F. Skinner regarded all behaviour as elicited by environmental factors and reinforced through its consequences in the sociophysical world. Skinner strongly contended the psychodynamic notion that disturbed behaviour is a 'mere by-product [of] fascinating dramas which are staged in the depths of the mind'.[13] In behaviourist thinking, so-called abnormal behaviour is understood as learned response patterns which are socially inappropriate or undermine the child's schooling. Since the behaviour – not the child – is the trouble, there are no problems other than those apparent in the objective environment. Individuals are not carriers of mental aberrations, nor are they hosts for destructive drives. A problematic repertoire, such as a boy's fighting, would prevail as long as its reinforcers are not removed from the individual's environment.

In this spirit, advocates of behaviour-modification techniques recommend treating exclusively the focal problem.[14] Behaviour modification prescribes structured programmes tailored to individuals' circumstances. Proper conduct is segmented into discrete behavioural items (working quietly for a certain period of time, completing assignments on time, being punctual, and so on), the fulfilment of each receives extrinsic rewards (e.g., praise, token points, exchangeable for agreed-upon 'treats'). Undesirable responses are either ignored or lead to punishment (e.g., isolation or 'time out', loss of points). If the programme is successful, the problematic behaviour decreases while desirable behaviour increases.

Sometimes, problems of adjustment may be due primarily to operant learning or habit. A natural 'chatterbox', for whom talking to classmates is intrinsically rewarding, may be slow to comply with the teacher's request to work quietly. Behavioural management of the kind described above may suffice; in time, appropriate conduct would become the habit. Behaviour modification might similarly reduce a boy's fighting in school, and thus alleviate his *teachers'* problem, but would it touch the root of the *boy's* problem?

A common concern among critics of behaviour modification, symptom substitution, arises from the belief that a focal problem behaviour or habit (e.g., nail-biting) is an expression of an inner state (e.g., anxiety) which is untouched by the behavioural programme. However, anxiety is itself a response to anticipated or imaged stressors. Behaviour therapy in general centres on the identification of anxiety-provoking situations and changing the client's maladaptive responses to those situations.[15]

Persistent focal problems often raise questions about their context. Does a boy always fight with certain peers? If so, the real problem might be disagreement or grudge. Disciplining the apparent culprit or applying a behavioural programme would not resolve the conflict, but might move overt clashes to another setting, or drive the conflict 'underground' to covert forms of hostility. Resolving the interpersonal conflict, i.e., dealing with the context of the focal problem, is more likely to remove the behaviour.

Should causes of problems be sought beyond the context

in which troublesome behaviours manifest? Educational psychologists inspired by ecological and systemic theories hold that it is meaningless to treat problems out of context. In broad terms, ecosystemic thinking in educational psychology is compatible with a behaviourist approach,[16] though it has a separate history.[17] It is derived from psychiatric systems theories, the innovation of which lies in the shift from psychodynamics to sociodynamics. Instead of fascinating dramas staged in the depths of the mind (to paraphrase Skinner), the systemic analysis concerns dramas staged in the interpersonal zone. The imperative, then, is to diagnose and treat the *relationship*, encouraging healthier interaction patterns. This may be achieved in joint or group counselling.

However, in treating the 'context' of the problem, we might overlook problems that transcend their specific context. For example, a boy might pick fights with almost anyone, and at the slightest provocation; the context seems hardly to matter. His reliance on aggression as a means of getting his own way is a residual problem. While his *fighting* can perhaps be abated with behaviour modification (or even more crudely, with punishment), or by resolving immediate conflicts so that current 'excuses' are eliminated, as long as the boy's strategy is not addressed, similar responses will arise in other situations. It is, then, a residual problem.

Residual problems are biases in either pupils' appraisal of school or in school appraisal of pupils, which originate outside the particular individual–school interface. On either side of the interface, biases are due to belief systems which are difficult to change, for they implicate self-fulfilling prophecies. Examples of school residual problems are discriminations which reflect race, gender or social class prejudices. Social attitudes can predispose a school's internal organization to the effect of discriminating against certain pupils or undermining their aspirations. Several years ago in a local comprehensive school, a girl's wish to play rugby was met with strong opposition; the school gave a number of practical reasons why she could not join the boys. However, one suspects that the insurmountable obstacle was the teachers' disapproval of female rugby, not administrative inconvenience.

The conceptual difference between residual and contextual problems rests on the generality of the beliefs or strategies which give rise to problems. In reality, separating residual from contextual factors may be impossible. This difficulty can be illustrated with reference to a problem which is not usually construed as reflecting 'maladjustment'. The reading difficulties of a child who has sufficient access to educational provision at school are taken to reflect child-residual problems – either constitutional (dyslexia), motivational, or biographical (social disadvantages). There is strong evidence that success in learning to read is linked to children's awareness of the phonological structure of spoken words. In a longitudinal study, Raz and Bryant investigated phonological awareness and progress in reading among children from middle-class homes and seriously disadvantaged backgrounds.[18] Before starting school, the phonological skills of the disadvantaged children did not fall behind those of the middle-class children; a gap rapidly widened in the later school years. Raz and Bryant trace the reading difficulties experienced by the socially disadvantaged children to a relatively slow phonological development on their part. But what happens during the primary school years to bring about divergent development? Parental attitudes to literacy are supposedly among the determinants of progress in school. Reading progress was significantly related to the number of books owned by the child and to the frequency of visits to a library. But these may be viewed as effects, rather than causes: a child who reads poorly is less likely to ask for books as presents, or to enjoy visiting the library. The questions remains open. It is a possibility, however, that the root of the problem is contextual or school-residual, to do with the way that the school system accommodates children from different social backgrounds. If this is the case, at least some instances of learning difficulties are primarily problems of adjustment.

Social disadvantages are regarded as risk factors, but should not be mistaken for residual problems. The point is elucidated below.

RISK FACTORS

The *risk* concept in education has been extrapolated from the health service. The basis for regarding an individual as being at risk is derived from epidemiological studies which describe recurrent associations of certain health, social or educational outcomes and personal attributes, lifestyle, or demographic factors. The potential utility of identifying risk factors is obvious:

> if teachers could predict with acceptable accuracy at an early age those children who were later likely to give cause for concern (be it delinquent, maladjusted, truants, or severe reading failures), preventative action might be taken.[19]

For example, many surveys demonstrated that attainment is correlated with socioeconomic background. Knowing this, teachers may be more alert to signs of learning difficulties among children from poor families. However, risk factors should not be confused with environmental determinants of a child's emotional and behaviour problems or learning difficulties.

Caution is necessary in generalizing from epidemiological findings, for several reasons. A trivial point is that the proportions of neurotic and conduct disorders found in one study – e.g., among children and adolescents in the Isle of Wight in the late 1960s[20] – might not be found in studies carried out with other generations of pupils or in other areas. Nevertheless, irrespective of percentages, many studies in different countries and decades have consistently shown the greater occurrence of school-related problems among pupils from disadvantaged backgrounds than among 'middle-class' pupils. Plausible explanations offered in the wake of surveys' findings narrow the risk factors. The Isle of Wight study points to the greater prevalence of deviant behaviour among children who lived in families characterized by discord at the time of the study.[21] Therefore the risk factor refers to *family circumstances*, not social class *per se*.

Similarly, a sociological explanation regarding educational outcomes is that adaptation to poverty accounts for low academic motivation: the financial needs of poor families would impel youngsters to seek employment instead of staying on at school.[22] There is evidence that pupils' socioeconomic and ethnic backgrounds generate diverse expectations about their own achievement. But even within a single sociocultural stratum, families differ greatly in the sense of priorities they convey to children – and the expectation of 'typical' attitudes from a family identifiable with a particular section of society cannot be condoned. Labelling a child as *potentially* needing help is itself a risk factor: teachers' expectations can adversely influence the child's adjustment or academic effort. This raises questions, again, about within-school processes which discriminate against pupils from certain backgrounds. Rutter *et al.* found that the incidence of behaviour problems was significantly correlated with differences in school processes, not with social background.[23]

Early identification of 'maladjustment' through statistical risk factors is not entirely possible or even appropriate. Epidemiological findings have an important role in policy-making, but being based on correlational designs, they cannot explain the aetiology of problems encountered in educational environments. Contexts of behaviour and development have been frequently, and wrongly, equated with familial and demographic variables; as a result, differences in children were 'explained' (or explained away) as attributes of the children's diverse socioeconomic stratum, cultural membership, or family composition.[24] Statistical regularities with which levels of attainment, conduct variables, or attitudes are associated with demographic factors do not disclose what it means to a child to be white or black, male or female, from a poor or a rich family, let alone how such experiences shape the child's adjustment in school:

> It is by no means clear that, for example, social class or race or climate, as these are defined by the sociologist, . . . do actually exist for the child in the relevant determining context of his behavior. On the other hand, it is clear that conditions vaguely identified by words such as *loneliness, parental overindulgence,* and the

227

oppressiveness of adult standards do exist in the contexts of behavior as coercive facts.[25]

OBJECTIVE CAUSES, SUBJECTIVE REASONS

Kellmer Pringle is not alone in stressing the 'multiplicity of interrelated and interfacing factors', the combination and impact of which are unique for each child.[26] In practice, the needs of an individual would be considered in their own sphere. But the practitioner (or teacher) needs guidelines. Are there any universal determinants of child–school interface problems?

Adjustment is usually contrasted with maladjustment. A continuum is thus drawn from behaviours which indicate smooth adaptation to the school environment to behaviours which suggest otherwise. When we hold in focus a behaviour setting or micro-setting – e.g., a school, a class, or a lesson – the existence of behaviour programmes is apparent: most people behave similarly (cf. Chapter 2). They pick up more or less the same affordances of the sociophysical environment (cf. Chapter 3). In the first instance, an objective measurement of adjustment compares a child's behaviour to that of most peers in the setting: does the behaviour depart from the setting programme? Focal problems occur mostly when a pupil's conduct deviates from the normative programme in ways which interfere with the goals or well-being of other inhabitants of the setting. Typical criteria are the pupil's manageability or prospering as seen by other people, especially teachers. This begs the question about teacher-subjective criteria: a teacher's own expectations, experience, tolerance, management skills and sensitivity to pupils' personal needs must enter the evaluation of adjustment (cf. Chapter 5). Nevertheless, if the behaviour in question is publicly observable, and there is an agreement that it constitutes a departure from a norm, we may regard the judgement as objective. The existence of behaviour programmes suggests that most people perceive a particular setting in similar ways. There are normative expectations about appropriate behaviour. Being *seen as adjusted* rests on others' inferences about the individual's awareness of these expectations: do individuals' actions suggest that their perceptions of the setting deviate from the consensus?

Objective causes of behavioural deviance may be sought in the child's environment. Behaviourists would single out circumstances in which troublesome response patterns are reinforced. In the psychodynamic perspective, early life experiences are believed to result in pathological mental dispositions. In both behaviourist and psychodynamic views, people are victims of their biographies. In contrast, explanations which attribute deviant behaviour to personal reasons centre on the meaning and significance of the behaviour in the person's viewpoint. Pupils may be 'anti-school' because this is the consensus among people with whom they identify; misconduct or 'role distance' can reflect a semi-deliberate attempt to create a certain image among peers. In the information-processing framework, individuals process input about their environments, and interpret the personal implications of events, in the context of self-organizing networks of knowledge (variously called schemas, scripts, personal construct systems, etc.). These networks develop in the course of the person's life. In a cognitive perspective, then, people are victims of their reasoning processes.

Children can become victims of internalized social expectations about them. Imagine an occasion when a teacher has to leave her class for a moment. When I asked junior school pupils to name something they usually do in this situation, 59 per cent of respondents with behaviour problems confessed to misconduct, from talking to running around, jumping on tables, or throwing things; 72 per cent of the controls, non-problematic pupils, said that they would carry on working, read a book, or paint; the difference is statistically significant. The truthfulness of children's answers is irrelevant here. One of the 'control' boys, having given the normative answer, indeed muttered, 'And I'm a good liar.' The point is that there is a 'naughty pupil' role, as there is a 'good pupil' role[27] – and children learn which is *their* role. In my study, although the children were not aware of the grouping, most 'control' respondents engendered an image of themselves as compliant pupils, whereas more than half of the 'problem' respondents positioned themselves as naughty; they were living up to expectations.

A child's initially innocent misconduct, due to temperament, high-spiritedness, early socialization or relative immaturity, can be reinforced by the way it is reciprocated by peers and staff. Nash interpreted incidents of disruptions he observed in a secondary school class as deliberately 'testing the teacher'.[28] A child may gain attention, a sense of peers' appreciation, and a sense of personal power over a teacher, from being defiant. If these consequences are salient to his or her self-esteem, the child has a good *reason* to be 'naughty'. The possibility that a school's disapproval may take second place to the gratification found in mischief and defiance was brought home to me by an 8-year-old boy I met during visits to a special needs class. On one occasion, coming in from the break, he suddenly declared cheerfully, 'I *love* being naughty!' Usually, we seek to explain others' behavioural deviance by postulating some frame of reference in which their behaviour makes sense, irrespective of whether we approve or disapprove of their behaviour or their reasons. The boy who loved being naughty made sense to me, though I do not condone his antics: he was pitting his wits against authority (he also told me how he outwitted a policeman in a motorbike chase). My brief work with him suggested that he could be guided to find challenge and satisfaction in positive goals. Unfortunately, his teacher at the time regarded him as a hopeless case. She could not see beyond the 'highly disturbed' product of a chaotic family (as was the case).

Behaviour which does not make sense to us personally prompts inquiries about its *causes*, not the person's reasons. 'Irrational' behaviour can be seen as symptomatic of psychotic and neurotic disorders – and those, in turn, are explained as caused by traumatic experiences or severe deprivation in childhood, brain dysfunction, even genetic dispositions which supposedly impede the person's ability to reason. Such cases sadly exist, but they are relatively few. Regarding the majority of troublesome pupils, it may be more useful to ask about the pupils' subjective reasons.

A multiplicity of perspectives is intrinsic in the evaluation of adjustment. An objective measure describes an individual's relation to a social context; therefore, the relevant context must be identified. That a delinquent boy may be well-adjusted to a street gang does not render his disaffection in school less real. Harré reviewed research describing 'activities which, interpreted from the teacher framework of theory, seem almost archetypes of disorder, [but] when interpreted from the pupil perspective are strictly within a systematic and rule-bound social order'.[29] Beynon and Delamont, in an ethnographic study of 11- and 12-year-old boys in one comprehensive school, concluded that school violence can only be understood through the eyes of the participants: 'much apparently brutal behaviour at Victoria Road School is actually hypothesis-testing, and deliberate display, on the behalf of pupils and teachers'.[30] Ravenette expounded a clinical application of this insight: he diagnosed problems of adjustment by comparing what 'problematic' children, their teachers, and their parents or guardians believed about pupil behaviour.[31]

Whose consensus constitutes the objective reality of school to which individuals adjust or fail to adjust? There is evidence that pupils do not share teachers' criteria for adjustment. Israelashvili asked Israeli teachers and 11- to 13-year-old pupils to rate the pupils' adjustment.[32] The teachers' ratings of their pupils correlated most strongly with the pupils' academic performance, whereas the pupils' self-ratings correlated with social criteria. Israelashvili[33] noted emergent implications on the outset of a new school placement: while the teacher seeks to define the pupil along a simple, single dimension of 'academically good/bad', the task facing pupils, as they perceive it, is multidimensional. It involves not only academic effort, but also peer relations. Some pupils might not invest sufficient energy in their work at the beginning of the school year, but 'postpone that until further into the year, when it is too late – the teacher has already formed his impression, and the implication is clear'.[34]

Conceivably, some pupils who are satisfactorily adjusted according to objective (teachers') criteria might feel socially rejected and isolated. If social acceptance is central to their self-esteem, they are likely to associate school with personal failure. *Subjective* maladjustment, the perception or feeling that one doesn't fit in, is an accurate observation on the person's part, in so far that it is based on personal criteria for adjustment. But how 'normal' are personal criteria?

Generally in psychology, objective criteria are based on publicly verifiable phenomena (behaviour), whereas subjective criteria are based on feelings, experiential knowledge or private beliefs (emotion or cognition). Another sense of the objective –subjective dichotomy pivots on the fact that most people perceive the world in similar ways. In scoring responses to the Rorschach inkblot test, for instance, there is a distinction between *popular* (common) and *original* (unusual) responses. Norman Wilkinson, who devised the Children's Object-Relation Test (CORT) for clinical usage, uses a similar distinction. In scoring a child's descriptions of ambiguous pictorial cards, Wilkinson looks to see whether the card is interpreted by the child '*objectively*, as it appears to most people', or in a very *subjective* and 'personalized way, drawing heavily on the child's way of resorting to an inner world of fantasy', among other things.[35] Since unusual responses could indicate originality, creativity and imagination, not necessarily a disturbed view of the world, Wilkinson recently revised the scoring system: the revision allows the clinician to rate separately responses which reflect 'harmony between the child's inner world and external reality', and responses which suggest a lack of harmony.[36]

DETERMINANTS OR CONSEQUENCES?

Jackson, concerned at the consistent proportion of American pupils who expressed a dislike of school in surveys, surmised that even children who said that they liked school might be dissatisfied and disgruntled some of the time.[37] Moreover, 'Not all children who like school can be described as being continually happy while there'.[38] Jackson's reflections imply that the prevalence of malcontended pupils is symptomatic of a flawed educational setting; therefore, the real issue is the organizational ethos. But a school's effectiveness is rarely evaluated in indices of pupils' happiness or their liking of school; educational and social outcomes take precedence (cf. Chapter 4).

Pupils' feelings tend to become topical when something is amiss. Then the inquiry is typically about causes of 'maladjustment'; the pupils' negative attitudes seem evident in their behaviour.

We may relate subjective factors to emotional and behaviour difficulties (EBD) in three ways. First, the perspectives of disaffected or troubled pupils may be taken simply as experiential accounts; clearly, individuals who experience school differently tell different stories as a result. Second, self-reports may be taken as reflecting attitudes and motives which cause the individuals to act differently in school. Third, individuals' responses in tasks designed to assess mental processes may be regarded as an indicator of their reasoning. When pupils' perceptions of school are looked into with a reference to EBD, there is a tendency to objectify subjective factors into predictors or markers of problems. In a comparative investigation of perceptual anomalies in EBD, children or adolescents whose objective 'adjustment' status is already known are asked to perform tasks designed to reveal their mental functioning. Do particular beliefs about school or cognitive schemas correlate with focal problems? Do pupils with EBD construe school differently than do pupils without apparent problems? If so, do divergent perceptions result from different experiences in school (e.g., the fact that they are singled out by teachers), or does their cognitive appraisal lead them to behave in ways which single them out?

It is a small jump from the discovery of a correlation between EBD and social-cognitive differences, such as reviewed below, to the conclusion that those differences cause or exacerbate problems of adjustment. Such conclusions are neither universally justified, nor necessarily fallacious; individual cases vary.

SOCIAL-COGNITIVE FACTORS

Despite the wide range of problems that the term EBD covers, studies have repeatedly shown that children and adolescents labelled globally as 'disturbed' tend to function at a lower level of interpersonal understanding than do non-problematic peers in the same age group. Early research centred on the identification of social-cognitive deficits. In Reker's study,[39] the performance of severely disturbed boys (aged 10–11) was poorer when they were asked to compare and contrast close-up photos of people than when they compared inanimate objects in an identical procedure. Reker concluded that disturbed children 'are not impaired in their ability to abstract but rather in their ability to interpret, anticipate, and predict their social environment'.[40] Hayden and Nasby used the same method to compare interpersonal conceptual systems used by 10- to 16-year-old boys in residential schools for the maladjusted with those used by normal boys; their findings replicated Reker's demonstration of what he called poor person prediction.[41] Long *et al.*, using a nonverbal test, compared self–other relations among adolescents, institutionalized because of behaviour problems, and normal peers.[42] Compared to the control group, the maladjusted group showed a greater distance between self and others, greater egocentricity, and lower self-esteem. Jackson and Bannister found that problematic children, relative to non-problematic peers, described themselves in shallower ways.[43]

Although these findings appear to imply a mental dysfunction, they could reflect basically the fact that children with EBD lag behind their non-problematic peers. In a longitudinal study, Gurucharri *et al.* compared the development of interpersonal understanding among boys in mainstream education (the 'normative' group) and boys who, at the beginning of the study, attended a day school for the emotionally and behaviourally disturbed (the 'clinical' group).[44] At regular intervals over several school years, covering Grades 1 to 6, the boys were asked to reflect on interpersonal issues and dilemmas, and to report real-life conflicts with friends. During the childhood years, both groups passed through the same sequential stages in developing social conceptions, but the disturbed boys lagged behind their normal counterparts in achieved level. As they approached adolescence, however, the clinical group on the whole began to catch up on the normative group, and in fact some individuals in the clinical group equalled or surpassed matched 'normative' subjects.

Gurucharri *et al.* point out some implications of developmental differences among individuals who display similar symptoms and appear to have similar problems. For example, two adolescents may suffer depression, partly because they lack friends and feel isolated. But if their respective developmental levels are different, a boy who reasons at a lower level may see the problem as 'not having friends "who do things for him" ', whereas a boy who reasons at a higher level may understand the problem as 'not having a friend "who is really close and intimate" '.[45] A further difference between low- and high-level adolescents is the type of situations perceived as indicating conflict, and the strategies used to solve the conflict. Youths who displayed a lower level of interpersonal understanding tended to perceive other people as a source of conflict, and therefore were likely to try to get rid of the other person, often physically. Youths with a higher level of understanding saw conflicts as stemming from differences of opinion about issues such as relationships and commitment to work, and therefore could accept responsibility for self-change more easily than could their low-level peers.

Immature functioning, relative to same-age peers, has clear implications for the child's social adjustment in school. In my research into perceptions of school among pupils with and without behaviour problems, the problem and control groups did not differ markedly in the ways peer interactions featured in their responses, except in two respects. First, throughout their responses to the three tasks used in the study, more control respondents mentioned peer interference with a child's work among characteristics of negative school settings, whereas more problem respondents mentioned peers spoiling *play* activities in the same context. Second, pupils with and without behaviour problems differed in their expectations about interpersonal relationships. In three out of the 24 items of the School Behaviour Game (a modified repertory grid), the respondent is asked to name something a friendly child does, something other children do that makes the respondent happy, and something that the respondent does which makes other children happy (see Chapter 6). Significantly more control respondents emphasized 'psychological' aspects (helping others, being friends), whereas more 'problem' respondents mentioned overt expressions (sharing sweets and crisps, lending stationery, joking or pulling faces 'to make people happy'). Teachers' evaluations of the respondents' social integration were remarkably congruous with those results. Most children who were regarded by their class teachers as both problematic and less socially integrated than most peers emphasized concrete expression of friendship. Most children who were regarded by their teachers as both non-problematic and fairly well-integrated emphasized psychological aspects.

If children who (for whatever reason) operate on a relatively immature level of interpersonal understanding are to be successfully integrated in ordinary classrooms, we need to know what part their cognitive appraisal of the school's social environment, their perceptions of peers and teachers, plays in the perpetuation of contextual problems. The development of interpersonal understanding and social agency depends on children's exploration of the social world – and what the world happens to offer them. Research suggests that 'problematic' pupils feel, more often than peers, that they have little influence over the events that affect them in school: as early as the infants school, non-problematic children tend to attribute their successes and failures to internal causes (effort or ability), whereas children identified as problematic tend to attribute outcomes to external causes.[46] Therefore, external locus of control among problematic children may indicate a developmental lag. But it does not follow that older pupils construe themselves as having influence in school. Regardless of psychological maturity, 'personal power' as a pupil refers to feeling involved in the school. A pupil's incorporation into school may depend on teachers' expectations.

PUPILS' PERCEPTIONS OF TEACHERS

A conscientious teacher may avoid gender, social class or ethnic biases; but in order to 'manage' a pupil with behaviour problems, the teacher must use control strategies that are not needed with well-behaved pupils. Pupils discriminated against in this way might well formulate different views on teacher–pupil relationships. What is the evidence that pupils with and without behaviour problems relate to their teachers differently?

Stahl asked adjusted and problematic Israeli 8th grade pupils to write two essays: an 'academic' essay, in which the pupils discussed the qualities of the good teacher, and an 'experiential' essay, in which they recalled a teacher they liked, and expressed their feelings about him or her.[47] The analysis of the essays' contents revealed quantitative and qualitative differences between the two groups. On average, the adjusted pupil touched on nearly twice as many topics as did the problematic pupils. The adjusted pupils emphasized matters related to teaching methods and styles, educational outcomes, and teachers' attitudes to curricular material; they also emphasized teachers' attitudes towards the class, and teacher attributes such as age and physical appearance. By comparison, the problematic pupils emphasized conduct/discipline matters, the importance of homework (homework plays a greater part in Israeli elementary education than in the British primary), and 'fun' aspects of school, such as trips. They seemed more sensitive than the adjusted pupils to tension in the classroom, and also commented more on the teacher's clothing. Difficulties related to home background, and the expectation that the teacher would help in that respect, were more conspicuous among the problematic pupils. Finally, Stahl notes that the adjusted pupils wrote in a generalized way, drawing from their experiences throughout their school years, whereas the problematic pupils tended to refer to their current teachers, and to draw from immediate experiences.

In Stahl's and similar studies, pupils were asked directly about teachers. But the extent to which teachers feature *spontaneously* in children's descriptions of school can itself be informative. The 75 junior school children in my study were not asked about teachers' actions or attitudes. Instead, they were asked to imagine and describe schools which were positively or negatively evaluated; the ways 'teachers' featured in those descriptions were looked at. In a separate task, the children were asked two questions alluding to teacher appraisal of pupil behaviour.

In the School Apperception Story Procedure (SASP), the

children chose suitable pictures from a set of thematic pictures depicting ordinary school situations. A teacher is pictured in several of the pictures. Children who selected those pictures usually focused on teacher–pupil interactions when explaining why they chose the picture. Children also mentioned interactions with teachers when describing pictures not showing a teacher (e.g., an apparently sad boy 'has been told off by the teacher'). In a second task, the School Rating Grid (SRG), the children were asked to state what, in their opinion, is most characteristic of a 'good school', 'bad school', etc.; in this case, references to teacher activities or personality were entirely spontaneous. A count of the references to teachers made in either the SASP or SRG gives an idea of teachers' salience in school reality as seen from children's perspective. Moreover, noting whether more references to a teacher were elicited in association with either positive (good, happy, liked) or negative (bad, sad, disliked) types of school can tell us something about the way children construe the teacher role. In both tasks, literal mentions of *teacher* (including *Miss* and *she*) were fewer than references to peer interactions (cf. Chapter 6). This was most conspicuous in the SRG (mean 'teacher' references: 0.27; mean 'peers' references: 1.69). Also in both tasks, teachers were mentioned in association with good, happy and liked schools more than with the 'negative' ones.

Interestingly, the *positive* school types elicited more references to teachers among children with behaviour problems than among non-problematic classmates, in either SASP or SRG, whereas the *negative* school types elicited more references to teachers among the controls than among the 'problem' respondents.

The SRG data are especially informative since the respondents were not 'cued' to refer to the teacher. Indeed, in all, only 35 children did mention teacher behaviour, attitudes or personality as the definitive feature of one or more of the school types, and seven other children mentioned pupils' behaviour towards teachers. The 'problem' and control groups were more or less equally represented among those children. However, the 'problem' group's greater inclination to associate teachers with the desirable kind of school is statistically significant. This does not mean that pupils with behaviour problems are more inclined to hold teachers in positive regard. In fact, the 'problem' respondents understated the teacher's *positive* role in undesirable school situations, such as helping to resolve conflicts between children and being a source of support.

The count of the children's references to teachers allowed an inference about the extent to which individuals regarded 'teachers' as personally salient. It was reasoned that a child for whom teachers are important would emphasize their roles in both desirable and undesirable environments, *irrespective of the given type of school*. Similarly, a child for whom teachers are unimportant would make few or no reference to teachers, or would only mention their role in one type of environment in which the teacher role seems most relevant, in the child's view. Therefore, by correlating the number of individuals' references to teachers in positive contexts with the number of their references to teachers in negative contexts, a group-level measure of the teacher's salience can be obtained. A striking difference was found among the 'problem' and control groups in this respect. Individual controls consistently emphasized or understated teachers; this is reflected in significant positive correlations in both SASP and SRG responses. In contrast, no consistent pattern emerged from the responses of the 'problem' children: some individuals mentioned teachers only in association with positive school types, whereas others mentioned teachers only in association with negative school types; the correlational analyses show a virtually random pattern.

The references to teachers ranged from laconic stereotypical statements to elaborations which describe the teacher as sensitive to children's personal needs. Predominantly, however, teachers were portrayed doing their job – teaching and disciplining – often in reciprocal relation to pupil behaviour. For example, one boy explained his reasons for selecting a certain SASP picture to describe a 'disliked school': 'She [the teacher] tries to put something on the blackboard but has to take a naughty boy to the headteacher.' And another boy, describing a picture he selected to show a 'liked school', said: 'They are working quietly and the teacher hasn't told them off yet.'

On the whole, both SRG and SASP responses reveal a consistent view. The teacher *helping* with work (or a pupil asking for the teacher's help) was most frequently mentioned as the definitive feature of desirable schools, whereas *disciplining* – telling off, shouting, etc. (or a pupil being told off, sent by the teacher to the headteacher) – often defined the undesirable settings. Other references were to aspects of teacher personality or attitude (kind, 'nasty', etc.) and liked or disliked behaviours (e.g., entertaining the class). It is worth mentioning that only three out of the ten children who mentioned teacher personality or their own liking or disliking of the teacher, in the SRG, were among the 'problem' respondents.

Due to the nature of the projective task, SASP responses also include 'neutral' descriptions of classwork activities depicted in the pictures: 'the teacher is reading a story' was a common literal description of one picture. It is noteworthy that the complementary references to pupils listening or not listening to the teacher are not so neutral!

A relatively small number of responses referred to the teacher's concern for the child (or lack of it, e.g., when a child is bullied). These references allude to teachers' responsiveness to children's personal needs, in contrast with the role stereotypic descriptions. The qualitative difference is clear in children's descriptions of one SASP picture, which shows a teacher leaning over a seated boy and pointing to a book open in front of him. Predictably, this picture was popular in association with good, happy and liked (imaginary) schools: 85 per cent of the whole sample used it to point out that the teacher is helping the boy (or that the boy asked her help) with work; only 15 per cent related it to either bad, sad or disliked schools, but they pointed out the boy's idleness or academic incompetence. Qualitatively, descriptions of this picture varied from flat statements ('she's helping him') and slightly expanded explanations ('the teacher helps him when he is stuck') to elaborations of a more personal nature:

> He probably likes the teacher – others sometimes don't like the teacher so they don't ask the teacher for help, or they're afraid that the teacher will shout at them.

... the teacher is there when you need her to help you, so you might have a struggle but they'll help you to learn, reading and all that.

This kind of description reveals something important about what a child expects from his or her relationship with teachers.

The responses of each child were coded for the presence or absence of references to teacher concern (irrespective of the number of codeable statements made by the child). Such references were made by about a third of the controls, but are virtually absent in 'problem' group. An even stronger difference was obtained when the sample was re-grouped according to age. Among the 12 younger children in the sample (Year 3), only one boy (control) referred to teacher concern. Out of the 63 older children (Years 5 and 6), clear allusions to teacher concern were made by 4 'problem' respondents, compared to 12 controls; indeterminable references were made by 11 'problem', compared to 7 control respondents. The age-related distribution could suggest a developmental lag among the children with behaviour problems. However, although references to teacher concern were absent (or indeterminable) in the responses of 90 per cent of the problem group, 64 per cent of the control group did not make clear (or any) references either. Therefore, the *absence* of this kind of reference cannot serve as a predictor of problems.

If pupils who are labelled 'problematic' experience a lack of rapport with teachers, they might well maintain an impersonal, distant attitude towards teachers. Effects of teachers' expectations have been substantiated mainly regarding pupils' attainment, not behaviour (see Chapter 5), but it might appear that the problematic pupils in my study reciprocated their teachers' disapproval with low expectations of what teachers, in general, can offer them. This coincides with the finding, reported earlier, that whereas the non-problematic children either emphasized or understated teachers, reflecting individual differences, the problematic children tended to associate teachers with specific kinds of school environments. When testing for correlations between individuals' references to teachers in desirable and undesirable settings, the *content* of the references was not considered (literal mentions were simply counted); in coding individuals' responses for the presence of references to teacher concern, *quantity* played no part (a single pithy statement sufficed; numerous 'role stereotypic' statements did not). Both sets of results, then, derived independently from correlational and thematic analyses, suggest that nearly all the pupils with behaviour problems perceived teachers 'impersonally', while at least some of the control group regarded teachers as personally important. Interestingly, in view of the expectancy effect hypothesis, the presence or absence of such references in a child's responses did not correspond to his or her teacher's ratings of the child's behaviour as being less or more problematic than that of most other pupils.

'Adjustment' in an Educational Context

Educational context implies a sociocultural context. Concern with official attitudes towards pupils' problems coincided with changing attitudes towards the disabled. In Britain, this climate of opinions precipitated the Warnock Report[48] and the subsequent Education Act 1981, which prescribed managing problematic pupils within the educational authority, rather than treating their problems as a health matter. In the wake of those documents, the debate was perpetuated by objections to the legal retention of the 'maladjustment' terminology.

The word maladjustment was used in British education as a generic term for problems including antisocial behaviours, emotional deprivation, neuroses, psychoses, and so on. Before the 1980s, teachers seeking advice about problematic pupils were usually directed to child guidance clinics, where the psychiatrist's view was dominant. Thus teachers consulted those whose conceptual model on pupil 'misconduct' was that of illness.[49] The view that problems which manifest at school must originate there, and should therefore be resolved within the educational system, has gained popularity since the late 1970s. A token of the conceptual shift was a change in terminology. To talk about maladjusted pupils has become politically incorrect. In current jargon, pupils who display worrying or disturbing behaviours are *disaffected*, suffer *emotional and behaviour difficulties* (EBD), or have *special educational needs* (SEN): 'disaffection' draws attention to pupil discontentment and alienation; 'EBD' retains the focus on psychological problems of the individual; 'SEN' reflects a concern with pupil receptivity to statutory provision. Sociology, psychology and education thus part.

The Warnock Committee acknowledged the common criticisms of the term 'maladjustment': it can stigmatize a child unnecessarily; describing a child as maladjusted is meaningless without details of the child's circumstances; it tends to suggest a permanent condition. But the Committee considered the term as 'serviceable', in view of its advantageous implication that 'behaviour can sometimes be meaningfully considered only in relation to the circumstances in which it occurs.'[50] Other workers in the field have attached a greater importance to the fact that the term 'had become and remained a label useful principally for the purpose of removing children to special schools'.[51]

The practice of setting up special units for problematic pupils was taken by some sociologists and psychologists to reflect unwarranted quasi-medical thinking.[52] A twofold emotive argument emerged. It was felt that the legal definition emulated the inclusion of problematic pupils in the pre–1981 ten categories of handicapped pupils. This insinuated that maladjustment is a condition caused by constitutional defects or unfortunate life events, similar in kind to sensory and motor disabilities, brain damage, etc. A complementary line of argument was to show that problematic behaviours in school are not symptoms of individual pathology, but reflect teacher expectations.

Is it justified to construe maladjustment as a disease or dysfunction? 'Disease' implies invasive agents which disrupt the child's development; treatment, in this case, means removal of the detrimental factor, or (more realistically) removal of the child from the deleterious environment. 'Dysfunction' indicates a failure to develop satisfactorily, partly due to maladaptive learning; intervention would mean a re-learning programme which involves modifying the child's environment. Instead (some argued), the focus should be on perceptions of deviance among teachers, psychologists, parents, and others who find the pupil problematic. Accordingly, it is attitudes that should be changed, not pupils' minds or their placement. In so far that pupils' educability is impaired, remedial measures (not therapy) are called for.

The shift from the reliance on medical opinion was explicit: 'The recommendation whether a child needs a special education . . . is primarily an educational matter rather than a medical one.'[53] This claim is generally in keeping with the view implicit in the Underwood Report, published twenty years earlier. The Underwood Report described the maladjusted child as 'developing in ways that have a bad effect on himself or his fellows, and cannot *without help* be remedied by his parents, teachers, and other adults in ordinary contact with him'.[54] The added emphasis points to the necessity for professional intervention. The point of contention was who is best qualified to provide help. It has been suggested that the vested interests of the various professional factions involved underlie the development of British special education.[55] How viable are criticisms of the medical model?

THE MYTH OF MALADJUSTMENT

The psychoanalytic view was influential in post-war child psychiatry and child guidance clinics. The prominent practitioners of the era – Anna Freud, Melanie Klein, D. W. Winnicott, and others – considered the troubled child as one who had not negotiated successfully the various intrapsychic and external conflicts faced in the process of maturation. Anna Freud described childhood problems, such as stealing and lying, as symptoms caused by 'delay or failure to attain or perfect specific personality traits'.[56] Winnicott asserted that 'most delinquents are to some extent ill [in that] the sense of security did not come into the child's life early enough to be incorporated into his belief'.[57] Thus behaviours which are essentially disturbing to others were discussed as symptomatic of a disturbed personality.

Proposing that children who steal, lie, and so on, are somehow ill is more humane than judging them as wicked. But the assertion of individual pathology diverts attention from the social context in which the behaviour is deemed abnormal. The relevance of a 'disease' frame of reference to the treatment and analysis of the mind was queried by Thomas Szasz, R. D. Laing and others who comprise the anti-psychiatry movement. In his book *The Myth of Mental Illness*, Szasz argued compellingly that since there are no reliable criteria for what is normal, judgements of what is abnormal are made within particular cultural frames of reference.[58] Definitions of normality and abnormality are therefore inevitably biased. Is maladjustment in the eye of the beholder?

In the education-oriented literature, opponents of the medical model pointed to teachers' *definition of the situation* when faced with disruptions to classroom routines.[59] There is ample empirical evidence that teachers evaluate their pupils' adjustment within a cultural context. Studies in Britain, the United States, Israel and Japan found that primary school teachers rated their pupils' adjustment in accordance with their own definitions of the ideal pupil temperament – and the teachers' definitions of that ideal consistently echoed the variation of cultural stereotypes across those countries.[60] Moreover, teachers' judgements are influenced by their perceptions of the behaviour setting. Safran and Safran demonstrated that teachers rate differently the severity of classroom disruptions if told that the incidents took place in a mainstream class or in a special class.[61] Teachers' professional frameworks also channel their judgements. Sharp and Green, in extensive classroom observations, noticed that the implementation of a progressive teaching method carried with it pragmatic problems for the teacher.[62] These problems led teachers to distinguish between children whose disposition or temperament was amenable to the new method – i.e., children who could be induced to busy themselves with teacher-approved activities – and the 'problem child', who could not readily be made to fit into the classroom routines.

The clinical literature of the 1970s likewise supports the idea that problems are construed within a sociocultural context. Stewart found that 'normal' and 'disturbed' children were more sharply differentiated in Britain than in the United

States, which suggests national differences in thresholds of recognizing problems.[63] Furthermore, English children identified as disturbed were more inclined towards avoidance of expressing feelings, were more anxious, and voiced more negative affect than their American counterparts. A study by Nachshon *et al.*[64] produced a host of differences, indicative of contrasts in socialization and values, between Israeli clients of a child guidance clinic and American child patients.[64] Draguns concluded that 'no disorder is entirely immune to cultural shaping'.[65] Regional variability in the incidence of pupils' emotional and behavioural problems was discovered in epidemiological studies in the Isle of Wight and a London borough.[66] Moreover, it was widely noted that children's socioeconomic background influenced the attribution of behaviour problems to a neurotic disorder. De Vos commented that middle-class delinquents seem to 'show more evidence of neurotic maladjustment', since their cases were typically brought to psychologists' attention, whereas social maladjustment featured more often in discussions about lower-class delinquent youths, because their cases typically drew the interest of sociologists.[67] Melanie Klein remarked that referral to a psychologist reflects the judgement of parents or other adults, whose routine interactions with the child are probably affected by the 'problem'.[68]

In conclusion, there is a widespread consensus that the *evaluation* of problems depends on the sociocultural frame of reference of the person who is affected by the child's behaviour. An objectionable corollary of the 'myth of maladjustment' is that such context-dependence hinders fair judgement. Should efforts to determine and ameliorate problems be abandoned because truly unbiased, context-free observations are unattainable? The common-sense solution is to abandon the quest for absolute syndromes, and to consider contingent problems in their real-world complexity. This solution was yet to come.

FOCI OF CONVENIENCE

The medical model of maladjustment was in a sense erected by its critics to make a point in argument. In the education-oriented literature, the gist of the debate was: does a pathological condition of maladjustment exist? Evidently, it cannot exist 'in' the child, as if independently of the environment into which the child fails to adjust, and not even the staunchest of orthodox psychiatrists would have suggested otherwise. Underlying the debate, there is some confusion about what exactly is being discussed.

Kolvin *et al.* relate anecdotal evidence that both antisocial and neurotic behaviour often subside spontaneously when the child is placed in a remedial class.[69] This may happen because the child is taken out of a crisis situation, or because certain features of the remedial class have positive effects on problematic children. In any case, the observations locate the origin of problems firmly in the person–environment relationship. For opponents of the medical model, this may suffice to query the existence of individual pathology. But the awareness that problems originate in a social context was not new in mainstream child psychiatry, and was not seen as inconsistent with the notion of individual pathology.

Theories of sociogenic aetiology in child analysis reflect the understanding that social and societal events might create obstacles to normal development.[70] Child analysts widely recognized that symptoms are sometimes a manifestation of nontolerance of the environment, a 'functional disorder'.[71] Writing in the *American Handbook of Psychiatry*, Leighton forwarded a view of children's 'Behaviours of Psychiatric Interest' as being manifestations of societal stress: 'psychological strain derived from experiencing the world as a sea of frustrations, terrors, and disappointments'.[72] Leighton encouraged a consideration of actual disturbances in the child's developmental milieu. A similar sentiment underlies Galloway and Goodwin's comment, made in support of the argument that EBD are not a clinical matter:

all teachers in special schools know many children whose disturbing behaviour can be reasonably viewed as a normal, or even healthy, reaction to highly abnormal and stressful conditions in their families or even in their previous schools.[73]

However, the psychiatric view involves the assertion that behaviours of clinical interest are reactive but not adaptive in coping with life stress: they do not remove the perceived threat, and they are not in proportion to the severity of the stressor. Such reactions might be understandable, but they are hardly 'healthy'. In psychiatry, a syndrome represents a personality type that 'endures beyond the precipitating events'.[74] For a 'Behaviour of Psychiatric Interest' to arise, the conflict between child and environment must be internalized. Freud conceptualized this as an inner conflict between the ego and the id; contemporary thinking focuses on maladaptive coping strategies.

Despite the evident overlap in the subject matter of child psychiatry, educational psychology and sociology of education, there is a crucial difference between disaffection as investigated by sociologists (who emphasize social implications of truancy, disruptiveness, or evasion of academic tasks), and problems which require clinical attention (and might involve truancy, etc.). Clinicians are interested in problems which transcend the educational setting in which the problem comes to light; educationalists are concerned with the impact of pupils' problems in the educational setting. Obvious as it is, the qualitative difference between problems imported into child/school transactions and school-endemic problems needs stating in essays about 'maladjustment'. A popular sociological thesis is that the school, representing middle-class values, favours children of a middle-class background. Regarding 'unconventional' home styles (e.g., single parenthood) as detrimental or as just different is a matter of opinion; emotional deprivation due to parental neglect cannot be dismissed as a case of parents' and teachers' differing ideologies.

Professionals have different foci of convenience, and therefore are not necessarily discussing the same issue when they talk about maladjustment. This point is perhaps too obvious, for it is rarely made explicit. Inadvertently, a misleading impression of a shared focus was created.

CONTEXT AND INTEGRATION

The idea that pupils' problematic behaviours originate in the setting in which they manifest has been widely asserted for several decades. In Britain, this view was extrapolated into special education policy, led to administrative changes, and thus affected the lives of many pupils and teachers. Initially, the explanation was that teachers inadvertently reinforce a pupil's response pattern by their own behaviour. This was based on the behaviourist premise that behaviour is controlled by objective events or features of the sociophysical environment. Over the years, there has been a subtle reformulation, influenced by sociological perspectives. The idea that behaviour can be understood in terms of its locus was far from abandoned or repudiated, but the definition of the locus was revised: the functional context of behaviour is not necessarily the concrete location in which it is observed – but the person's reference group.

Most of our actions serve a social function, they are *communicative acts* directed at significant others, prior or in addition to whatever immediate purposes an action may serve, or how it was learned. Therefore, setting-specific behaviours (problematic or otherwise) cannot be understood from a description of the objective environment; there must be an account of the frames of reference in which the behaviour is interpreted. Currently, it is held in social and clinical psychology that people collectively, by virtue of their mutual transactions, construct the functional context of their action; people maintain the relationship systems in which they act and interpret their reciprocal actions. Although classroom relationships have received considerable research attention since the 1960s, psychologists' interest in pupils' frames of reference is relatively recent and sporadic. Empirical evidence, such as mentioned earlier in this chapter, identifies pupils' social-cognitive functioning as a residual problem, and seems to point at individual deficit. More research on the implication for the child–school interface would be timely.

More than a decade ago, the Warnock Report recommended that pupils with EBD, notwithstanding severe cases, would be cared for in the mainstream school. This has been the practice since the implementation of the 1981 Act. In contemporary special education the sentiment, if not quite the practice, is that 'all children have the right to be educated alongside their peers in a "normal" environment'.[75] In practice, the integration of children with special needs can take place on three levels:

(1) *locational* integration means physically locating a special school on the same site as the mainstream school;

(2) *social* integration means incorporating a special unit or class into the organization of the ordinary school; special and mainstream pupils may share school dinner times, breaks, assemblies, and other extracurricular settings;

(3) *functional* integration is achieved when individuals' special needs are met in the ordinary classroom.

The emphasis is on *rights*. Is integration really in the best interests of a particular child, classmates and teachers? Before demanding global functional integration, the nature of children's needs ought to be understood. Children's psychological needs are not their educational needs. The most controversial, and perhaps least understood in education, are the needs of pupils formerly classed as maladjusted. The accommodation of physical, sensory and mental disabilities is straightforward in principle: educational programmes and specially designed resources can be used to enable these children to actualize their academic potential, and, in an ideal world, these will be provided in ordinary classrooms alongside provision for the able-bodied. But what educational programme can we design for pupils who refuse to study, who are frequently absent, are hostile and disruptive? Whatever personal troubles or private circumstances cause a child's disaffection, the *child–school interface* needs remedying before educational needs can be met.

Notes and References

1 Cf. Department of Education and Science. *Special Educational Needs*. London: HMSO, 1978.

2 Cf. Upton, G. and Cooper, P. 'A new perspective on behaviour problems in schools: the ecosystemic approach'. *Maladjustment and Therapeutic Education*, **8**, 3–18, 1990.

3 Jackson, P. W. *Life in the Classrooms*. New York: Holt, Rinehart and Winston, 1968, p. 26.

4 Cf. Sharp, R. and Green, A. *Education and Social Control*. London: Routledge and Kegan Paul, 1975.

5 E.g., the Elton Report: Department of Education and Science. *Discipline in Schools*. London: HMSO, 1989.

6 Achenbach, T. M. and Edelbrock, C. S. 'The classification of child psychotherapy: a review and analysis of empirical efforts'. *Psychological Bulletin*, **85**, 1275–1301, 1978; see also Stott, D. *Helping the Maladjusted Child*. Milton Keynes: Open University Press, 1982.

7 Achenbach, T. M., McConaughy, S. H. and Howell, C. T. 'Child/adolescent behavioural and emotional problems: implications of cross-correlations for situational specificity'. *Psychological Bulletin*, **101**, 213–232, 1987.

8 Landau, S., Milich, R. and Widigier, T. A. 'Conditional probabilities of child interview symptoms in the diagnosis of Attention Deficit Disorder'. *Journal of Child Psychology and Psychiatry*, **32**, 501–513, 1991.

9 Humphrey, L. L. 'Children's and teachers' perspectives on children's self-control: the development of two rating scales'. *Journal of Counselling and Clinical Psychology*, **50**, 624–633, 1982.

10 Achenbach, T. M., *et al.*, 1987, op. cit.

11 Edlebrock, C., Costallo, A. J., Dulcan, M. K., Conover, N. C. and Kala, R. 'Parent-child agreement on child psychiatric symptoms assessed via structured interview'. *Journal of Child Psychology and Psychiatry*, **27**, 181–190, 1986; Kadzin, A. E., Esveldt-Dawson, K., Sherick, R. B., and Colbus, D. 'Assessment of overt behaviour and childhood depression among psychiatrically disturbed children'. *Journal of Counselling and Clinical Psychology*, **53**, 201–210, 1985.

12 Kellmer Pringle, M. *The Needs of Children*, 2nd edn. London: Hutchinson, 1980, p. 76.

13 Skinner, B. F. *Beyond Freedom and Dignity*. New York: Jonathan Cape, 1971, p. 12.

14 E.g., Herbert, M. *Behavioural Treatment of Children with Problems*, 2nd edn. London: Academic Press, 1987; Upton, G. (ed.), *Educating Children with Behaviour Problems*. Cardiff: Faculty of Education, University College Cardiff, 1983.

15 Wolpe, J. *The Practice of Behaviour Therapy*, 2nd edn. New York: Pergamon, 1973.

16 Blackman, D. E. 'Images of man in contempory behaviourism'. In Chapman, A. J. and Jones, D. M. (eds), *Models of Man*. Leicester: British Psychological Society, pp. 99–1121, 1980.

17 Cf. Upton, G. and Cooper, P., 1990, op. cit.; Barker, P. *Basic Family Therapy*. London: Granada, 1981; Apter, S. J. *Troubled Children/Troubled Systems*. New York: Pergamon, 1983.

18 Raz, I. S. and Bryant, P. 'Social background, phonological awareness and children's reading'. *British Journal of Developmental Psychology*, **8**, pp. 209–227, 1990.

19 Davie, R. C. *Children and Families with Special Needs*. Faculty of Education, University College Cardiff, 1975, p. 7.

20 Rutter, M., Tizard, J. and Whitmore, K. *Education, Health and Behaviour*. London: Longman, 1970.

21 Wolkind, S. and Rutter, M. 'Children who have been "in care"'. *Journal of Child Psychology and Psychiatry*, **14**, 97–105, 1973.

22 Wedge, P. and Prosser, H. *Born to Fail?* London: Arrow, 1973; Essen, J. and Wedge, P. *Continuities in Childhood Disadvantage*. London: Heinemann, 1982.

23 Rutter, M., Maughan, B., Mortimore, P. and Ouston, J. *Fifteen Thousand Hours: Secondary Schools and Their Effects on Children*. London: Open Books, 1979.

24 Cf. Bronfenbrenner, U. *The Ecology of Human Development*. Cambridge, MA: Harvard University Press, 1979.

25 Wright, H. F. 'Psychological habitat'. In Barker, R. G. (ed.), *Habitats, Environments and Human Behaviour*. San Francisco: Jossey-Bass, 1978, p. 23; his italics.

26 Kellmer Pringle, M., 1980, op. cit., p. 79.

27 Calvert, B. *The Role of the Pupil*. London: Routledge and Kegan Paul, 1975.

28 Nash, R. 'Pupils' expectations for their teachers'. *Research in Education*, **12**, 47–61, 1974.

29 Harré, R. 'Notes on childhood conceptions of social order'. *Educational Review*, **30**, 1978, p. 113.

30 Beynon, J. and Delamont, S. 'The sound and the fury: pupil perceptions of school violence'. In Frude, N. and Gault, H. (eds), *Disruptive Behaviour in Schools*. London: John Wiley and Sons, 1984, p. 150.

31 Ravenette, A. T. 'Personal constructs theory: an approach to the psychological investigation of children and young people'. In

Bannister, D. (ed.), *New Perspectives in Personal Construct Theory*, London: Academic Press, pp. 251–280, 1977.
32 Israelashvili, M. 'Did the pupil adjust to the school?' Paper presented to the Psychological Association of Israel on 8 February 1989, Haifa.
33 Israelashvili, M., in personal correspondence, 1990.
34 Ibid., my translation from the Hebrew.
35 Wilkinson, N., in personal correspondence; his emphasis, 1990a.
36 Wilkinson, N., in further correspondence, 1990b.
37 Jackson, P. W., 1968, op. cit.
38 Ibid., p. 57.
39 Reker, G. T. 'Interpersonal conceptual structures of emotionally disturbed and normal boys'. *Journal of Abnormal Psychology*, **83**, 380–386, 1974.
40 Ibid., p. 384.
41 Hayden, B. and Nasby, W. 'Interpersonal conceptual structures, predictive accuracy and social adjustment of emotionally disturbed boys'. *Journal of Abnormal Psychology*, **86**, 315–320, 1976.
42 Long, B. H., Ziller, R. C. and Bankes, J. 'Self-other orientations of institutionalized behavior-problem adolescents'. *Journal of Consulting and Clinical Psychology*, **34**, 43–47, 1970.
43 Jackson, S. R. and Bannister, D. 'Growing into self'. In Bannister, D. (ed.), *Issues and Approaches in Personal Construct Theory*. London: Academic Press, pp. 67–82, 1985.
44 Gurucharri, C., Phelps, E. and Selman, R. 'Development of interpersonal understanding: a longitudinal study of normal and disturbed youth'. *Journal of Consulting and Clinical Psychology*, **52**, 26–36, 1984.
45 Ibid., p. 35.
46 Fry, P. S. and Grover, S. C. 'Problem and non-problem children's causal explanations of success and failure in primary school settings'. *British Journal of Social Psychology*, **23**, 51–60, 1984.
47 Stahl, A. 'The good teacher as perceived by advantaged and disadvantaged children'. *Havat Daat: Israeli Journal of Psychology and Counselling in Education*, **14**, 47–66, 1981. Hebrew, untranslated.
48 Department of Education and Science. *Special Educational Needs*. London: HMSO, 1978.
49 Laslett, R. *Changing Perceptions of Maladjusted Children 1945–1981*. Portishead: Association of Workers for Maladjusted Children, 1983.
50 Department of Education and Science, 1978, para. 3.27.

51 Galloway, D. and Goodwin, C. *The Education of Disturbing Children.* London: Longman, 1987, p. 15.

52 E.g., Lewis, I. and Vulliamy, G. 'The social context of educational practice: the case of special education'. In Barton, L. and Tomlinson, S. (eds), *Special Education: Policy, Practices and Social Issues.* London: Harper and Row, pp. 53–70, 1979.

53 Department of Education and Science, 1975, quoted by Laslett, R., 1973, op. cit., p. 26.

54 Department of Education and Science, 1955, quoted by Laslett, R. *Educating Maladjusted Children.* London: Crosby Lockwood Staples, 1977, pp. 2–3; my italics.

55 Cf. Tomlinson, S. *A Sociology of Special Education.* London: Routledge, 1982.

56 Freud, A. *Normality and Pathology in Childhood.* Harmondsworth: Penguin, 1965, p. 99.

57 Winnicott, D. W. *The Child, the Family, and the Outside World.* Harmondsworth: Pelican, 1964, p. 229.

58 Szasz, T. S. *The Myth of Mental Illness.* London: Paladin, 1960.

59 Cf. Stebbins, R. A. 'The meaning of disorderly behaviour: teacher definitions of a classroom situation'. *Sociology of Education,* **44**, 217–236, 1970.

60 Ballatine, J. H. and Klein, H. A. 'The relationship of temperament and adjustment in Japanese schools'. *Journal of Psychology,* **124**, 229–309, 1990; Klein, H. A. and Ballantine, J.H. 'The relationship of temperament to adjustment in British infant schools'. *Journal of Social Psychology,* **128**, 885–595, 1988.

61 Safran, S. P. and Safran, J. S. 'Classroom context and teachers' perceptions of problem behaviors'. *Journal of Educational Psychology,* **77**, 20–28, 1985; Safran, S. P. and Safran, J. S. 'An ecological analysis of cognitions of behavioral deviancy'. *Psychology in the Schools,* **23**, 288–294, 1986.

62 Sharp, R. and Green, A., 1975, op. cit.

63 Stewart, P. *Children in Distress.* Beverly Hills, CA: Sage, 1976.

64 Nachson, *et al.,* 1972, reviewed in Draguns, J. G. 'Psychological disorders of clinical severity'. In Triandis, H. C. and Draguns, J. G. (eds), *Handbook of Cross-cultural Psychology,* Vol. 6, Boston: Allyn and Bacon, pp. 99–174, 1980.

65 Draguns, J. G., 1980, op. cit., p. 155.

66 Rutter, M., Cox, A., Tupling, C., Berger, M. and Yule, W. 'Attainment and adjustment in two geographical areas'. *British Journal of Psychiatry,* **126**, 493–509, 1975.

67 De Vos, G. A. 'Cross-cultural studies of mental disorder'. In

Arieti, S. and Caplan, G. (eds), *American Handbook of Psychiatry*, 2nd edn. Vol. 2. New York: Basic Books, 1974, p. 562.

68 Klein, M. *The Psychoanalysis of Children*. London: Hogarth, 1948.

69 Kolvin, I., Wrate, R. M., Wolstonholme, F. and Hulbert, C. M. 'Seriously disturbed children in special settings and ordinary schools'. *Maladjustment and Therapeutic Education*, **5**, 65–81, 1987.

70 E.g., Erikson, E. *Childhood and Society*. London: Paladin, 1963.

71 E.g., Smirnoff, V. *The Scope of Child Analysis*. London: Routledge and Kegan Paul, 1971.

72 Leighton, A. H. 'Social disintegration and mental disorder'. In Arieti, S. and Caplan, G. (eds), *American Handbook of Psychiatry*, 2nd edn. Vol. 2. New York: Basic Books, 1974, pp. 416–417.

73 Galloway, D. and Goodwin, C., 1987, op. cit., p. 31.

74 Achenbach, T. M. and Edelbrock, C. S. 'The classification of child psychotheraphy: a review and analysis of empirical efforts'. *Psychological Bulletin*, **85**, 1978, p. 1294.

75 Ramasut, A. 'Paving the way for change – Warnock and the 1981 Act'. In Ramasut, A. (ed.), *Whole School Approaches to Special Needs*. Lewes: Falmer, 1989, p. 10.

CHAPTER 9
Living Child, Whole School

As members of crowds, as potential recipients of praise or reproof, and as pawns of institutional authorities – students are confronted with aspects of reality that at least during their childhood years are relatively confined to hours spent in classrooms.[1]

This book has been dedicated to showing ways in which the school constitutes a unique reality, a complex whole in which the living child operates. It is my contention that the scope of the ecosystemic metaphor in education is not yet fully realized. Studies into diverse aspects of the child-school interface abound, and several theoretical models exist; but they represent isolated fields of inquiry, and sometimes divergent theoretical frameworks. An integrative model still awaits development.

There is at least one good reason why such a model is needed. Without a coherent conceptualization of how different aspects of the child–school interface interrelate, school improvement and curricular initiatives remain a hit-or-miss affair.

Questions about school environments are typically raised in order to explain and predict behaviour or learning. In research, it is necessary to isolate variables in order to ascertain their relationships. We cannot understand why certain classroom environments are associated with better performance, without identifying precisely which features make one environment better than others. Likewise, we cannot understand why children develop differently in ostensibly the same environment, unless individual differences are identified. But having broken down both school and child into clusters of variables for the sake of research, we need a framework in which they can be put back together again.

The starting-point for an ecological perspective in psychology is the premise that behaviour must be explained in a relevant context. My thesis, unfolded in this book in a very global way, is that the functional context is sometimes not the setting in which the child is observed, but the personal frame of reference in which the child interprets what is going on in that setting.

There are several stages to an ecological or systemic inquiry. An initial step towards mapping a psychological habitat is to observe which environmental phenomena children react to in a given setting. This kind of endeavour is embodied in the school of ecological psychology founded by Barker and his associates, described in Chapter 2. The fact that different children react to different events, or react differently to the same event, leads to the assertion of subjective reality, the 'functional world': what is it about those phenomena, and not others, which attracts the attention of these children, and not of others? However, unless observers share or can comprehend the frame of reference within which a child makes sense of what is going on at school, they might not be able to infer the subjective significance of some child-school interactions. 'Except for the immediate satisfaction of biological needs, man lives in a world not of things but of symbols'.[2] As seen in Chapter 5, the ecosystemic approach in educational psychology looks at the world of symbols, though still keeping to the social context of behaviour. Interpersonal exchanges (especially verbal) are analysed in terms of what a child's actions and reactions communicate to others in the classroom, what their actions and reactions communicate to the child, and how those interlocked perspectives sometimes bring about discord. Sociologists and social psychologists point out that people's actions may be political, designed to negotiate one's position in the group, or have a historical function, to do with finding meaning in one's life (or both). Looking at children's perceptions of school means taking into account the ways in which they present themselves to others and to themselves in the educational setting.

Being at school is more than participating in interpersonal relationships. It is also having to comply with certain rules and regulations, to carry out prescribed tasks, and so on – and schools have their own unique ethos. Each child and school is a dynamic whole, different from the sum total of its 'isolated' parts. When those two systems are taken together, they comprise *another* dynamic whole, with its own evolution. Attention was drawn in Chapter 1 to the two interpretations of the ecosystemic metaphor. In biology, synecology is the study of a community of organisms and their habitat, such as a forest, as a unit (ecosystem). Autoecology is the study of an organism or a species in relation to an environment (e.g., an oak tree, or oak trees in general, in a forest); in this kind of study, 'attention is sharply focused on a particular organism for the purpose of seeing how it fits into the general ecological picture' and 'life histories and behaviour as a means of adaptation to the environment are usually emphasized'.[3] Similarly, we may focus on the school or classroom group, or even on the relationship between a teacher and one pupil (a subsystem of the classroom group), as a unit – or focus on how a child (or a particular age group, background, ability, etc.) fits into the school.

Two qualifications are in place. The one point has been raised earlier, especially in Chapter 7: the living child has a life outside school. Moos' social-ecological model, reviewed in Chapter 4, encapsulates the idea of a reciprocal interaction between the personal and the environmental systems, allowing for the fact that the personal system is partially detached from the environmental. A child's integration into school should be described holistically, but this does not mean imagining children as if they were totally immersed in the school. It means looking at children as *persons whose realities include the school.*

Second, regarding a child–school interface as analogous to an organism–environment fit might not be entirely appropriate, because the educational setting is not a naturally evolving system. Unlike natural systems, a social organization maintains its integrity by consensus and power relations among the people who constitute it. Its evolution indicates 'true finality or purposiveness . . . determined by the foresight of the goal' on the part of its 'elements'.[4] The 'foresight of the goal' on the part of teachers and others determines the reality a child finds at school.

Whether a school becomes a 'reality bubble', detached from the community in which the child grows, or an integral part of that community, depends largely on how the school is managed. A 'whole school' approach, a phrase increasingly heard in education, mirrors the ecosystemic metaphor at the operational end. If a school is a complex in which all processes are interconnected, then any school-improvement, educational or social initiative must be implemented with an awareness of how the changes may affect the rest of the system. For instance, the integration of children with special needs in the mainstream school (cf. Chapter 8) requires attention not only to the classroom environment, but also to the playground ethos. It is 'special' children who become a target for bullying and name-calling. I have a vivid memory of a sad Down's syndrome child in a primary school playground. On the positive side, on that occasion it was a couple of 'mainstream' girls who alerted us to her plight. There are perhaps untapped resources among pupils to ameliorate social problems. The pragmatic challenge is to incorporate pupils into anti-bullying and similar projects without lecturing them about it. As I discovered from comments children made to me about their school's initiatives, pupils can be very cynical. Some enter a game of wits with the school authority, whereby they make all the 'correct noises' in class and deliberately do the opposite in the playground. The parallel agendas, the two worlds of childhood, should be taken into account (see Chapter 6).

Generally, I have refrained from making recommendations. Teachers are inundated with practical advice. In offering a psychologist's perspective on the world within the school, I have aimed to complement the 'applied' literature. This book, if successful, has raised sensitivity to the importance of well-substantiated evidence. The point is not just academic scrupulousness or finicking; it has ramifications for how teachers carry out their work. All too often, I suspect, potentially effective methods which have been devised and tried out by experienced workers are executed in a cookbook manner by novices.

An encounter in a college common-room comes to mind.

Joining my friend, who was a student teacher there, I was drawn into a group discussion about a course assignment concerning the role of the primary school teacher. A young student earnestly proposed that the teacher ought to be like a mother. I commented that it was a sad state of affairs if a child needed teachers to fulfil that role. Most children in the nursery schools in which I had worked did not appear to need a mother during the preschool sessions; if they showed persistent distress, the staff suspected problems of adjustment. Furthermore, as a mother, I did not send my children to school (or preschool) for someone to substitute me; I expected other things from my children's teachers. It was my impression that the student, conscientious and keen though she was, spoke received wisdom which lost something in the translation. Teacher trainers quite rightly stress TLC, Tender Loving Care. Child education does entail an element of custodian care; and any human relationship ought to be based on empathy and unconditional respect. But in the harsh reality of classroom tedium, daily encounters with pupils one might feel deserve to be called 'obnoxious little brats' can erode humanistic sentiments. It is therefore crucial to realize that TLC and similar clichés are not mere idealism. We have seen that surveys reveal that 'teacher concern' – that is, responsiveness to pupils' personal needs – is among the predictors of the effective learning environment.

The teacher's craft does not call for mothering the dozen or more children in a class. On the contrary, it entails creating an environment that enables the children to become self-reliant, responsible individuals.

Notes and References

1 Jackson, P. W. *Life in the Classrooms.* New York: Holt, Rinehart and Winston, 1968, pp. 10–11.
2 Von Bertalanffy, L. *General Systems Theory: Foundations, Development, Applications.* New York: Braziller, 1968, p. 228.
3 Odum, E. P. *Foundations of Ecology,* 3rd edn. Philadelphia: W. B. Saunders, 1971, p. 6.
4 Von Bertalanffy, L., 1968, op. cit., p. 79.

Name Index

Name Index

Subject Index